Male
Spiritual
Leadership

Special Study Edition

D1470430

F. LaGARD SMITH

MALE SPIRITUAL LEADERSHIP

Published by:
21st Century Christian,
2809 Granny White Pike, Nashville, TN 37204.

With Appreciation

The manuscript for this book was reviewed at various stages by a number of people whom I want to thank for their insight, dedication, and honesty: David and Sally Davenport, Deon Dunaway, Tracy Hanson, Bill and Laurette Henegar, Linda King, Tania McKinney, Ann McMurray, "Chip" and Sharon Moore, Tom and Dorothy Olbricht, Kim Parker, Lora Postelwait, Bob Rowland, Cynthia Rowland-McClure, Kathy Shores, Billie Silvey, Karen Smith, Howard White, John and Claudette Wilson, Bob and Sherry Woodroof, and Jim and Louine Woodroof.

Not all of them agree fully with the conclusions expressed in this book. Several of them, in fact, were sought out specifically for having significantly different perspectives from mine. Because of their unselfish contributions, all of us have been richly blessed.

Dedicated to the memory of my grandmother,
Eva Mae Stirman Smith—

A woman of God who, as a young widow,
led her five sons
to be men of strength.

Table of Contents

Introduction

It has been almost a decade since I first wrote *Men of Strength for Women of God*, which was published in a later edition under the title, *What Most Women Want*. Ten years ago, we were hearing the first faint whispers of a movement for greater involvement of women during our times of gathered worship. Many questions were being asked, but none more often repeated than this: What role may women play in the church?

In the intervening years, much discussion has ensued at every level, whether in books, or on the university campus, or—most crucially—at the congregational level where the questions being asked have their greatest practical impact.

Among scholars, the case for a wider role for women has been articulated principally in terms of comparative cultural studies and the original meaning of the Greek language. Elaborate cases have been presented in an effort to demonstrate either 1) that Paul's writings were merely a reflection of the first-century patriarchical culture in which he lived, or 2) that the role of women in the early church was never as restrictive as traditionally understood. It seems not to matter that the two positions are mutually exclusive.

Under the latter approach, Paul's statement in Galatians 3:28 that there is "neither male nor female" has been touted as a great Emancipation Proclamation eliminating Old Testament notions of women as second-class citizens. Just as the civil rights movement was necessary to overcome the evils of slavery (following the rubric, "neither bond nor free"), we are being told that the feminist movement is necessary to bring the church into line with what surely was God's intended freedom for Christian women. If the practice of the early church was far more gender-inclusive than traditionally understood, our responsibility today is to re-dig the ancient wells and drink freely from the water of apostolically-approved liberation.

If, on the other hand, Paul is not to be viewed as the great Liberator of women, but rather as their arch Nemesis, then the ancient wells of patriarchical ignorance, intolerance, and bigotry must be blocked up with the enlightened understanding of a modern age. Under this approach, Paul's clear instructions that "a woman is not to teach or to have authority over men" must be dismissed as the vestigial remains of cultural practices which either should never have existed at all or which were never intended to be perpetuated beyond their time.

Regardless of which of the two inconsistent arguments one chooses to accept, the conclusion is the same: Distinctions between men and women in the church are suspect, if not outright unbiblical.

In the pew, the argument for a wider role for women is far less sophisticated. For many younger Christians, particularly, it's simply a matter of equality and perceived fairness. "Why is the Lord's church the only realm in which women do not yet have equal rights?" comes the question from a generation of women (and men) birthed in an era when gender equality is seen as an inalienable right. Even to suggest that women might be restricted to roles otherwise played by men smacks of glaring discrimination. The stain-glassed ceiling is seen as no less deplorable than the corporate glass ceiling.

Yet, despite all the discussion and disquiet regarding gender roles over the past decade, little actual change has taken place in worship assemblies . . . until now. At last, the seeds of discontent which have been lying dormant for nearly a decade are beginning to sprout up in congregation after congregation. It began as a trickle, with women participating in so-called "chain prayers" in a home-church setting. Then came the inclusion of women in the highly-visible "worship teams" which have become popular in leading (sometime supplanting) congregational singing. Next, came women teaching gender-mixed classes at Bible lectureships and then, predictably, in the local church. Now (seemingly everywhere), the push is on for women to participate fully in the worship hour, in leading prayers, reading the Scriptures, and serving—even presiding—at the Lord's table.

If those moves seem unremarkable to many (and, to others, inexcusably no more than a token response), they are nevertheless revolutionary in the light of historical practice.

That the line, so far, is being drawn at pulpit preaching and the eldership can be seen either as a matter of principle or pragmatism. Many are genuinely convinced as a matter of principle that women may be permitted to do everything but be an elder or a preacher. Others believe that women ought to be able to serve in every role or capacity in the church, but are convinced that wisdom dictates a creeping incrementalism which would permit current thinking to catch up to an ever-widening sense of inclusion.

The somewhat more intermediate question of whether a woman may serve as a deaconess promises to severely test both of those approaches. Already, a number of congregations have begun the process of discussing this option. If similar discussions in the past are any indication, it is inevitable that deaconesses will soon be appointed.

Those who believe that only the "top-echelon" positions in the church are biblically reserved for men have left themselves vulnerable indeed. Having already conceded that there is no pervasive principle of male spiritual leadership which would address the participation of men and women across the board, they are left with nothing more than legalistic line-drawing set adrift from a more generalized framework. And because such line-drawing suggests a whiff of power politics, the day is probably coming when even the secular courts will seize upon such line-drawing as arbitrary and discriminatory.

In the meantime, everyone seems to be asking, "Where, in fact, is the line to be drawn?" But asking that question is an exercise in futility as long as there are those who remain unconvinced about a divinely-commanded principle of male spiritual leadership. Why all the wasted talk about where to draw a line when so many people believe that no such principle exists in the first place?

Unfortunately (and far more important), we are surely missing the whole point when we ask the original question, "What role may women play?" The question is not what women may or may not do. The crucial question is, What has God called men to do which, by and large, we have not been doing?

If there are roles that God has forbidden women to exercise, it is only because he has purposely assigned that responsibility to men for reasons of his own, wholly unassociated with the talents and abilities of women. The role of women, therefore, is hardly the focus of a principle which calls men to a special task. Once seen in that light, drawing lines about what women may or may not do is a side issue at best, and a wasteful distraction at worst.

The principle of male spiritual leadership which is explored in this book has nothing to do with rules for inhibiting women, and everything to do with encouraging men to be more responsible, more participatory, and more spiritual in their worship and service before God. It is not meant as a red light to arrest the spiritual energy already exercised by most women, but rather as a green light to encourage the often-reluctant male believer in the pursuit of a spirituality that may not come as easily to a man as to a woman.

Applied pervasively, the principle transforms the home, the church, and society at large by permeating every aspect of a man's life. Rules and "lines" and titles and positions become entirely secondary—virtually irrelevant. If there are rules, they are meant to free us from conflict. If there are lines, they are drawn as boundaries against abuse. But the principle itself calls us higher. The principle speaks to men about duty, responsibility, service, and submission.

If that last word, submission, seems surprising in light of its normal use with reference to women, it is nevertheless true that, ultimately, male spiritual leadership is all about man's submission to God, not to mention his submission to the needs of his wife and children. That being the case, you can forget any notions of honor, privilege, position, or power being attached to man's headship role. He who would lead as a man must do so with the same humility as Christ himself, our ultimate spiritual leader.

As we begin our study of the Scriptures, it should be noted that the principle of male spiritual leadership suffers to some degree from a sense of the obvious. As with any number of other issues where we might wish for more direct and fully-articulated doctrinal statements, the matter of gender roles is virtually assumed in the Bible. Attention often focuses upon what women are forbidden to do only because centuries of Scripture and religious practice presuppose an ageless call of God for men to exercise spiritual leadership in their immediate family and among God's people.

It remains, then, for us to "come through the back door," as it were, to piece together that ancient call to men. It was not some revolutionary first-century issue, much less some newly-discovered twenty-first-century issue. Male spiritual leadership goes all the way back to the Garden, back to the origin of all things. And so it is there that we, too, must go—back to Creation, back to the future.

1 *As It Was in the Beginning*

Gender Principles from Creation Accounts

Several summers ago I sat on the grassy banks of a small, peaceful lake on the edge of the quaint village of Kemerton in the English countryside, reading a book in which the author, Oxford scholar Richard Dawkins, made the most cogent arguments I had ever read in support of amoeba-to-man evolution. His writing of *The Blind Watchmaker* was masterful and persuasive—so persuasive, in fact, that it was alarming. Carefully scrutinizing every word, I wrestled and fought through his book with an intellectual intensity that I had rarely been forced to muster.

If as a nonscientist I was venturing into unfamiliar territory, as a lawyer employing logic to test the author's theories I was still on home turf. My reading was like a game of cat and mouse. At each step along the way, at first I would gasp uncomfortably at the compelling evidence he presented, then finally manage to recognize the logical flaw in what had appeared to be an airtight argument based on that evidence. It happened paragraph after paragraph, page after page.

The extraordinary exhilaration I felt in reading the book was heightened by Dawkins' intellectual honesty—to a point, at least. Just when I discovered the flaw in each argument,

Dawkins invariably conceded, "But, of course, there is this weakness in my argument . . . ." So back and forth we went in this mighty, if unnoticed, battle of wits—with his neatly printed words on the page and my pencil-scrawled rebuttals in the margins.

Because I had been able to sniff out in advance every other weakness he was willing to acknowledge, I felt confident that, when he reached the bottom line in each chapter, I had also found the major weaknesses he had refused to acknowledge. What was so troublesome about Dawkins' book was that it looked so good, felt so right, and rang so true—at least on the surface. That's when the alarm bells went off: This is a *very* dangerous book!

Recently I have been hearing those same alarm bells going off when I read the arguments being made in support of a major shift in the role of women in the church. They seem to be *very* good arguments. They look so good, feel so right, and ring so true. But I sense that beneath the surface there are giant leaps of logic taking place. And rarely do I see us asking the tough questions which simply must be asked before we can rest content that we have pursued the truth with unrelenting fervor.

If it is alarming how the flawed theory of Evolution can be dressed up to look so respectable to a faithless world, it is even more alarming to think how people of faith can be led to radically new understandings of God's will on the strength of misleading biblical exegesis.

Just a Tiny Bit of Omniscience?

As I closed Dawkins' book and lay back on the grass, I looked out over the lake and watched the ducks as they bobbed for underwater delicacies. There were also several mother geese gliding gently across the mirrored surface, followed by their precious little yellowish goslings struggling awkwardly to keep pace. Why the thought ever crossed my mind I'll never know, but it suddenly dawned on me that I didn't have any idea what happened to ducks and geese when they die. I admit that this is a strange curiosity, but I really didn't know. After all, you don't see a lot of dead ducks lying around.

Then it occurred to me how little I knew about anything, really—clouds, gravity, earthworms. Thousands of life forms existed together in perfect harmony in and around that lake, just as their predecessors had done for centuries. Yet I didn't have a clue what made it all work. And there I was, a staunch creationist, preparing to wage battle against the teaching of Evolution. How was I supposed to do that if I didn't even know about dead ducks?

It is not just a matter of answering all the standard questions: Were the "days" of Creation literal 24-hour days or representative periods of time? How did the various races of humankind get their start? How could the earliest men and women live for hundreds of years? Was the Flood local or global?

It's also the *details* I wanted to know about: When God thought of light, what prompted him to give it motion and speed? During the time that "the earth was formless and empty," were the seven continents ever one unified mass of land, as a casual glance at the globe might suggest? If so, was there "continental drift" or did God expand this terrestrial ball, causing the continents to spread apart into their present positions? How did God create a single blade of grass, which we couldn't duplicate if our lives depended on it? And what ever possessed God to make something as useless and menacing as flies!

Lowering my head, I talked to God in the informal way that I normally pray. Only half-facetiously I told God that I desperately needed his omniscience for, say, five minutes or so. I wouldn't be greedy. I would give it back to him once I had the answers I needed. I thought of Tevya in "Fiddler On the

Roof," asking God what would be so wrong if he were a rich man. Likewise, thought I, what would be so wrong in having just a *few* minutes of omniscience in aid of a godly cause!

More serious reflection reminded me that I probably was wrong in assuming that I *needed* to know everything there was to know about how and why God created the universe. In my less-frustrated moments I am confident that God has told us all we need to know for now. Otherwise he surely would have told us more.

Equal But Different

All this leads me to believe that God's frustratingly brief revelation about his Creation has greater significance than we might have suspected at first. Compared to the vastness of what he has *not* told us, which would have taken endless volumes, what he *has* told us in one volume must be incredibly important. And this brings me to the male-female relationship and what we know about it through the Genesis accounts of Creation.

I say "accounts," of course, because there are two complementary records of God's creation of humankind. The first, found in chapter 1, gives a vertical, Creator's-eye view of male and female mankind ("Man") along with every other creature, object, force, and power in the universe. As for Man (to be distinguished from God on one hand and animals on the other)—

Then God said, "Let us make man in our image, in our likeness, and let them rule over the fish of the sea and the birds of the air, over the livestock, over all the earth, and over all the creatures that move along the ground."

So God created man in his own image, in the image of God he created him; male and female he created them.

God blessed them and said to them, "Be fruitful and increase in number; fill the earth and subdue it. Rule over the fish of the sea and the birds of the air and over every living creature that moves on the ground" (Genesis 1:26-28).

Distinct from all other creatures, Man was made in the very image of God—not just *male* Man but *female* Man as well. Here again I feel the urge for omniscience. In *what way* are we created in God's image? Physically or spiritually? In personality or simply in the ability to make moral choices? Having a sense of aesthetics, passion, compassion, even humor? A capacity for creativity? Or is it simply that we rule in our sphere as he rules in his?

Closer to our concern, why did God choose to make Man in two separate forms, male and female? Solely for purposes of reproduction, as is generally true in the animal kingdom? Obviously, separate genders would not have been necessary for that reason alone, because we know that there are other life forms which reproduce androgynously without gender differences.

If *both* male and female are created in God's image, are we to believe that God is also both male and female? Are we not told elsewhere that God is spirit? Wouldn't "spirit," even if referred to almost exclusively in masculine terms, imply that God is without gender? If God is neither male nor female, why are we—both created in his image—either male or female?

Years ago in a lecture on Christian sexuality, I suggested that in the male there is something of the female; in the female there is something of the male; and in each there is something of God. Was I right about that? It sounds good, but is that what God intended to convey?

There's so much we simply don't know. And what a grand understatement that is! But perhaps God's silence on so many of our questions is intended to magnify all the more the significance of what little he *has* revealed. And what is that? What in fact has God told us about himself and Man, man and woman, male and female?

First, the most obvious fact is that, for whatever reasons, God has chosen to create us as male and as female.

We are different. Our bodies are different, our emotional makeup is different, our interests are often at odds. Even if we are not always certain *how* we are different, the fact remains that we are not the same. And that difference between us is God's choice. It is not evolutionary accident, a quirk of nature, or divine afterthought. We are male and female—different—because God *wanted* it that way.

Second, even though we were purposely created to be different, there is also some very special sense in which we are alike, equal. We are *both* equally like God in some way. In whatever way we were created in God's image, we were created equally as male and female. We must not assume that *male* Man was created in God's image but that *female* Man was somehow created in the image of maleness, or else woman would never have been different from man. As for our created natures, then, we are *equal* as man and woman.

Yet a fascinating implication flows from the fact that we were created in the image of a being so superior to us that he could bring into existence human beings who have difficulty learning how to tie shoelaces: Despite being *like* God we are *not* God. If we are similar, we are nevertheless also vastly different. If we are alike, we are by no means exactly the same. If we are in some way equal, we are clearly and resoundingly unequal as well.

When we see that we are like God but different, alike in image yet different in position, we start to get a picture of the male-female relationship. Neither sex is superior to the other, as God is superior to Man, but clearly we are different from each other—equal, yet different. It's such an important point: Men and women are alike with reference to God, but different with reference to each other. Men and women are equal with reference to God, but unique with reference to each other—that is, *different*. We are not interchangeable.

Neither our differences nor our equality has anything to do with ego, political power, custom, culture, tradition, or preferred translations of obscure Greek words. It is the way God made us—different but equal. Equal but different.

For all the things we don't know, this one thing we do know: We *are* different; we *are* male and we *are* female— and surely for a reason. The first reason which suggests itself is *relationship,* one of God's best gifts. But what reason might there be beyond relationship?

The combination of obvious physical differences together with such a strong statement of divinely ordained equality suggests a difference only in function or purpose. We see this difference in dimension demonstrated even in Genesis 1. For example, basic differences in sexual functions would have played a vital role in God's first command—that the male and the female should "be fruitful and increase in number." Man and woman each bring something unique to the sexual encounter. Like horse and carriage, and love and marriage, in procreation you can't have one without the other.

Likewise, gender differences may contribute significantly to successful compliance with God's second command—that the male and the female rule jointly over the earth. As with procreation, in the ruling of the earth there is something unique that men and women each bring to that task. It would not be reasonable to assume that separate genders were needed solely to increase the numbers of those who would rule over the earth. Surely the idea of gender has more to do with quality than quantity, distinctive contributions than mere aesthetics.

A sexually androgynous reproducer would likely have been one-dimensional in its nonsexual attributes as well. Apparently God saw wisdom in having sexual reproducers who could contribute more than one dimension to their nonsexual earthly task together. To that task of ruling over God's creation the male brings one dimension and the female brings another.

Male and female: equal in God's image but different; equal in procreation but different; equal in rulership but different.

Different. But *why?* Surely there are reasons why! *Different.* But *how?* Surely we are told how!

Beyond the Headlines

With each step of Creation, my curiosity is heightened all the more. What about those two incomparable moments when God made the first male and the first female? If all we had was Genesis chapter 1, we probably would assume that God just zapped man and woman into existence at exactly the same moment in time. But that is where the second account comes in.

Where Genesis chapter 1 was a vertical, Creator's-eye view of mankind's relationship to God, Genesis chapter 2 is a more horizontal view of the relationship between man and woman, male and female. Unexpectedly, however, we discover that God creates *man—male* Man—before woman is ever on the scene. Surprisingly, their appearances on earth were not simultaneous. This is the account of man's appearance:

> When the Lord God made the earth and the heavens . . . the Lord God formed the man from the dust of the ground and breathed into his nostrils the breath of life, and the man became a living being (Genesis 2:4, 7).
>
> The Lord God took the man and put him in the Garden of Eden to work it and take care of it (Genesis 2:15).

But what are the *details?* Many curious children have wanted to know what Adam would have looked like without a bellybutton. Personally I'm curious about that "dust of the ground." Man surely doesn't *look* like dust or dirt. If indeed it is from dust that we come and to dust that we return, are we simply being told that man's physical body is composed of the same basic chemical elements as found within the earth, the same elements which decay and deteriorate upon death?

Or is the account to be understood more literally— that, had we been standing there, we would have seen a cloud of dust rising from the ground and transforming itself into a male physical body right before our very eyes? That, all of a sudden, a great wind swept down from the heavens and his body started breathing, and seeing, and hearing? That it began smelling, tasting, and touching?

What was the first thing Adam saw—the trees of Eden, the river? Unlike the rest of us, whose entrance into this world was as immature infants, Adam came as a full-grown man. Would he not have been absolutely overwhelmed by his first view of the world? How did he react to the first sounds he heard—the rush of the river, the chirping of the birds, the roar of the lion? What did he think about? How did he relate to God? Wouldn't it be fascinating to know the details!

But we are not given the details—only, I suggest, what is terribly important for us to know. And what is that? What facts are we to take away from this selected reporting of the events?

For openers, this first man we know as Adam is— unlike God—of the earth, earthly. Adam therefore was more than just spirit, as God is spirit; he was flesh and blood, like other earthly creatures. In his fleshly humanity he was different from God.

Yet Man was also different from animals, which, like Man, were "living beings." The flesh-and-blood beasts of the field were capable of breathing and reacting to the common senses of touch, taste, smell, sight, and sound. But, unlike Man, animals were not created in the image of God.

Perhaps in that distinction we are moving closer to understanding how Man is created in God's image—as a soul in whose bosom rests the potential for eternal existence, a "living being" with a morally conscious spiritual self unknown to lower creatures.

When Adam is placed in the garden to *work* it, we begin to see design and purpose for his creation. Man is task-oriented. He is put into a position of authority over the garden. He is given responsibility for its well-being. He is meant to take initiative, to exercise his skills and abilities for whatever purposes God has directed.

The Suitable Helper

The last significant clue we are given about the nature of Man is the fact of man's *aloneness*. But that will not last long. What would bring about the change? Was Adam unable to carry out his work in the garden by himself, simply in terms of work load? Was he incomplete in other, more personal ways? Did he himself actually long for companionship? If so, would he have been just as happy to have another man in the garden to talk with? Or did he sense the need for another dimension in his life? Was that dimension sexual? If so, was it *merely* sexual or might it also have been spiritual? Whether Adam himself sensed a need for personal companionship or perhaps assistance in his task, God recognized that something very important was missing.

> The Lord God said, "It is not good for the man to be alone. I will make a helper suitable for him."
>
> Now the Lord God had formed out of the ground all the beasts of the field and all the birds of the air. He brought them to the man to see what he would name them; and whatever the man called each living creature, that was its name. So the man gave names to all the livestock, the birds of the air and all the beasts of the field.
>
> But for Adam no suitable helper was found. So the Lord God caused the man to fall into a deep sleep; and

while he was sleeping, he took one of the man's ribs and closed up the place with flesh. Then the Lord God made a woman from the rib he had taken out of the man, and he brought her to the man.

The man said, "This is now bone of my bones and flesh of my flesh; she shall be called 'woman,' for she was taken out of man."

For this reason a man will leave his father and mother and be united to his wife, and they will become one flesh (Genesis 2:18-24).

Most people want to know about the scar. Did Adam have a scar where God removed the rib? Did Adam feel any residual pain from this supernatural operation? Other questions crowd my mind. Was he surprised at what he saw when he woke up with Eve next to him? Was he *pleased?* And what of Eve—what did she think as she looked around the garden for the first time and discovered a bearded, groggy Adam getting to his feet? Wouldn't you just love to know what their first words were to each other? Perhaps more intriguing—how were they able to instantly communicate with each other? What did the first human language sound like?

Their personal relationship also raises interesting questions: Were Adam and Eve shy, or was it love at first sight? Whatever in the world made them think of kissing each other the first time? I assume they kissed somewhere along the way. Did they feel a bit silly being romantic? You get the idea from Genesis 2:25 that everything was warm, comfortable, and natural from the very start, but who knows for sure?

More pertinent to our inquiry, did they have a division of labor in the garden? Did Adam say to Eve in the morning, "Honey, I've got to go to work. I'll be back for lunch at noon"? If so, did Eve respond to Adam, "What do you want for lunch, dear?" On the other hand, might she have said, "Wait, I'll go with you. I want to show you a better way to trim those trees"?

(With a winsome smile, of course.) I don't know about you, but I'd give a month's salary to know!

There is so much to speculate about, so many questions to ask. Wouldn't it be great to have five minutes of omniscience? My curiosity about what happens to ducks when they die is peanuts compared with the scoop we would have if the details of Creation could be known! But once again I suspect that if those details were important for us to know, God would have revealed them to us. As suggested before, what he *has* told us must be terribly significant for us. So what *has* God told us? What are the known facts of Creation regarding the first man and woman?

To begin with, God saw that man's aloneness was not good. Whether that meant sexually, emotionally, spiritually, or just productively we are not told. Perhaps all of the above. In some way man needed a "helper." A servant? No, a helper. A master? No, a helper. A *suitable* helper, who could meet the needs of man's aloneness.

Because the English word "helper" can mean everything from "Mother's little helper" to a "plumber's helper," the word can too easily suggest the idea of inferiority. But it need not. The best examples are found in the Psalms, where God is seen as man's helper:

> God is our refuge and strength,
>   an ever present help in trouble
>   (Psalm 46:1).
> Surely God is my help;
>   the Lord is the one who sustains me
>   (Psalm 54:4).

Many a husband has had appreciative thoughts of his wife's strength in their marriage that closely parallel the sentiments of David reflecting on God's help:

On my bed I remember you;
> I think of you through the watches of
> the night.
Because you are my help,
> I sing in the shadow of your wings.
I stay close to you;
>> your right hand upholds me
>> (Psalm 63:6-8).

When men are heard to say, "I couldn't have done it without my wife," too often this sounds trite, but virtually always it is nevertheless true. If in the imagery of being a helper the woman is not always in the spotlight, she does not lose her identity, nor her capacity for strength, wisdom, or courage. In fact it is precisely in her strength, wisdom, and courage that we may find her greatest identity.

The King James Version uses the expression "help meet," which originally meant "help suitable" but has degenerated into "helpmate." I've never felt good about the connotation attached to this term in reference to a wife. It never quite captured the nobility of man's helper being "just right" for him, "a perfect match." Woman was to be a help *suitable* for man—appropriate, fitting, all he could ever ask for and more than he could have expected.

The proof of that proposition comes in the parading of the animals before Adam, as if any of them might be a suitable helper! The unusual scenario simply drives home the point that what man needed was nothing less than someone on his own level—of equal position, not inferior. Otherwise "man's best friend" might have been a sufficient companion!

There is one other interesting detail of the animal parade that surfaces as possibly significant: The *naming* of the animals. Unusual, isn't it? Are we to believe that at least one of every kind of creature on the earth found itself at Adam's feet, waiting for him to think up some name for it? How would

Adam have come up with all those different names on the spur of the moment? How would he ever *remember* all their names?

On the strength of its inclusion in God's revelation, I believe just what the account says about Adam naming the animals. However, surely there must be something more significant here than what first appears. Perhaps it has something to do with pointing out man's comparative status with the animals. God's status as Creator naturally gave him the right to name Adam, which he did by calling him "man" (*"adam"* in Hebrew). In turn, Adam's status as ruler over the animals gave him the right to name *them*. Likewise, when Adam's companion is finally formed and *Adam*, not God, says, "She shall be called 'woman'"—and later names her Eve—we must ask if Adam's status is in some way different from Eve's.

It is possible, of course, that too much can be made of this. After all, everything else points to equality between the man and the woman. But that may not be the end of the story. For one thing, the word "man" (Adam) is apparently related to the Hebrew word for earth or ground *(adamah),* and the Hebrew for "woman" apparently sounds somewhat like the Hebrew for "man."

Therefore even their names are a reminder of the different ways in which man and woman were created— man from the dust of the ground, woman from man. Equality notwithstanding, in that difference in sequence and source there is also potential for a difference in status as well—certainly not the qualitative difference between God and Man, or between Man and the lower animals, but perhaps a functional difference in status between two equals. For example, the very name "Eve," meaning *living,* was related to the first woman's role in childbearing and perpetuation of faith, as noted in Genesis 3:20, where "Adam named his wife Eve, because she would become the mother of all the living."

What must not be lost in all of this is the joy that seems to exude from Adam when he calls his companion "woman." Not only does he use a word which shares common features with the word for "man" (even apart from the similar-appearing English words), but he relates that name to the unity which he has with the woman. She is "bone of my bones and flesh of my flesh," he fairly shouts!

"Unlike all these animals and birds with which I have been surrounded," you can almost hear him say, "the woman is *like* me. She is made of the same stuff, the *right* stuff! I can communicate with her and exchange ideas. She knows how I feel and cares what I think. And I can share in *her* feelings and thoughts as well. We are *both* rational, *both* emotional, *both* physical, *both* spiritual. She is someone I can relate to as an equal. After all, it was out of me that she was taken. She is the *very* helper I need!"

Even marriage, which is instituted with this first couple, is predicated upon the unity which they share. It is all very mystical, of course, but the man and the woman are to become "one flesh" because, in Adam, they once *were* one flesh! At this stage in God's revelation it is too early to fill out all the intricacies of the relationship. However, we are later given the idea that what becomes one is not simply the physical bodies during sexual relations but the couple's spirit-selves which intermingle in the union of two personalities.

Yet note the symbolism of partnership: "For she was taken out of man" is followed immediately by "For this reason . . . they will become one flesh." Two complementary dimensions of the human personality are united as one for the optimum combination of God's creation!

First Born and First Created

When God created man and woman, he could have accomplished it in one of three different time sequences:

1) He could have created both the man and the woman simultaneously; 2) he could have created woman before man; 3) he could have created man before woman. That God chose neither of the first two options, but instead created the man before the woman, may have special significance. God's choice in this detail of Creation is all the more intriguing in light of the equality between man and woman stressed in Genesis chapter 1.

We are drawn, then, to the temporal priority of man's creation as being parallel with the principle of firstborn that is proclaimed later in the Bible. Even within the first few chapters of Genesis, we find family lineage being traced through the firstborn son (see, for example, Genesis chapter 5). More importantly, birthright—the right of inheritance—came through the firstborn: "That son is the first sign of his father's strength. The right of the firstborn belongs to him" (Deuteronomy 21:17). Since responsibility for the family was always that of the firstborn son, he inherited a double portion for his trouble.

You will recall the story of Esau, who "despised his birthright" by selling his right of inheritance to his brother Jacob for a bowl of stew. In that case the significance of being the firstborn son was emphasized by the fact that they were twins. Any thought that the privileges and responsibilities of being the firstborn rested in the superior wisdom of age and experience is dismissed in this case. Jacob was so close behind Esau in exiting the womb that his hand was actually grasping Esau's heel (Genesis 25:24-34)! The headship of the firstborn, then, was a matter of arbitrary designation without reference to any subjective factor of qualification for the role.

The principle of firstborn had much more to do with the spiritual realm than the material. Under the laws of Moses the firstborn were to be consecrated to God: "The Lord said to Moses, 'Consecrate to me every firstborn male. The first offspring of every womb among the Israelites belongs to me, whether man or animal'" (Exodus 13:1, 2).

As early as Genesis chapter 4 we see Abel offering a more acceptable sacrifice than his brother Cain, which was noted to be "fat portions from some of the *first born* of his flock" (Genesis 4:4). One gets the idea that the principle of firstborn sacrifices had been expected by God even of this first family, long before the laws of Moses formally required it. It should also be noted in passing that Cain's role of spiritual leadership as firstborn son obviously would not have been by virtue of his superior spirituality, but rather, solely because of his designated role of responsibility.

This point is highlighted in Jacob's repudiation of his firstborn son, Reuben, who had slept with his father's concubine Bilhah:

> Reuben, you are my firstborn,
>> my might, the first sign of my strength,
>> excelling in honor, excelling in power.
> Turbulent as the waters, you will no
>> longer excel, for you went up
>> onto your father's bed,
>> onto my couch and defiled it
>> (Genesis 49:3,4).

Firstborn or not, Reuben was stripped of his right of inheritance (1 Chronicles 5:1, 2). Add the wicked firstborn sons of Aaron (Numbers 3:2-4), Samuel (1 Samuel 8:2, 3), David (2 Samuel 13), and Judah (1 Chronicles 2:3), and you quickly realize that personal spiritual strength was not the basis of the firstborn's position of headship or of the privileges and authority which accompanied it. The principle of firstborn was more important than any individual. The principle ensured continuity of lineage both physically and materially, and—at least by design—spiritually.

The importance of the firstborn's role as spiritual head of the family is seen most graphically in the selection of the Levites to assist in the work of the tabernacle. "Take the Levites for me in place of all the firstborn of the Israelites," was the command from the Lord. In this unusual transition of personnel, the relationship between the Levites and the firstborn was one of *spiritual* responsibility, not simply lineage or the protection of family inheritance.

Combine the principle of firstborn with its almost exclusive association with firstborn *males* or *sons* and you begin to make sense of the priority of creation relating to man and woman. The pattern is consistent: The man had to come *first,* and the firstborn had to be the *man.*

Adam's status as "firstcreated" suggests similar implications as with his "firstborn" successors—that is, that responsibility for family leadership befell Adam; that family headship was on his shoulders; that the guarantee of spiritual heritage to unborn generations should flow from his special consecration before God as the "firstcreated." Adam's "firstcreated" responsibility for spiritual leadership heralds the clearest indication yet of how man and woman were equal but different: equal before God, and equal as partners in marriage, they were different in spiritual responsibilities.

As the spiritual leader of his own immediate family, Adam—the first man—became the prototype for the patriarchal spiritual leader in each succeeding family, whether or not the husband and father had been the firstborn among his own brothers. Through Adam, male spiritual leadership became inextricably tied to the marriage and family relationship.

However, there is this important caution to be noted: Just as experience proved regarding the role of the firstborn, the responsibility for male spiritual leadership was no guarantee of superior personal spirituality on the part of those who were given that responsibility. Nor, more importantly, can it be concluded that the responsibility was given *because of* spiritual superiority. In fact, as we are soon to see, that would be a highly questionable conclusion even regarding Adam.

To the contrary, it appears that God must have had reasons of his own for instituting the principle of firstborn wholly apart from any idea of male spiritual superiority. Therefore neither can the principle of male spiritual leadership be automatically associated with any supposed male ascendancy. In fact we may discover that imposed spiritual leadership has more to do with *responsibility* than privilege, with *requirement of exercise* than recognition of ability.

Christ, The Firstborn over All Creation

Of course the ultimate Firstborn is Jesus Christ, who not only would be Mary's "firstborn, a son" (Luke 2:7) but also "the firstborn over all creation" (Colossians 1:15). His would be the supreme spiritual leadership over the entire family of man. "He is before all things, and in him all things hold together. And he is the head of the body, the church; he is the beginning and the firstborn from among the dead, so that in everything he might have the supremacy" (Colossians 1:17, 18).

It is hard to miss the striking parallel with Ephesians 5:23, 24: "For the husband is the head of the wife as Christ is the head of the church, his body, of which he is the Savior. Now as the church submits to Christ, so also wives should submit to their husbands in everything." In this analogy the husband's spiritual headship is drawn full circle back to the principle of the firstborn's spiritual leadership.

Even the picture of the church (as the bride of Christ) being Christ's body parallels the fact that Eve (the bride of Adam) was almost literally the body of Adam, from whose body she was created. Therefore the principle of spiritual headship by the husband has its roots deeply embedded in both the imagery of Creation and the image of Christ and the church.

Male Spiritual Leadership: God's Idea

Through inspiration, the Genesis account was written by Moses hundreds of years after Creation. Some say it was written in order to correct and heal the wrong relationships which humans had introduced and maintained in the intervening centuries. Later revelations use the Creation accounts as a basis for maintaining the principle of male headship even in centuries far removed.

If our understanding of these Creation origins is correct, it must be emphasized that the principle of male spiritual leadership was established before custom or culture ever came into existence. It was not initiated by woman-denouncing Jewish religious leaders in the intertestamental period or by suppressive third-century church fathers. It did not result from misunderstandings of the original languages of the Scripture text. It did not come in response to unique situations facing a few congregations of Christians thousands of years from Creation. To the contrary, the principle of male spiritual leadership came from God, in the beginning, with the first man and the first woman.

First in creation, first in headship, first in spiritual responsibility—would the man be worthy of his calling? Would he bow his own head in submission to God? Would he faithfully tend the garden? Could he adequately tend it alone, or would he, even in the exercise of his spiritual responsibilities, need a "suitable helper"? Would he need someone who, though different in dimension and having different responsibilities, would be "a perfect match" for such a task? Would he need a partner in faith, a co-worker, a fellow servant, a companion who would share equally as a joint heir of God's rich inheritance?

Study Questions

1. Given all the things about our universe that we do not understand, what should we appreciate about the brief account of Creation which we are given in Genesis?
2. What significance is there in the fact that God created both man and woman in his own image?
3. Other than the obvious distinctions between male and female, what should we learn from the fact that we have been created different?
4. Why do you suppose that God chose to create Adam before creating Eve?
5. What do we know about the responsibilities which were later given to firstborn sons?
6. In what kind of ways might we think of one who is said to be a "helper"?
7. When someone *names* another, what is implied?
8. If all we knew about spiritual headship came from the first two chapters of Genesis, what would we conclude?
9. Do you believe that the principle of male spiritual leadership was established at the dawn of Creation?
10. In what way does an understanding of gender roles in the Garden speak to the argument that first century apostolic teaching merely reflected the patriarchical norms of that culture?

2 From the Garden to the Cotton Patch

The Abandonment of Spiritual Leadership

In trying to understand the implications to be drawn from the story of Creation, we are likely to see in the Genesis account what we have always believed. Tradition has a way of putting colored glasses over our eyes, so that we miss details we've never seen before. Evidence has a way of being what we always *thought* it was. My experience as a trial attorney has made me a bit more skeptical of "cut-and-dried" cases.

Two weeks before I was due to leave office as District Attorney for Malbeur County, Oregon, I had misgivings about my decision to make a change in my professional career. Being a trial attorney and the chief law enforcement officer in a small eastern Oregon county had been the most challenging and rewarding experience of my life. At the age of 25 it was exciting to roll out in the middle of the night to the scene of a crime or to direct a gambling raid on the local Elk's Lodge. But most exhilarating of all were the murder cases that came my way.

I walked from my small, institutional-green office on the second floor of the courthouse to the desk of my irreplaceable secretary, May Hussey. For years May had run the office through a succession of young, inexperienced district attorneys. She had been our mentor, guide, and most fervent supporter. It was another case where the men were up front getting all the glory but a woman was working quietly behind the scenes to make it happen. And naturally I had to kick and scream at the County Commissioners to get even the most modest salary increases to reward her efforts.

"May," I said, "I'm sure going to miss doing trials. If only I could have just *one more* murder case before I leave office." May looked at me sternly as if to say, "LaGard, do you realize what you're asking?" I walked back to my office, appropriately rebuked.

At 1:00 the next morning the phone rang in my bedroom. It was the police. There had been a homicide. You can guess what my first thought was and, even knowing it had to be coincidence, I couldn't help but think I was responsible for the killing.

I got up, got dressed, and drove out into the night. The scene of the homicide was a farmhouse north of the town of Ontario. When I arrived, officers from the Oregon State Police were already sifting through the evidence. The pools of blood throughout the house told a grisly story. Sergeant Baker was taking a statement from the owner of the house, who apparently had done the shooting.

It seems that the deceased, a friend of the homeowner, Robert Turner, had come to the house earlier that night to drink and play cards. The typical scenario had followed: Drinking had led to intoxication, and card-playing had led to an argument. It was a volatile combination.

According to Turner, he had grabbed his shotgun and ordered his friend out of the house. A struggle ensued, "the gun just went off," and before he knew what was happening his friend was bleeding to death. Mortally wounded, the deceased managed to drag himself outside to his car, where with his last breath he begged God not to let him die and then slumped over the steering wheel.

Forensics later confirmed that the deceased's fingerprints were found on the end of the barrel. Yet that simply compounded the conflicting evidence. *Why* were his fingerprints on the barrel? Had he grabbed the gun to take it away from Turner and use it against him? Or had he simply been trying to push the gun away from a homicide-intent drunken friend? My best guess was that it was a case of accidental death—that when the deceased grabbed the gun to pull it away from his friend, he had caused the trigger to be pulled in the opposite direction, resulting in the blast which hit him in the stomach. But it was only a guess. Because the physical evidence could have pointed either way, I thought the case was a loser and suggested as much to my successor. For reasons of his own, he decided to charge Turner with murder. The jury returned a verdict of Not Guilty.

Evidence is a funny thing. We tend to assume that it is always objective and trustworthy. But one thing I have learned as a trial attorney is that "obvious evidence" can fool you. It often changes in light of the theory or perspective with which you approach it. For example, two completely honest witnesses can see the same accident—one witness testifying that the light in the intersection was red, the other that it was green—and both be right, at least at the time they saw it and from the different positions where they were standing.

My experience with "shifting evidence" leaves me with less confidence than I would like when I approach certain passages in the Bible. What seems so clear to many people is less clear to me, and, I'm sure, vice versa. My understanding of the Genesis account, with which one certainly may disagree, is an attempt to bring a fresh biblical perspective to significant events in the garden.

Confusion at the Crime Scene

Genesis chapter 3 and its account of Adam and Eve's encounter with the serpent's temptation is one of those difficult passages. Everyone seems to be so sure what the story is telling us about the spiritual roles of men and women. But I wonder . . . and all the more so when I see advocates on *both* sides using the same story in support of vehemently contradictory positions!

My respect for the ambiguity of the passage begins with the serpent's talking to Eve. Let's face it—apart from temptation itself, we are not dealing here with the normal, fairly predictable circumstances with which we are all familiar! Furthermore, I suspect that we don't know all we would like to know about the devil or Satan, whom we assume to be speaking through the serpent, and certainly very little about how serpents and human beings could talk with each other. But there we have it, in black and white:

> Now the serpent was more crafty than any of the wild animals the Lord God had made. He said to the woman, "Did God really say, 'You must not eat from any tree in the garden'?"
>
> The woman said to the serpent, "We may eat fruit from the trees in the garden, but God did say, 'You must not eat fruit from the tree that is in the middle of the garden, and you must not touch it, or you will die.'"
>
> "You will not surely die," the serpent said to the woman. "For God knows that when you eat of it your eyes will be opened, and you will be like God, knowing good and evil."
>
> When the woman saw that the fruit of the tree was good for food and pleasing to the eye, and also desirable for gaining wisdom, she took some and ate it. She also gave some to her husband, who was with her, and he ate it (Genesis 3:1-6).

Let me see if I have this straight. Somehow the serpent is aware of God's command to Adam and Eve that, at the risk of death, they are not to eat fruit from the tree of the knowledge of good and evil. So he comes up to Eve and matter-of-factly engages her in conversation about that fruit. Lying to her outright, the serpent tells Eve that she should not worry about God's command, that in fact she will *not* die if she eats the forbidden fruit. But Adam was there *with* Eve when this conversation took place (Genesis 3:6). So why did the serpent choose to talk to Eve first? What is God telling us in this story?

If you listen to those who reject a wider role for women in the church, you are likely to hear some of them say that Satan knew that Eve was more vulnerable to sin than Adam, that she was not only a seducer of her husband, but also more easily seduced into sin herself. She was the "weaker vessel." But in light of the ease with which Adam also was induced to sin, and with the record of centuries of sin and wicked seduction on the part of men seen throughout the Bible, it is hard to say that the female prototype, Eve, had any edge on the male prototype, Adam, in the categories of either moral weakness or inherent seductive abilities.

Yet there must be something unique about the nature of Eve's sin that it should be given so much dishonorable press in the Genesis account. Centuries later, one of the apostle Paul's divinely inspired letters would refer back to this scene as scriptural justification for excluding any authoritative role for women in the church. 'Adam was not the one deceived," he wrote; "it was the woman who was deceived and became a sinner" (1 Timothy 2:14).

Deception. Is that the key to Eve's sin? Clearly she *was* deceived. She readily bought Satan's lies! But when put that way it looks as if she did it with callous defiance of God's command—as if she were just waiting for an excuse to do what she had wanted to do all along. Yet notice the detail with which we are told of Eve's deception. She did what most of us do all the time: She looked at the fruit and it seemed okay to eat, she was impressed with how it looked aesthetically,

and she felt that it would be a good thing to have the wisdom
it could bring.

"How could something with all that going for it possibly not
be God's will?" she probably asked herself.

If there is any clue as to how men and women might differ
in their approach to temptation, it might be found in Eve's
openness and trust. Why should she have believed the serpent? He was "more crafty than any of the wild animals." It is
possible, of course, that what we have here is nothing more
than distrust of God and intentional disobedience. That is how
most of us sin every day. Yet Eve may have *wanted* to believe
the serpent—not his *message*, which, had she thought about
it, was directly contradictory to God's, but the serpent *himself.*

Eve may have overlooked the obvious command of God
because, being guileless herself, she couldn't imagine someone else having guile. Pure herself, she did not fully appreciate the serpent's capacity for craftiness. And her every instinct
seemed to confirm his message. It *looked* right, it *felt* right.
Having spiritual wisdom seemed to align with her own sense
of spirituality. So through sincere openness and innocent trust,
she suddenly finds herself in sin—*deceived.*

Who is to say that Adam might not have reacted the same
way? Men too are often easily deceived. So we may not have
reached the bottom line regarding men and women and the
threat of temptation. But it appears that God is telling us *something* significant when, by contrast with the details of Eve's
sin, God simply and abruptly notes that "she also gave some
to her husband, who was with her, and he ate it."

If you listen to some people who would promote a wider
role for women in the church, you would hear them suggest
that, in her sin, at least Eve acted intelligently and decisively,
whereas by contrast Adam just took the fruit and crammed it
down his throat! As if to say the woman's sin somehow comes
off looking better than the man's! (As if to suggest that woman
is more capable of making bad moral choices?) Why is it then

that we punish more severely murder which has been pre-meditated and deliberate than murder which results from callous neglect of life-threatening risks? Does well-thought-out sin really speak better of a sinner than thoughtless sin done in haste?

On the other hand, if you listen to some of those who would *reject* a wider role for women in the church, you are likely to hear that Adam's sin was in following the lead of a woman—no more, no less. After all, what other reason would Paul have for using this passage to support his teaching that women are not to take the lead in spiritual matters? By their reasoning, women obviously are not trustworthy leaders!

But if that were the correct analysis of the evidence, neither would women be trustworthy mothers, whose more important role as childbearers surely is not in making babies but, together with fathers, in making sure those babies come to know God. Women are the first and arguably the most influential leaders of little boys on their way to becoming men!

At this point I am back to speculating as to who shot whom and why. With so little hard evidence, one can only hypothesize regarding all the implications that might have been intended. But there are two obscure clues which are often overlooked in this most famous of all cases.

The first clue is that God never told Eve directly not to eat of the forbidden fruit. At least there is no record of it. It was *Adam* whom God had told about the prohibition even before Eve was created. We may fairly assume, therefore, that Adam had passed on to Eve the commandment regarding the fruit.

When Eve gave the fruit to Adam, it was not as if Adam were less aware of God's prohibition than was Eve. In fact, Adam would have been even *more* aware of it than Eve. If we may draw from Adam's status as "firstcreated," that is exactly the point: Adam bore the responsibility for *two* sins—his sin in eating the fruit and his sin in failing to exercise spiritual headship. Certainly Eve was also responsible for her own sin, as the text will soon tell us. But it appears that Adam's sin of disobedience may have been compounded by his failure to exercise a separate responsibility for protecting Eve from spiritual danger. Protection, after all, is the duty owed by the firstborn to those over whom he has headship.

Adam was neither stronger nor weaker than Eve in the moral-decision department. That is evident from the fact that *both* of them sinned. Nevertheless, as "firstcreated," Adam was the *designated spiritual protector* of his family. Dictator? No, *protector.* Autocrat? No, *protector.* He was to be the spiritual protector just as man has always been a physical protector of the woman against physical threat. And had Adam faithfully exercised his role as protector, neither he nor Eve would have succumbed to the serpent's temptation.

This brings us to the second clue, which is found in Romans chapter 5. There, in verse 12, Paul wrote that "sin entered the world through one man," whom he later identified as Adam. But was not Eve the first to sin and therefore the one through whom sin entered the world? It would be easy to reconcile the apparent gaffe by citing the necessary parallel construction of Paul's contrasting picture: Whereas by one *man* (Adam) sin entered the world, by one *man* (Jesus) came justification. Use of the word "woman" not only would have ruined the parallel structure of his argument but also potentially could have been seen as pejorative toward women—as if sin predictably came because of a woman and salvation thankfully came by a man.

Conceivably, any desire for parallel construction could have been satisfied by referring to a genderless "humankind" or "mankind." Paul also might have referred to "Adam and Eve" together or "the couple" through whom sin entered the world. There is more than one way to preserve parallel thoughts. One should not read too much into the structure of this passage one way or the other, but my guess is that Paul was not overlooking the fact that Eve was the first to eat the forbidden fruit. I also suspect that his parallel use of the word "man" was more than coincidental. I suspect that Paul was pointing to yet another clue in this difficult case: If Adam had properly exercised his role as spiritual protector, sin may *not* have entered the world, either through himself or through Eve. At least the chances of Eve's sinning on her own would have been diminished.

The "obvious" evidence may have misled us once again. The first sin may not have been Eve's when she took the fruit and ate it. In priority of time, the first sin actually may have been *Adam's* sin in failing to exercise his responsibility as a spiritual protector.

It was the same sin which Abraham committed on two separate occasions (Genesis 12 and 20), when he not only lied about Sarah being his wife but told *her* to lie as well. (Imagine his saying to Sarah, "This is how you can show your love to me: Everywhere we go, say of me, 'He is my brother'"!) Sarah's lies would have been preceded by Abraham's abdication of spiritual responsibility. For fear of his own personal safety, Abraham had willingly put Sarah in jeopardy both physically and spiritually. In so doing, Abraham had failed miserably in his role as designated protector of the family.

This was also the sin of Ananias, that first-century Christian who, instead of supplying moral strength and direction to his wife, Sapphira, conspired with her to lie about the gift they were giving to the apostles (Acts 5:1-11). It hardly matters which of them conceived the plan. It is important to note here that, despite Ananias' failure to be a proper spiritual leader in his family, Sapphira herself bore the fatal consequences of her personal sin.

The man's designated role as spiritual protector does not eliminate personal responsibility on the part of the woman. As with the spiritual leaders of Israel (Ezekiel 33:7-9), it is man's responsibility to watch and to warn, but neither to dictate moral choice nor to shield the woman from the consequences of any wrong choices she might make.

Under Closer Light

The evidence in this case, though persuasive, is far from convincing beyond doubt. Therefore we must proceed cautiously. However, there appears to be further confirmation of these initial conclusions when God sits Adam and Eve across from himself in the interrogation room and asks them what their story is. You can bet that no criminal defendants were ever more nervous than Adam and Eve at that point.

> "Have you eaten from the tree that I commanded you not to eat from?"
> The man said, "The woman you put here with me— she gave me some fruit from the tree, and I ate it."
> Then the Lord God said to the woman, "What is this you have done?"
> The woman said, "The serpent deceived me, and I ate"
> (Genesis 3:11-13).

Of course finger-pointing is a classic defense tactic, and both Adam and Eve did their best to focus the spotlight of suspicion elsewhere. I keep hearing from some quarters that Adam's cop-out was despicable weaseling while, by contrast, Eve demonstrated greater moral courage by standing up and readily confessing her guilt. Of course that interpretation overlooks the fact that Eve too acknowledged only indirect responsibility. Her reference to the serpent mimics the classic reaction among accused co-conspirators, where A points to B, who quickly points to C.

But I have to agree about Adam's weaseling. It *was* despicable. Whatever happened to his excited "This is bone of my bone and flesh of my flesh"? Now the story is, "I never asked for her in the first place"!

It is not particularly odd that Adam would have tried to divert guilt from himself. Sin invariably attempts to spread the blame. What is significant about Adam's copout is that he pointed to Eve rather than to the serpent, as he might have done. That thought is especially worth remembering, because we are soon to see how God specifically reacts to Adam's attempt to further abdicate his responsibility toward Eve as her spiritual protector.

The most disturbing aspect of Adam's defense is the potential blame he directed toward *God!* If only we could have heard the inflection in his voice. It would have been bad enough for him to say, "The *woman* you put here with me" is the reason I sinned. But imagine God's reaction if what Adam actually said was, "The woman *you* put here with me" is the reason I sinned! Regardless of his inflection, Adam seems to be implicating God, whether directly or indirectly. Eve may have said, "The devil made me do it," but Adam was at least inferring, "*God* made me do it." Dangerous ground indeed!

When we think of man's natural role in the protection of the woman from physical harm, we are likely to focus on his superior physical strength as the reason he finds himself with that responsibility. By contrast, Adam's weak, sniveling, and potentially blasphemous response is further evidence that his designated role as spiritual protector is not based upon any inherently superior moral strength. The truth is that we may find he has been given sentry duty on the front line to make sure that he himself stays awake in the face of the enemy.

Facing the Consequences

As a prosecutor, I always thought I had the easier job. All I had to do was prove guilt. Never would I have wanted to shoulder the judge's burden of having to determine the appropriate sentence. Would the sentence be too lenient and make a mockery of the justice system? Would it be too harsh and break the spirit of a valuable human being? Would it have any possibility for rehabilitation, or would it only serve to warehouse someone we didn't know what else to do with? How could you ever be sure that the punishment fit the crime? What, for example, would have been the appropriate punishment for the man who shot his friend with the shotgun? I doubt that we all could readily agree.

In the case of Adam and Eve, as well as the serpent, we have a rather unusual Judge sitting on the bench. His judgment is always just, and the punishment he imposes always fits the crime. A look at the court reporter's transcript of the sentencing reveals some very interesting judgments. First, in the case of Serpent Doe:

> So the Lord God said to the serpent, "Because you
> have done this,
>
>> "Cursed are you above all the livestock and all
>>   the wild animals!
>>
>> You will crawl on your belly
>>   and you will eat dust
>>   all the days of your life.
>>
>> And I will put enmity
>>   between you and the woman,
>>   and between your offspring
>>   and hers;
>>
>> he will crush your head,
>>   and you will strike his heel"
>> (Genesis 3:14, 15).

What are we to make of this? Are we to understand that the serpent walked on two or more feet while talking with Adam and Eve? And was the serpent literally the early progenitor of the modern-day snake? Are we to take it that if Satan hadn't used the serpent as his instrument of enticement the serpent would never have crawled around on the ground—that in fact we might have been free of snakes altogether?

All of this is interesting curiosity, but the key to our concern is what God meant when he spoke of putting enmity between the serpent and the woman, and between his offspring and hers. Surely we are no longer talking about snakes here, but Satan himself. Virtually all Christians agree that in this passage is the first reference to the coming of the Messiah. Jesus the Christ, born of a woman, would bring reconciliation between God and Man, and would eventually overthrow Satan's power which he uses to alienate Man from God.

It is a picture of spiritual warfare that would be waged because of what Satan had done in destroying the harmony of the garden. But in what way was that warfare related to "the woman" as opposed to "man and woman"? Is there a reference here simply to Eve, who had allowed herself to be deceived? Certainly Eve would no longer have any goodwill toward the serpent!

Is this instead a reference to Mary, who would bear the incarnate Messiah? Mary is clearly the offspring of Eve through whom the Deliverer would come to crush the serpent's head. Furthermore, if a singular use of the word "offspring" (meaning "seed") is intended, there would be some support for strictly limiting application of the passage to Mary and her son Jesus. Speaking of the promises given to Abraham, for example, Paul wrote: "The Scripture does not say 'and to seeds,' meaning many people, but 'and to your seed,' meaning one person, who is Christ" (Galatians 3:16).

Nevertheless there seems to be some support for the proposition that the word "offspring" is used in the plural. If that is the case, God may also be telling Satan that the human race would not always be such pushovers—that, taking a cue from Adam and Eve, they would be more suspicious of Satan's ploys. Even if he managed to be successful with most people, Satan would not be entirely successful with all. This might further suggest a reference to a more limited number of Eve's "offspring" and some special role they would play in the battle against Satan.

Might we who are believers be Eve's offspring in this sense? We know, for example, that our faith has made us the offspring of Abraham. "Consider Abraham," Paul told the Galatians:" 'He believed God, and it was credited to him as righteousness.' Understand, then, that those who believe are children of Abraham" (Galatians 3:6, 7). In the same letter Paul changes the picture to a comparison between Hagar, the slave woman, and Sarah, her mistress—the former having given birth in the ordinary way, the latter having given birth by the power of the Spirit. "Therefore, brothers," Paul concludes, "we are not children of the slave woman, but of the free woman" (Galatians 4:31).

We believers, then, trace our faith back to Abraham and Sarah, and even farther back to Eve, the mother of all the living. If there is meant to be any play on the word "living," an interesting symbolism appears: In contrast to Adam, whose failure to exercise his responsibility as Eve's spiritual protector brought both physical and spiritual *death* into the world, even in her name Eve is greatly honored as being the mother of all those who have found spiritual *life* through their faith.

The battle between spiritual life and death is the enmity which has come between Satan and those who believe. Through the one seed, Christ, the many offspring in faith join in the chorus of the faithful through the ages. They sing the often-overlooked verse of Charles Wesley's famous carol "Hark the Herald Angels Sing":

> Rise, thou woman's conquering seed,
> Bruise in us the serpent's head!

Adam and Eve, sinners though they were, should not suffer the cruel and unusual punishment of unmitigated villainy. If the wicked can trace their origins to that first couple, so can the righteous. Satan alone was sentenced to eat dust!

Same Evidence, Different Conclusions

Many years ago I left the practice of law in order to teach law. One of my favorite courses is Trial Advocacy, in which the students perform mock trials while I sit on the bench acting as the judge. Over the years I have been amazed at how the same cases can be presented in such radically different ways, with creative arguments surfacing on each side. The evidence is always the same, but the strategy and the issues which are emphasized are wildly different!

When it comes to the "sentencing" of Adam and Eve, I am equally amazed at how so many novel conclusions can be drawn from the same evidence. Here is the record of what transpired:

To the woman he said,

"I will greatly increase your pains
in childbearing;
with pain you will give birth
to children.

Your desire will be
for your husband,
and he will rule over you."

To Adam he said, "Because you listened to your wife and ate from the tree about which I commanded you, 'You must not eat of it,'

"Cursed is the ground
because of you;
through painful toil you will
eat of it all the days of
your life.

It will produce thorns and
> thistles for you,
> and you will eat the plants of
> the field.

By the sweat of your brow
> you will eat your food
until you return to the ground,
> since from it you were taken;
for dust you are
> and to dust you will return"
> (Genesis 3:16-19).

Right away there are those who would question my use of the word "sentencing," urging that God here is not a judge dispensing punishment for sin, but a prophet *predicting* what would happen in a fallen world. In other words, it was not God's will that the husband would rule over the wife. Far from being a divine ordinance, male headship would be the result of man's own sinful actions. Therefore woman's submission is not a God-imposed *consequence* of sin, but a human-imposed *manifestation* of sin.

The problem with this interpretation is that when we look at what God said to Adam about *death*, we remember that the consequence of death had been promised to Adam from the very beginning as a God-imposed penalty for eating of the forbidden fruit: "You must not eat from the tree of the knowledge of good and evil, for when you eat of it you will surely die" (Genesis 2:17). For Adam, death was not something that God merely *predicted* would happen in the ordinary course of human events as a result of the Fall; death was a God-imposed *consequence* of Adam's sin.

Although Adam's *physical* death-sentence would be suspended for the 930 years that Adam was on the earth, ultimately his *spiritual* death would be nothing less than the imposition of capital punishment. Nor did Eve escape the ultimate punishment of death. Even though her "sentencing" does not specifically include a reference to death, she too had eaten of the forbidden fruit, well aware that God had set a death penalty for violation of his command. The sobering fact is that, by following in the rebellious footsteps of Adam and Eve, we find ourselves facing the same death penalty!

When we look at what God said to the serpent about crawling on his belly, and about enmity coming between the serpent and the offspring of the woman, it was also more than a prediction. "I, *God*, will put the enmity between the two of you," he was saying. It won't happen by chance or by the actions of fallen mankind.

Even when we look at what God said to Eve about the pain of childbirth, this surely must have been more than a mere prediction. If God himself had not determined the consequence, what force *resulting from the Fall* would have increased the pain?

Therefore when we look at what God said to Eve about her desire being for her husband, and about her husband's rule over her, it hardly makes sense that these two statements alone should be taken as mere *predictions*, while each of the other statements unquestionably referred to God-imposed, God-willed *consequences* of sin. It is one thing to question the meaning of "desire" and "rule"; it is another thing altogether to dismiss their significance by selectively changing the nature of God's words in order to bolster a weak case.

Acknowledging that the Fall brought about radical changes even in our own lives, we must ask what *natural* result of the Fall would necessarily dictate that the serpent become a snake. Likewise, what *natural* force would have brought about the woman's "desire for her husband"? We might predict that men would use their physical superiority to impose masculine rule over women, but why would a woman herself want her husband to rule over her?

God's "sentencing" of Adam and Eve was not merely pre-
dictive: It was punishment; it was penal. To say that the rule
of man over woman represented a *perversion* of human conduct rather than God's perfect will comes closer to the truth,
but is still misleading. If Adam and Eve had not sinned, they
would have continued to live in the garden without the *sweat*
of labor, the great *pain* of childbirth, or the fearful prospect of
death. And Adam's role as spiritual leader would have been a
lasting precedent for *servant* leadership.

Like Adam and Eve, we share in the consequence of death
because of sins which we ourselves commit. We also share in
the consequences of toiling for our sustenance, experiencing
pain in childbirth, and serving God through specified gender
roles. God permits us to prolong life through medical science,
to make our workday easier by use of computers, and to use
anesthetics to ease the pain of birth, but he has never altogether eliminated any of those consequences. While we may
ameliorate harshly imposed male domination, it is yet to be
seen whether gender roles are interchangeable.

Above all, if God had *disapproved* of the man's spiritual
headship as being merely a perverted result of the Fall, it
would have been unthinkable for God thereafter to have instituted a male-oriented society and religious system for both the
patriarchs and the nation of Israel.

Same Text, Different Interpretations

That fact alone makes me skeptical of supposedly superior
Hebrew translations of the traditional reading of God's statement to Eve. For example, "I will greatly multiply your pain in
childbearing" is said by Hebrew scholar Katherine Bushnell
(*God's Word to Women*) to be more correctly translated: "A
snare has increased your sorrow and your sighing." Her interpretation of that translation is that Satan's lying in wait to
deceive Eve resulted in Eve's oppression from both Satan and

the man who would "rule over her." Therefore, Bushnell contends, there was no curse at all against Eve.

I will let the Hebrew scholars decide about such a radical departure from the widely accepted traditional reading. It is always possible, I suppose, that male-dominated translating committees have perpetrated a skewed picture of what God actually said. My greater concern is whether we are to believe that two out of the three co-conspirators received punishment, but that the third, Eve, got off scot-free! No curse, no rebuke, no adverse consequences—just a sympathy card and a reassuring hug! The fact that Eve had to leave the garden along with Adam is by itself insignificant compared with Adam's sentencing.

Another concern is the implication that Eve had been just a helpless victim when she was deceived, so that in fact she bore no personal responsibility for her sin. It is ironic that such an interpretation of the evidence actually makes Eve out to be a weak, gullible, mindless individual. It would not change in the least whatever it was that God actually said to Eve, but I personally would hope for a translation that attributes to Eve the dignity of having made an intelligent decision, even if it was the wrong decision.

In the opposite camp, some conservative Hebrew scholars are suggesting that in order to properly understand the statement "Your desire shall be to your husband," we must fill in a less-than-obvious blank with words that they are willing to supply. The new version would read: "Your desire shall be to *control, manipulate,* and *possess* your husband." The interpretation is that this new urge which God gave woman actually instituted class warfare and began a struggle for the supremacy of wills which led ultimately to male domination, exploitation, and suppression of women—a problem to be solved only through Christ.

I am not a Hebrew scholar, but again I wonder if this novel interpretation really intends to accuse God of having instigated class warfare and with being responsible for centuries of abuse in the name of male leadership. Are we really to believe that a new desire in woman to control her man was God-imposed in order to draw man's irate reaction as a penalty against woman's insubordination? This seems to be a fairly outrageous attempt to rid men of guilt for the all-too-common abuse of their spiritual headship: "After all, women asked for it!"

No, man's now-formalized headship did not result from a conspiracy between man and the devil to dominate and oppress the woman. Nor did it result from some scheme of God to ensure that Eve got what was coming to her. Closer to the idea is Irving A. Busenitz' suggested translation: ". . . you will still desire [as you did before the Fall, though now tainted by sin] your husband, and he will still rule [as he did before the Fall, though now tainted by sin] over you." (Grace Theological Journal 7.2, p. 212.)

Before the Fall, Adam had already been cast in the role of Eve's spiritual leader. Male spiritual leadership was God's intention from the very beginning. But in the wake of the Fall, God's insistence on male spiritual leadership was reiterated with a renewed *emphasis*, about which there could be no ambiguity whatsoever. This formalization of the pre-Fall principle was apparently designed to help prevent in the future the very situation which had led to the Fall—namely, Adam's failure to be strong in the face of spiritual danger to his wife.

We are told in the New Testament that the laws of Moses were "added because of transgressions" (Galatians 3:19). They were intended to keep the people of Israel from self-destructing after their unfaithfulness to the covenant God had made with Abraham. Similarly, we may surmise that the formal recognition of male headship was added "because of transgression" in the garden, when Adam was unfaithful as Eve's protector.

Emerging Patterns

Discovering a pattern of repetition is often helpful in interpreting evidence. For example, if a known suspect had been observed alone at the scene of the crime at the same time each week for six weeks, by factual inference he was probably the same man who was observed there at that same time the seventh week as well. When we look closely at God's statements to our three co-conspirators, we see some definite patterns emerging.

First, in each case there is both a *physical consequence* and a *spiritual consequence*. Physically, the serpent would become a crawling creature, Eve would experience great pain in childbearing, and Adam would have to earn his living by the sweat of his brow. Spiritually, the serpent would be crushed by the woman's offspring, Eve would be subordinated to her husband's headship, and Adam (together with Eve) would forfeit his right to life.

Second, in each case there seems to be a *natural connection* between the physical consequence and the spiritual consequence. With the serpent, his relegation to crawling along the ground put him in just the right position so that the woman's offspring could crush his head and the serpent in turn could strike his heel. With Eve, the tie is between woman's two respective roles as wife (husband's rule) and mother (pain in childbearing). With Adam, he would have to exert toil and effort to work the ground, which itself had been cursed because of him, and then upon death return to that very ground!

Third, in each case the curse relates to what appears to be the *dominant role played by that individual.* The serpent is cast as the great tempter and antagonist, Eve as the prototype wife and mother, and Adam as the prototype "breadwinning" husband and father.

Finally, in two out of the three cases the punishment is presented as *fitting the crime.* The serpent is punished as a tempter "because you have done this" (Genesis 3:14). Done what? In the immediately preceding sentence Eve had told God that the serpent had deceived her. So it was his *deception* that brought him punishment in the role of tempter.

What was the reason for Adam's punishment? "Because you listened to your wife and ate from the tree . . ." (Genesis 3:17). Since eating from the tree would itself have been sufficient to warrant the death penalty, the part about listening to his wife takes on added significance. Had God told Adam *not* to listen to Eve? Was there something wrong in a man listening to his wife?

The point is that Adam had followed Eve in her sin when instead he should have taken the initiative to act as her spiritual protector. At a critical time in the life of his family, Adam was listening rather than speaking the caution he should have given Eve. His punishment of *physical* death therefore fit perfectly his crime of permitting *spiritual* death to enter into their lives.

It is here, with Eve, that the pattern fails to play itself out, at least explicitly. But the consistency of the pattern up to this point makes the appropriate implication all too clear. As with the serpent and Adam, the nature of the punishment points to the nature of the crime. However, I wish it were without further complication. Unfortunately I am aware that others have made a similar deduction and decided that Eve's crime was in enticing her husband to eat the forbidden fruit, and that therefore her husband was to be put into a position as warden over her imprisonment in subordinate confinement!

The first problem with such an analysis is that there is no evidence that Eve *enticed* Adam. Adam apparently was present when the serpent was talking to Eve ("She also gave some to her husband, *who was with her* . . ."). He heard all the same lies that Eve heard. The only difference was that Eve ate the fruit first and then passed it on to Adam with a favorable recommendation, as it were. So the idea of making the husband a thumbscrew to keep an enticing and seductive wife under control simply does not fit the facts. It also puts a misleading, dangerous, and unnecessary connotation on the word "rule."

If man is meant to be elevated in a particular responsibility, woman is not meant to be beneath him; if man is meant to be the leader, woman is not meant to be behind. Man's position is not to be an *elevated* position of power and ego, but rather a *celebrated* position of union with one's very self. Two "better-halfs" make one "better-whole."

But there appears to be a definite connection between the husband's "rule" and the woman's sin, and the connecting idea is *headship—spiritual* headship, and in particular *conscientious* spiritual headship. "Rule" in Scripture essentially means to be *responsible* for, to be a *servant* to the person being "ruled."

Even before the Fall, as the "firstcreated" person Adam had been given the responsibility of being Eve's spiritual protector. And he would continue to be this, but the picture now focuses on a more structured headship, perhaps owing to the fact that the informal designation had proved to be an inadequate safeguard. In exploring roles and relationships reflected in this first couple we can only read between the lines of an all-too-brief Creation account. But it appears that Eve had not looked consciously to her husband for spiritual leadership, and Adam had too easily overlooked the importance of his protective role.

In situations of shared power, there can be balance, cooperation, and mutual consideration. Yet political scientists would recognize in a union of shared power the principle that interdependence erodes the autonomous governments' ability to act independently. The rest of us are more likely to recognize the fact that doubles tennis gives you twice the number of players per side, but also opens up the possibility of letting the ball whiz through the center of the court while the partners give those classic I-thought-*you*-were-going-to-get-it looks at each other. Recognized roles always put the ball of responsibility in the right court.

Therefore it makes sense that God would set into place specific, normative, easily identifiable roles for the marriage relationship. Each party can know in advance what to expect from the other. The husband's spiritual headship, exercised properly, will ensure greater protection for the wife, and her desire to seek his spiritual guidance, exercised willingly, will bond the two together in a symbiotic spiritual partnership stronger than the sum of their individual parts.

On the Brink of Repeating History

Like Adam and Eve, we too seem to be headed for unexpected disappointment, ironically for some of the same reasons. There are many people today telling us that God's commands regarding the roles of men and women in the home (and, by extension, in the church) are not set in divine concrete, as Christians have believed for centuries. And because most of these people are apparently sincere, committed Christians, doing good work in the kingdom, we *want* to believe them. Why should we think they are not telling us the truth?

So we look at the call for a significant change in roles for women in the church, and it looks right. It seems consistent with the unity we have in Christ. It reflects our growing concern for human rights and the important movements toward equality in our society. It recognizes the talents of Christian women and provides new opportunities for those talents to be utilized.

Like Eve, who assumed that gaining wisdom would be desirable, we think to ourselves how desirable it would be to tap the rich spiritual resources and insight of godly Christian women. An expanded role for women in the church looks so good, feels so right, and sounds so spiritually true, so how in the world could it ever be contrary to God's will?

But God had indeed said, "You shall not eat of the fruit." And God through Paul has also said, "A woman should learn in quietness and full submission. I do not permit a woman to teach or to have authority over a man; she must be silent" (1 Timothy 2:11, 12). Eve, for all her good intentions and comfortable feelings, ignored what God had plainly commanded her. Are we, with good intentions and comfortable feelings, tempted to ignore what God has commanded of us?

And if we do ignore what God has told us, who will bear the greater responsibility? Is it not those who are in positions of spiritual leadership over God's spiritual family, the church? Like Adam, they are our spiritual protectors. Their headship is not the authoritarian rule designed to maintain unbiblical traditions or to preserve their own power base, but the heavy burden of responsibility for leading us toward God's will—for reminding us of what God has told us, for warning us about the dangers of being enticed by what seems right in our own eyes, for telling us over and over the story of Adam and Eve—and the wily serpent who tempts us with seductive distortions of what is good for us.

As we contemplate changing roles and experience the influence of a growing cultural shift, are we headed toward the restored unity and harmony of the garden before the Fall, or in these changing times are we on our way to a cotton patch of pain, trouble, and unfulfilled expectations?

Study Questions

1. Is there any sense in which woman is a "weaker vessel" than man? If so, might her "weakness" also be a strength?

2. In what way was Eve deceived by the serpent? Is it possible that we today might be deceived about the very subject addressed in this book?

3. What, if any, significance should we attribute to the fact that Adam apparently was with Eve when she was talking to the serpent?

4. Who do you think committed the first sin: Adam or Eve? What was that first sin?

5. In what different ways is man to be a protector for woman?

6. Does man's responsibility as a protector relieve woman of her own spiritual responsibility before God?

7. What do you think God meant when he said to the serpent, "I will put enmity between you and the woman, and between your offspring and hers; he will crush your head, and you will strike his heel?" Did it have anything to do with the current question of gender roles?

8. Is there any message for women today in the twofold penalty given to Eve: 1) "With pain you will give birth to children; 2) "Your desire will be for your husband and he will rule over you?'

9. Is there any message for men today in the twofold penalty given to Adam: 1) "By the sweat of your brow you will eat your food; and 2) "for dust you are and to dust you will return?"

10. What significance is there in the fact that male spiritual leadership was set in place *prior* to the Fall?

3 *According to the Pattern*

Male Spiritual Leadership in the Old Testament

Before we go one step farther away from the Garden of Eden to explore what the Scriptures have to say about men and women beyond that point, we need to pause briefly to consider why it is that we are turning to the Scriptures in the first place. How important *are* the Scriptures? Are we giving them too much emphasis? Are the Scriptures themselves the product of male bias? Were they the product of custom or influenced by the cultural context in which they were written? There is no use appealing to the Scriptures unless we first decide that they constitute our ultimate authority in deciding the issues with which we are confronted.

I wish you could have known my dad. He was a preacher of the old school. Without formal education beyond the eleventh grade, he knew the Book backward and forward— much of it by memory, all of it by heart. More important, he knew the God of the Book.

In the pulpit Dad was not exactly a fire-and-brimstone preacher, but he was not above pounding the pulpit or thumping his Bible to make a point. Some of my earliest memories of Dad were at outdoor "Gospel Meetings," as they used to be called. It would be a hot Texas or Oklahoma night, and

Dad would be in shirtsleeves, sporting one of those superwide ties of the forties and fifties. The bare light bulbs strung from precarious poles around the makeshift podium were like blinking neon signs inviting wayward winged creatures, which would drone around Dad's bald head as he worked his way through a simple but earnestly presented lesson.

We children would squirm on the rickety wooden folding chairs, while Mother would fan us with those advertisement-laden cardboard fans provided by the local funeral home. Looking at their colorful paintings of Bible characters and scenes helped to pass some of the time before we would take a nap or scribble on scraps of paper from Mother's purse. It was better to keep busy and quiet than risk being whisked out to the shadows for a switching.

Who knows how old I was when Dad's sermons started sinking into my young mind? My earliest recollections seem to be of Old Testament texts which told about the ancient heroes of faith—Moses and Elijah, David and Daniel. Dad had a gift for making biblical characters come alive, as if he knew each one of them intimately. It fit Dad's personality. He loved people—old codgers, babies, city slickers, country folk. For him the Gospel was *for* people and *about* people.

If there was any one word that stood out in my dad's preaching it was the word "pattern." He was deeply committed to the belief that the Bible was a *pattern*, not just a collection of stories and wise sayings. I remember well one particular sermon in which Dad focused on a passage in Exodus where God was telling Moses precisely how he wanted the tabernacle built. Amid the many detailed instructions, God cautioned Moses: "Make this tabernacle and all its furnishings exactly like the pattern I will show you" (Exodus 25:9). Dad would then read some of the specific instructions, carefully noting each detail.

"See that you build according to the pattern," Dad would emphasize once again. No detail was too insignificant for God.

Everything had a purpose. If God said it, it was our job to do it—exactly according to the pattern!

To bring the pattern principle into New Testament credibility, Dad would then turn over to Hebrews chapter 8, where the writer speaks of Christ serving in the heavenly sanctuary, "the true tabernacle set up by the Lord, not by man" (Hebrews 8:1, 2). Comparing our high priest, Christ, with the high priests of Israel, the writer continues: "They serve at a sanctuary that is a copy and shadow of what is in heaven. This is why Moses was warned when he was about to build the tabernacle: 'See to it that you make everything according to the pattern shown you on the mountain'" (Hebrews 8:5).

Divine pattern! The message of the sermon was that doing God's work in God's way was the only safe way to proceed. How else are we to have any assurance that we are on the right track, that we are really doing God's will?

The apostle Paul had used the same word—*pattern*—in writing to Timothy: "What you heard from me, keep as the pattern of sound teaching, with faith and love in Christ Jesus" (2 Timothy 1:13). The pattern principle dovetailed nicely with Paul's observation just a few paragraphs later that "all Scripture is God-breathed and is useful for teaching, rebuking, correcting and training in righteousness, so that the man of God may be thoroughly equipped for every good work" (2 Timothy 3:16, 17).

When I was no longer the little boy who used to squirm in his seat while his dad proclaimed the virtues of following biblical patterns, I studied the Scriptures for myself. And when I did, I did not always agree with Dad about what in fact the pattern was in every case. But I came to treasure his dogged determination to stick to the pattern as he saw it to be. I had no doubt that the pattern principle itself was valid.

I must admit that from time to time I have been more skeptical about "pattern theology" because too often I have seen it being given lip service along the road to justifying this or that human tradition. However, more and more I keep seeing that departures from obvious biblical patterns have led to trouble both for the church and for society.

Whether it be radical changes in morality (such as the sexual revolution of the sixties and seventies), or open acceptance of homosexuality, or laxness in divorce and remarriage, we have had nothing but suffering. Broken marriages, psychological counseling, and AIDS are stark testimony to the whirlwinds we have reaped in abandoning clear biblical patterns for righteous conduct.

Even in matters pertaining to the church, too often we have left the pattern and suffered the consequences. Local congregational autonomy has given way to hierarchical, institutionalized church government which has suffocated spiritual life at the local level. We have substituted for the church a multitude of parachurch ministries, many of which have become an embarrassment to the entire Christian community and to the cause of Christ. We have abandoned the pattern of Christian conversion and found ourselves in a world of nominal Christianity where "Christians" are baptized but unconverted.

Biblical patterns matter because they are *God's* patterns. Why would God have revealed himself to us in historical context except to set forth the way that works—the way his *church* best functions, the way *we* best function? As our Creator, surely he must know!

I prefer to think of Dad's *pattern* as the manufacturer's operating instructions. Who better knows how frequently we ought to change the oil and lubricate the joints than the manufacturer who designed and made our car in the first place? When we fail to follow the manufacturer's instructions, we do so at the risk of unexpected trouble and exorbitant repair bills. Why should we expect any less when we choose to ignore the Creator's pattern for successful living?

Throwing Away the Pattern

Today I fear that many people in the Christian community have abandoned the pattern principle altogether. Perhaps in reaction to extreme legalism, today we are more comfortable with "the biblical story," "general Christian attitudes," "broad principles," and trying to do "the loving thing."

However, let me give you an example of how even well-intentioned Christians get into trouble by following this approach. I recently read a special issue of a local church newsletter devoted to the subject of women in ministry. The minister was writing to explain to his congregation the circumstances under which he felt it would be acceptable for women to be called to public ministry, including pulpit preaching. (A woman counselor on staff with the church had recently been invited to preach for the first time in the history of the congregation.)

I was struck by the precarious position assumed by someone who generally took rightful pride in being led by the Word. His reliance on the Word was threatened when he wrote "I want to talk, not of theological positions, but of real people who desperately desire to move in fullness of ministry."

Are we to believe that "theology" (if indeed it is God's) somehow fails to meet the needs of "real people who desperately desire to move in fullness of ministry?" And if Scripture-based theology and people's desires happen to come into conflict, which should prevail?

In the margin beside the minister's disclaimer about theology I scrawled a note saying, "Trouble ahead!" Sure enough, within a couple of paragraphs the minister wrote something that sounded great and seemed to capture the spirit of the Scriptures but ended up supporting conclusions quite contrary to specific passages. His observations turned out to be what he would *like* for God to have said on the subject, or perhaps what others would like him to say. "The key word is *release*," he wrote. "One of the functions of the pastoral office is to make possible the release of ministry." And from there he went on to justify the full inclusion of women in leadership roles within the church—including pulpit preaching—all based upon his concept of "release."

Remarkably, the idea of "release" is never associated with any of the passages relating to the function of the pastoral office, as he suggested. Nor is there any biblical basis for the minister's requirements that the decision to release ministry must be based upon the three factors of character, skills, and assignment. The minister's entire discussion was grounded upon a concept he had made up out of well-intended rationalizations.

That is the inevitable direction we head when we prematurely dismiss "theology" and proceed too quickly to what we perceive to be "bigger issues at stake." The biggest issue at stake is whether we are willing to be obedient to the Word, even when we don't fully understand its purposes or agree with its injunctions.

When a theology of headship and personhood allows for the full release of men and women to serve within biblical guidelines, then we have captured "the spirit" of what God intends. But when "release theology" conflicts with both specific prohibitions and a consistently maintained principle of male spiritual leadership, as we shall see, then it becomes *our* theology, not *God's.*

We are not dealing here with mere abstract theology. There is documented danger in replacing specific biblical guidelines with contemporary wisdom. For example, it is with the same inventive "God-speak" (in fact the very same) that others—including the Episcopal Church's first woman bishop, Barbara Harris—have justified the public ministry of practicing homosexuals in the church! The cry there too has been to *release* the oppressed into God's ministry.

If it is possible for "book, chapter, and verse" to erode into too much emphasis on a single verse taken out of context and applied capriciously (and this does sometimes happen), it is also possible for the abandonment of a "Thus says the Lord" to lead to any kind of rationalizing in which one might wish to indulge. I speak from experience, for I have done it myself with embarrassing ease.

The sad fact is that it is only because of widespread biblical illiteracy even among Christians that someone can get away with such creative and subtle amendments to the Bible. Since the people in the pew have so little personal knowledge of what the Bible says, they are reduced to blindly trusting whatever the local preacher tells them. Unfortunately, there is nothing new about this phenomenon. "My people are destroyed from lack of knowledge," said God through the prophet Hosea (Hosea 4:6).

Nor is this the first time that biblical illiteracy has been an ally of attempts to artificially bolster the role of women in the church. The deity-like veneration of Mary would never have been successful had not the church first taken away the Bible from the common person. That experience alone ought to give us great caution never to say that biblical theology takes second place to the spiritual desires of people. Along with Samuel (speaking to King Saul who thought he was doing something that would please God) we too must say, "To obey is better than sacrifice" (1 Samuel 15:22), and to hearken than to "release" those whom God has never released in ways that we might have hoped.

It's not that I don't sympathize with what seems to be the natural urge in cases like this. Along with the abrogation of the Mosaic laws comes the thought in our minds that God's caution about strictly following his pattern was somehow nullified. After all, Christian doctrine doesn't deal with blue curtain loops and gold clasps, which were details included in the pattern for the tabernacle. And with the passing of 2000 years from the first-century church comes the thought that surely the New Testament pattern regarding women in public worship is outdated for us. After all, women today permeate the professional workplace as doctors, lawyers, and corporate presidents. "Surely," we think, "with changing circumstances we too must change."

Most Christians feel obliged to retain the teachings that fit comfortably into our own time and culture, but, for more and more Christians, attempting to strictly maintain the pattern principle seems to be backward-thinking Christianity and counterproductive theological nostalgia.

How Can We Know the Pattern?

Lately I hear people putting down the pattern principle by asking, "*What* pattern? The pattern of the church in Rome, or the church in Corinth, or the churches in Galatia? And the pattern *when?* During the ministry of Jesus, during the first years following the establishment of the church on Pentecost, or decades later, at the end of the first century?" The implication—particularly with regard to the roles of men and women in the work and worship of the church—is that the pattern is somehow different from place to place and time to time.

If one were talking about changes in pattern from the Old Testament to the New Testament, that observation would take on added validity. But *within* each of those contrasting systems of worship, one would be hard-pressed to find evidence of differing patterns fluttering in the capricious breezes of time and place.

To the contrary, in the midst of key passages relating to the issues at hand we find Paul saying, "If anyone wants to be contentious about this, we have no other practice—nor do the churches of God" (1 Corinthians 11:16). And again, "*As in all the congregations of the saints*, women should remain silent in the churches" (1 Corinthians 14:33, 34). Nowhere is there any hint that some of the churches limited the public role of women but that other churches gave great latitude to their participation.

The problem with abandoning the pattern principle is that we hardly ever do a complete job of it. Invariably we find ourselves following *some kind* of a pattern—*someone's* pattern. Paul puts his finger on it when he urges:

"Do not conform any longer to the pattern of this world, but be transformed by the renewing of your mind. Then you will be able to test and approve what God's will is—his good, pleasing and perfect will" (Romans 12:2).

Someone correctly might suggest that societal changes from the Old to the New Testament are virtually nonexistent compared to the societal changes from the first to the twentieth century. But this only brings us back to the question "Which pattern are we following—the Bible's or the world's"? If we are not following closely the *biblical* pattern, the odds are good that we are probably following the *world's* pattern. And that is a very risky proposition in a culture which is rapidly exchanging traditional male-female patterns for new ones, based on reasons having little to do with biblical concern.

When we cut our ties with the biblical pattern, we have no plumb line against which to compare our Christian worship and practice, no means of verifying our judgments or validating our decisions. Your idea of what might be good for the church becomes just as valid as mine, and mine becomes just as valid as yours. Situational theology is a first cousin (if not a twin) of moral relativism. They are both ships without rudders.

Not All Patterns Are Precedent

Of course there are cautions to be observed in applying the pattern principle. For example, it must never be used to perpetuate human tradition, even if the tradition is ostensibly based upon Scripture. If in fact the tradition is *not* based upon Scripture, then it should not be promoted as a proper pattern. Mere tradition is not precedent; divine *pattern* is precedent. If a limited public role for women were found to be nothing more than time-honored, *man*-made tradition, it would have to be abandoned. Right now. Today!

Another caution is that the divine pattern in one dispensation of God's dealing with the world may not necessarily be his divine pattern under another dispensation. For example, the pattern of animal sacrifices under the old law gave way to a pattern of spiritual sacrifices under the rule of Christ, whose death upon the cross became our blood atonement for sin. Similarly, other specific practices associated with worship under the laws of Moses—including circumcision, temple worship, and the Jewish priesthood—have been replaced in the Christian era.

Nevertheless, sometimes there are patterns within patterns, or general patterns and specific patterns, lasting patterns and temporary patterns. Referring back to the change from animal sacrifices to spiritual sacrifices, for example, we can see where one specific worship pattern replaced another. Yet with regard to sacrifices generally, there is a consistent, permanent, overriding principle of offering "the best" to God. Under the old law the animals were to be "without defect or blemish" (Leviticus 22:17-25). Likewise, under Christ, the pure sacrifice, we are to offer ourselves as living sacrifices.

As Paul put it, "I urge you, brothers, in view of God's mercy, to offer your bodies as living sacrifices, holy and pleasing to God—which is your spiritual worship" (Romans 12:1). And it is noteworthy that by contrasting the sacrifice of holy lives with the "pattern of this world" (to which he refers in the very next sentence), Paul indicates that individual holiness and purity is itself a divine *pattern* that God has always expected. If the *outer form* changes, the *intrinsic principle* does not.

Perhaps the most difficult task in applying the pattern principle is in sorting out divine pattern from common custom. For example, when Paul concluded each of his letters to the Romans, Corinthians, and Thessalonians with the exhortation that they "greet one another with a holy kiss" (e.g. Romans

16:16), the question arises as to whether his instruction constitutes a divine pattern that would require *all* Christians to greet one another with a holy *kiss*.

The answer, of course, is both yes and no. Virtually everyone agrees that the pattern relates to the *greeting*, not to the *form* of the greeting. The pattern of Christian love and fellowship would apply to whatever customary greeting might be common to a given culture, whether it is a kiss or a handshake.

But determining the difference between mere custom and divine pattern is rarely that easy, and unfortunately some of the most difficult passages relate to the issues under present consideration. We will take a closer look at each of those passages as we come to them. But we should reaffirm the importance of the basic "pattern principle" before we begin to make critical decisions about what might or might not have been custom rather than pattern.

Perhaps the most important factor in distinguishing the limited significance of *custom* from the pattern precedent of an overarching spiritual *principle* is the frequency and priority given to a particular view in the big picture. In an overview of the Bible, we must ask ourselves what principles we see expressed again and again, even if the outer trappings happen to change from one dispensation to another.

Indeed, what principles take on the nature of divine pattern for the *very reason* that they survive transitions in form? If someone were asked to serve in a politically appointed position under both Democratic *and* Republican administrations, we would sit up and take notice. That would be a pretty special individual! Likewise any principle found repeatedly and prominently throughout both the Old and New Testaments ought to cause us to sit up and take notice.

In the remainder of this book we are going to survey the Old and New Testaments to glean anything that might shed light on the social and spiritual roles of men and women in the centuries before the coming of Christ and in the first century of apostolic teaching. Was there a pattern? If so, what was that pattern?

We have already covered in detail the Genesis accounts of Creation. If those accounts were required to stand alone, their sparse factual record, containing a number of extraordinary factors, might tend to make our conclusions tentative at best. Were we correct, for example, in seeing Adam as Eve's "spiritual protector" even before the Fall? Did we presume too much in drawing a parallel between the "principle of first-born" and Adam's status as "firstcreated?" On the other hand, if these Creation principles are corroborated by the testimony of the remainder of God's revelation, then the strongest case possible will have been proved.

There is another pattern which we must not overlook as we continue our study regarding roles and relationships. In the New Testament, the real focus is on the pattern of Christ's servanthood. "If anyone would come after me, he must deny himself and take up his cross and follow me" (Matthew 16:24). Whatever functional leadership role we might discover will have to be understood as *servant* leadership.

The Gender-Neutral Father God

An overview of the scriptural depiction of God's nature can help us both begin our search and examine how the pattern principle works.

In the second verse of the Bible the Creator is referred to as "the *Spirit* of God." In the very next verse God created light, and "*he* separated the light from the darkness." Within only four sentences the Bible seems to hurl us into a paradoxical quagmire about the nature of God. Is God *genderless spirit* or in fact *male?* The answer is *both!*

As spirit, God is the genderless Creator in whose image both male and female were created. But *as revealed*, God is couched overwhelmingly in male terms. There is no need to quibble about which personal pronoun ought to be used with reference to God. Look at the *roles* in which God comes to us: He is our father, not our mother; our husband, not our wife; our king, not our queen. And these are not simply generic words being given a masculine cast by male Bible translators. These words come complete with contextual pictures which portray masculine attributes.

No matter how blasphemously some people attempt to make the biblical texts gender-neutral in order to bolster their cause, the words and meanings of the originally inspired text remain the same. God is a "parent," yes, but he is a *father*, not a mother. God is a "spouse," yes, but he is a *husband*, not a wife. God is a "ruler," yes, but he is a *king*, not a queen.

To say that God comes to us in male imagery is not to say that he is never attributed with qualities which tend to be associated with women—for example, tenderness, passion, vulnerability, creativity, and self-giving. In fact there are several passages which present God metaphorically graced with feminine characteristics. Note the following, for example:

> You deserted the Rock, who fathered you;
> > you forgot the God who gave you birth
> > (Deuteronomy 32:18).
>
> For a long time I have kept silent,
> > I have been quiet and held myself back.
> But now, like a woman in childbirth,
> > I cry out, I gasp and pant (Isaiah 42:14).
>
> Can a mother forget the baby at her breast
> > and have no compassion on the
> > child she has borne?
>
> Though she may forget,
> > I will not forget you! (Isaiah 49:15).

If in some respects God is *like* a mother, as indicated in the last passage there are also ways in which he is *unlike* a mother. Yet for every passage that might suggest that God has feminine as well as masculine qualities (which should not be surprising, since God in fact is a genderless or perhaps gender-*inclusive* spirit), there are literally scores of other passages which emphasize male traits.

Certainly God *could have* revealed himself to us through gender-neutral terminology—such as "force," "power," or "it"—or indeed in the female images of mother, wife, and queen. But for God's own reasons he chose male terminology and predominantly male imagery. If ever there were serious doubt about how God has chosen to present himself to us, surely the clincher is found in his incarnation. There too God had at least two options: male or female. In the male Person of Jesus of Nazareth, who called himself the *Son* of God, and who addressed God as his *Father,* we have the clearest assurance that God has chosen maleness through which to reveal himself to us. The male personhood of Jesus is no error of translation!

Does this mean that Jesus looked only through dominating Jewish male eyes? No. With the tenderness of a mother he cried out, "0 Jerusalem, Jerusalem, you who kill the prophets and stone those sent to you, how often I have longed to gather your children together, as a hen gathers her chicks under her wings, but you were not willing" (Matthew 23:37).

Nor was Jesus unique among men in using female imagery. We hear Moses asking God, "Did I conceive all these people? Did I give them birth? Why do you tell me to carry them in my arms, as a nurse carries an infant, to the land you promised on oath to their forefathers?" (Numbers 11:12). And there is Paul writing with tenderness, "My dear children, for whom I am again in the pains of childbirth until Christ is formed in you, how I wish I could be with you now . . ." (Galatians 4:19, 20). And again, "As apostles of Christ we could have been a burden to you, but we were gentle among you, like a mother caring for her little children" (1 Thessalonians 2:7). All men share some of the qualities found more predominantly in women.

Jesus was neither the effeminate half-man that artists sometimes portray nor a man whose masculinity was threatened by the welling up of sympathetic tears in his eyes. But this is no time for game-playing—Jesus our Lord was *all man*, complete with Jewish circumcision.

In light of the obvious alternative options, the "maleness" of our gender-free spiritual God (as he presents himself to us in both revelation and incarnation) must be a matter of significance. Hypothetically it could mean that, between male and female, God's *favorite* was male—like a parent who has a favorite child. But only someone who might be looking for such favoritism would get that impression from the Scriptures. There simply has to be another reason.

At the risk of assuming the conclusion to be drawn, there appears to be a correlation between Jesus, the ultimate spiritual leader, and the role of spiritual leadership that we have observed in Adam. If we are right about Adam's special responsibility as spiritual leader in the family, then the principle of male leadership plays itself out perfectly in the maleness of Jesus. In such a case the gender factor is no mere coincidence. And looking retrospectively from Jesus back to Adam, the conclusions about Adam's responsibility as spiritual leader take on added credibility. Each of them was firstborn, each of them was male.

Of course Jesus, as a man, was neither a husband nor a father. But Jesus, as Christ, is the head of the church, which is his bride, and claims his family from among those who believe. As a spiritual leader, Adam was the developmental prototype. Jesus became the perfect model.

Pattern Versus Policy—The Crux of the Issue

God's very nature as revealed in Scripture becomes a pattern for the way in which he calls us to leadership. As we proceed through the Bible we will find that same pattern established again and again, whether it be in the laws of Moses, the worship of Israel, the ministry of Christ, or the history of first-century Christian thought. Are we prepared to accept that pattern—however we might find it to be—as our guide even today? Are we willing to yield our own instincts to God's divine guidelines?

I believe this is the most crucial chapter in the entire book. How we perceive the authority of Scripture will dictate ultimately what we believe God has said to us about roles and relationships in a time of great social change. The remainder of the book is predicated upon two assumptions: 1) that God has revealed a consistent, identifiable pattern of roles and relationships within both the home and the church; and 2) that the pattern is still applicable to us today.

Some of us who accept the Bible as constitutionally authoritative may disagree as to what the biblical pattern was in each case. We may also differ in our understanding of how that pattern is to be applied in our own culture. This book is designed to bring us closer together in our quest to be true to the pattern principle which we each honor.

A much different perspective will emerge for those who see the Scriptures more as the source of "broad principles for Christian living." Almost automatically, they will disagree with the conclusions which we will be led to draw. For them the search for specific biblical authority will be of only secondary concern. It is more a matter of overriding policy. For them the general principle of Christian equality will outweigh any specific instructions found in the biblical pattern and will lead to radically different conclusions.

Basic differences in biblical interpretation are neither new nor easily resolved. As a law professor, I encounter much the same conflict between liberal and conservative views of Constitutional interpretation. While it is not within the scope of this book to attempt a bridge between such frustrating differences in outlook among us, I suggest that all of us can prof-it from a close look at what pattern does exist. If we then choose to take a different path of understanding, at least it will not have been by default.

Lord, be with us in our study of your Word. Give us the insight to wisely discern the meaning of your revelation to us as it has been preserved by people of faith down through the centuries. Thank you for honoring us through your Creation and for guiding us by your written Word. Let it be to us a path of faith for our lives and a blueprint for your church. May we commit ourselves to your leading so that we might all truly be conformed to your image.

Study Questions

1. Why should biblical patterns matter when we are determining issues of doctrine?

2. How can we be sure that we are finding a "pattern" as opposed to simply finding something that is recorded in Scripture which may not have been intended for us to follow?

3. If we are not following a biblical pattern, what other kinds of patterns might we be following?

4. What effect does one's particular hermeneutic have on the way he or she interprets Scripture?

5. Is God's Word ever in conflict with honoring people and "doing the loving thing"?

6. How do we know when a biblical practice is mere custom, as opposed to eternal principle? (Consider, for example, footwashing, greeting one another with a kiss, and women wearing veils as part of their daily attire.)

7. Is God to be thought of as male, female, both, or neither?

8. Once a biblical pattern is established, can we know with assurance how that pattern ought to be applied in our own culture?

9. How important is it to firmly establish a principle before asking where lines of application ought to be drawn?

10. Is it possible to draw correct biblical lines regarding gender roles, and yet still not honor the principle of male spiritual leadership?

4 *Surprising Honor in a Man's World*

Women Among the Patriarchs

I doubt if anyone is surprised to learn that the world of the Old Testament was definitely a man's world. However, because of the many notorious cases in which women were abused at the hands of men, we may have overlooked a divine pattern of mutually supportive interaction. Even in the Old Testament, roles and relationships had a good side as well. As we start through the Old Testament, let's get the correct overall picture, including both good and bad.

We are familiar with the sons of Adam and Eve—Cain and Abel, and later Seth—but do we know the names of their sisters, who apparently also doubled as their wives? The unnamed sisters (and other unnamed brothers) are given only passing mention in the genealogical record (Genesis 5:4).

In fact, throughout the many Old Testament genealogical lists, only rarely do we find a daughter's name recorded for posterity. Ostensibly the lists were kept for the purpose of ensuring the inheritance of clan property.

That alone would explain why only the names of firstborn sons—the family heads through whom the property was passed on to succeeding generations—would be recorded.

Yet because the firstborn sons were specially consecrated to God (Exodus 22:29, 30), it is equally noteworthy from the male-oriented genealogical records that firstborn spiritual leadership was male. Firstborn daughters did not assume the mantle of that special responsibility.

Circumcision, A Male Ritual

Here is a quick test for you. What is the recognized symbolism of the following items?

A.   Dove
B.   Skull and crossbones
C.   Hammer and sickle
D.   Cross
E.   Swastika
F.   Six-pointed star
G.   Mushroom-shaped cloud

How did you do? (See answers below.)* If the list had included the Jewish rite of circumcision, what symbolism would you have guessed? Merely Judaism, like the six-pointed Star of David? Or perhaps covenant relationship with God? Certainly the latter would be a very good answer. Circumcision memorialized the institution of God's covenant relationship with Abraham and his descendants in the nation of Israel. The record of that act of covenant is worth a close look.

> Then God said to Abraham, "As for you, you must keep my covenant, you and your descendants after you for the generations to come.
> This is my covenant with you and your descendants after you, the covenant you are to keep: Every male

---

*A. Peace; B. Poison; C. Communism; D. Christianity; E. Nazism; F. Judaism; G. Atomic bomb.

among you shall be circumcised. You are to undergo circumcision, and it will be the sign of the covenant between me and you. For the generations to come every male among you who is eight days old must be circumcised, including those born in your household or bought with money from a foreigner—those who are not your offspring" (Genesis 17:9-12).

Circumcision symbolized God's covenant relationship with his chosen people. This gracious covenant extended to all of Abraham's descendants and even to those who became members of their households as indentured servants. Therefore, whether slave or free, male or female, God's covenant was with an entire nation of people—a people who later would become known as Jews.

But circumcision was symbolic of more than the covenant relationship itself. The covenant with Abraham was *racial,* and race is tied to genealogy, and genealogy (in the ancient Near East) was tied to lineage based on males. Moreover, circumcision was undoubtedly the most graphic symbol of male spiritual leadership. Once again, God obviously had alternative choices in deciding what would be the symbol of his covenant with the Jews. Because the covenant extended to all of Abraham's descendants—women as well as men—it would have been logical to the human mind for God to have chosen a covenant symbol that could be participated in by both men and women—perhaps pierced ears, dyed hair, or special headbands. Instead, God chose an act related exclusively to males.

Again comes the question, Why? Certainly not because women were any less a part of the covenant. They received the same blessings of spiritual atonement as the men and were under the same obligations of righteousness before God. The obvious answer is that circumcision was a symbol of male headship. On a spiritual level, women had the same relationship with God as did the men. In terms of covenant, they stood equal with men before God. But their *identity* with God was found through man, vicariously. Therefore once again we see the principle: alike but different—equal in status in relation to God, but different in status in relation to man.

I suspect that your mind has already raced across the centuries to the coming of Jesus and of Christian baptism, which, experienced by both men and women, would replace male-only circumcision as the identifying symbol of God's covenant with the faithful. You also may have thought of Paul's statement in the Galatian letter that in Christ "there is neither Jew nor Greek, slave nor free, male nor female" (Galatians 3:28). If so, it might have occurred to you that the principle of male spiritual leadership, like circumcision's racial exclusivity, may also be subject to change in the Christian era.

However, at this point it would not be safe to assume that we will find a one-for-one tradeoff in the transition between Jewish circumcision and Christian baptism. Neither the outer forms nor the intrinsic principles they represent will be exchanged in neatly tied, predictable packages. Looking at the symbols themselves, for example, whereas circumcision was administered to faithless infants, Christian baptism would become a chosen act of faith on the part of adult believers.

Nor does it necessarily follow from the abandonment of circumcision's vicarious covenant identity for women that in the Christian era the more encompassing principle of male spiritual headship was eliminated along with circumcision. But more on Galatians chapter 3 later.

Veiled Submission

With but few exceptions, such as Miriam and Deborah, wherever we turn in the Old Testament we see that women are cast in the supportive role. Their honor was almost always based upon personal qualities rather than position or title (for which, if we stop to think about it, there may be more to be said than might first appear). A sprinkling of passages will give us the flavor of male-female relationships in ancient culture.

You remember the story of Abraham sending his servant to Abraham's homeland to find a wife for Isaac. When Rebekah was found pursuant to the servant's prayer, it was Rebekah's father and brother who made the decision regarding the marriage, although they did consult with Rebekah concerning the timing of her departure. When Rebekah first saw Isaac, her husband-to-be, "she took her veil and covered herself" (Genesis 24:65).

In this rather obscure incident we find the first biblical reference to the use of the veil as the ancient symbol of submission—the wife reserving her very visage for her husband. What prompted its use so early in the history of human culture is unknown, but its early use does beg questions: Who was the first woman to don a veil, and what prompted her to do it? Was it her own idea or a man's? What made the idea catch on? Why was it more than just a passing fad?

More intriguing, how did the woman's veil ever become related to the idea of submission? Was the physical covering of the woman's head somehow related to the spiritual headship of her husband? These questions will take on added importance when we discuss Paul's instructions regarding veils in his first letter to the Corinthians.

Who Really Counts?

It's not really true, but if all you had read about the men and women in ancient times was the numbering of the Israelites just prior to their entering the land of promise, you likely would have gotten the idea that only the men really counted. The Lord told Moses: "Take a census of the whole Israelite community by their clans and families, listing every man by name, one by one" (Numbers 1:2). Apparently the women *did* count; however, they were not listed by name. Yet there appears to be nothing particularly sinister about this because the listing of the men by name was limited to "all the men twenty years old or more who were able to serve in the army." The listing of men's names constituted the first military draft registration!

Nevertheless, when it came to numbering the priesthood clan of the Levites, the instructions were: "Count the Levites by their families and clans. Count every male a month old or more" (Numbers 3:15). Just as it was the male who "counted" in terms of military defense, it was also the male who "counted" in terms of spiritual headship of the nation.

Challenges to Male Superiority

If women were in the background officially, they did not always comfortably take a back seat. It is difficult to know all the dynamics of what occurred in the incident involving Caleb's daughter Acsah, but it appears that she made an end run around her husband, Othniel, to whom she had been given in marriage by her father as a prize of battle.

> One day when she came to Othniel, she urged him to ask her father for a field. [The narrative which follows implies that Othniel ignored her request and that she went directly to her father.] When she got off her donkey, Caleb asked her, "What can I do for you?"
>
> She replied, "Do me a special favor. Since you have given me land in the Negev, give me also springs of water." Then Caleb gave her the upper and lower springs (Judges 1:14, 15).

But female initiative did not always pay off so handsomely. Take the case of Michal rebuking David's immodest dancing following his joyful return with the ark of God.

> When David returned home to bless his household, Michal daughter of Saul came out to meet him and said,

"How the king of Israel has distinguished himself today, disrobing in the sight of the slave girls of his servants as any vulgar fellow would!"

David said to Michal, "It was before the Lord, who chose me rather than your father or anyone from his house when he appointed me ruler over the Lord's people Israel—I will celebrate before the Lord. I will become even more undignified than this, and I will be humiliated in my own eyes. But by these slave girls you spoke of, I will be held in honor."

And Michal daughter of Saul had no children to the day of her death (2 Samuel 6:20-23).

What is surprising about this heated exchange is that one would think Michal had justifiable cause for rebuking David. From our perspective, not only was her husband acting less than modestly before other women but he also seemed to be demeaning his position as king. Yet the concluding comment about her barrenness seems to suggest that it was punishment for her behavior on this occasion. What had Michal done wrong?

In David's time, his conduct was a way to show hearty commitment and joy. So Michal's problem may have been in thinking David was *too* spiritual. Incredibly, there are women who belittle male spiritual leadership, not because they want to put *men* down, but because they want to put *God* aside.

The implication of this story is that Michal had turned aside from giving proper deference to God. This could also imply that she "didn't know her place" with regard to David, or—far from *having* a "place"—she had approached David with the wrong attitude. That the latter interpretation is a more accurate assessment is suggested in an earlier statement that "when she saw King David leaping and dancing before the Lord, she despised him in her heart" (2 Samuel 6:16).

Certainly God had no thought that the wife was so subordinate to her husband that she was to have no mind of her own. In fact on one occasion God specifically told Abraham to listen to what Sarah said.

> Sarah saw that the son whom Hagar the Egyptian had borne to Abraham was mocking [Isaac], and she said to Abraham, "Get rid of that slave woman and her son, for that slave woman's son will never share in the inheritance with my son Isaac."
>
> The matter distressed Abraham greatly because it concerned his son. But God said to him, "Do not be so distressed about the boy and your maidservant. Listen to whatever Sarah tells you, because it is through Isaac that your offspring will be reckoned" (Genesis 21:9-12).

It would have been easy enough for God to have said, "Don't bother listening to your wife, for after all she was the one who brought on the trouble in the first place by suggesting that you take Hagar as a concubine." But you never get the idea from Scripture that God intended wives to be silent, unseen shadows somewhere back in the kitchen. He honored the wisdom of too many women for anyone to draw that narrow conclusion.

Dark Sides of Male Leadership

I wish I could tell you that male leadership always presented itself nobly. Unfortunately, that is far from true. We have already seen where Adam laid the blame for his sin on Eve, if not on God himself! And we have seen where, for his own safety, Abraham twice forced Sarah to lie about their marriage. But it gets even worse—far worse.

You probably don't need to be reminded about Lot's "generous offer" of his daughters to the evil men of Sodom in exchange for the safety of complete strangers in his home! But here is a second look:

> Lot went outside to meet them and shut the door behind him and said, "No, my friends. Don't do this wicked thing. Look, I have two daughters who have never slept with a man. Let me bring them out to you, and you can do what you like with them. But don't do anything to these men, for they have come under the protection of my roof" (Genesis 19:6-8).

Lot would claim, undoubtedly, that in the hierarchy of values during his time the protection of guests took priority. But were not Lot's daughters under the protection of his roof *even more so?* And years later in a far less familiar passage this scenario is repeated virtually verbatim. It is the story of the Levite and his concubine who were sharing the overnight hospitality of an old man in a Benjamite town through which they were passing.

> While they were enjoying themselves, some of the wicked men of the city surrounded the house. Pounding on the door, they shouted to the old man who owned the house, "Bring out the man who came to your house so we can have sex with him."
>
> The owner of the house went outside and said to them, "No, my friends, don't be so vile. Since this man is my guest, don't do this disgraceful thing. Look, here is my virgin daughter and his concubine. I will bring them out to you now, and you can use them and do to them whatever you wish. But to this man, don't do such a disgraceful thing."
>
> But the men would not listen to him. So the man took his concubine and sent her outside to them, and

they raped her and abused her throughout the night, and at dawn they let her go (Judges 19:22-25).

The homeowner and his guest had tragic—terribly male-oriented—definitions of acceptable conduct! Nor did the story end there. When the concubine was discovered dead on the doorstep the next morning, in outrage (!) the Levite cut her body into 12 pieces and sent a piece to each tribe in Israel, instigating a civil war that all but wiped out the Benjamites.

Another of the less-familiar passages of the Bible gives us rich insight into ancient male attitudes regarding their superiority to women. Abimelech, one of Israel's military leaders (who by our terminology were mislabeled as "judges"), stormed a tower in a city he had sieged. "But as he approached the entrance to the tower to set it on fire, a woman dropped an upper millstone on his head and cracked his skull. Hurriedly he called to his armor-bearer, 'Draw your sword and kill me, so that they can't say, "A woman killed him"'" (Judges 9:52-54).

Still another obscure reference points to how such male superiority would be thrown in the faces of God's unfaithful men who would find themselves in foreign captivity. In promising to restore the nation of Israel, God first characterizes Israel as an unfaithful daughter, then says something quite remarkable:

> How long will you wander,
>   0 unfaithful daughter?
> The Lord will create a new thing on earth—a
>   woman will surround a man
>   (Jeremiah 31:22).

This "new thing," this departure from the recognized pattern of human conduct, was that a woman would "surround"—that is, *protect*—a man! Unheard of! Unthinkable! But God declared that what he was going to do in restoring the nation of Israel would be just as revolutionary as the thought that a woman would be a man's protector. I suspect that *this* got the men's attention!

What we have seen in these several passages is also a biblical pattern regarding male leadership—but it is *man's* pattern, not *God's*. Man's abuse of woman clearly and unmistakably is an abuse of God's pattern as well. And it is an abuse that has persisted throughout the centuries down to our own time. Male spiritual leadership, when abbreviated by the omission of the word "spiritual," has invariably transformed the *biblical* concept of male leadership into the *world's* concept of male domination.

Man the *protector* has become man the *abuser*—physically, emotionally, and spiritually. Headship was not thought of as servant leadership but as power. And as suggested regarding political power, male power corrupts and absolute male power corrupts absolutely.

It would be this corruption of the principle of male spiritual leadership that would catch the attention of Jesus during his ministry. His treatment of women with dignity and respect would stand in sharp contrast to the denigrating, even institutionalized Jewish disregard for women in his day.

Although he would not overturn the principle of male spiritual leadership itself, as many would like to believe, he would restore its proper focus and show us more clearly that leadership and headship have more to do with difference in responsibility than superiority of role—more to do with conscientious spiritual watchfulness and guidance than chauvinistic power-based domination.

Honor Through Childbearing

If men were honored through military, political, and spiritual leadership, the women were honored through their childbearing. It is significant that on the very occasion of instituting male-oriented circumcision as the sign of his covenant with Abraham, God said to him, "As for Sarai your wife, you are no longer to call her Sarai; her name will be Sarah. I will bless her and will surely give you a son by her. I will bless her so that she will be the mother of nations; kings of peoples will come from her" (Genesis 17:15, 16).

If for men relationship with God would be formalized through the pain of circumcision, women would be blessed through the pain of childbirth. The renaming of Sarah, together with its implications regarding childbearing, is a clear flashback to Eve, mother of all the living, and to God's reference to her pain in giving birth. If Abraham were to be the spiritual father of all the faithful—even faithful Christians—then Sarah was to be their spiritual mother. In the change of her name to Sarah, meaning princess, she was greatly honored along with Eve as a mother of the faithful.

Unfortunately, there were negative spinoffs from the honor which accompanied childbirth. If bearing children was a woman's honor, the failure to bear children—especially *male* children—was considered a disgrace. Nowhere, of course, does Scripture suggest that God either started this rumor or incorporated the disgrace of barrenness as part of his pattern of male headship. The likely source would be traceable directly to perpetuation of lineage through a man's sons.

In the childbearing competition between Jacob's two wives, Rachel and Leah, we see an example of how much trouble such disgrace could bring. "When Rachel saw that she was not bearing Jacob any children, she became jealous of her sister. So she said to Jacob, 'Give me children, or I'll die!'" (Genesis 30:1). You can almost hear Jacob's hostile response: "I've fathered four sons by your sister, so it's obviously not *my* problem!" As it turned out, it may well have been his problem!

As Sarah had done before her, Rachel believed the answer to her shame would be to give her maidservant to Jacob to have children on her behalf. It worked, but only served to give

Leah the same idea. She too gave her maidservant to Jacob. At the end of the competition between these two sisters and their surrogate stand-ins, there were 10 sons and a daughter, Dinah. Only then did Rachel conceive and bear a son of her own: "She became pregnant and gave birth to a son and said, 'God has taken away my disgrace'" (Genesis 30:23). She named her son Joseph. Later she bore another son, Benjamin.

Jacob's 12 sons and their descendants became the 12 tribes of Israel, Jacob's changed name. (It is significant that there were only 12 tribes, not 13. There was no tribe of Dinah.) Thus the irony is that the nation of Israel came about as the direct result of the shame attached to a woman's inability to bear children.

There would also be a certain irony in the fact that at least four of the most outstanding women in Scripture suffered the disgrace of barrenness until their children were born later than would have been expected: Sarah and Rachel, of course, and also Hannah the mother of Samuel, and Elizabeth the mother of John the Baptist.

The disgrace attached to barrenness was fostered as much by other women as by the sonless father, particularly where the man had more than one wife. The touching account of Hannah's longing for a son shows how compassionately her husband, Elkanah, tried to convince her that no real shame attached to her barrenness:

> Whenever the day came for Elkanah to sacrifice, he would give portions of the meat to his wife Peninnah and to all her sons and daughters. But to Hannah he gave a double portion because he loved her, and the Lord had closed her womb. And because the Lord had closed her womb, her rival kept provoking her in order to irritate her. This went on year after year. Whenever Hannah went up to the house of the Lord, her rival provoked her till she wept and would not eat. Elkanah her

husband would say to her, "Hannah, why are you
weeping? Why don't you eat? Why are you downheart-
ed? Don't I mean more to you than ten sons?" (1
Samuel 1:4-8).

As you probably are aware, the story has a happy ending.
God answers Hannah's fervent prayers, and Samuel is born. In
gratitude, Hannah dedicates Samuel to God's service and he
uniquely becomes the last of Israel's judges, one of its many
prophets, and the anointer of its first king.

In God's eyes, the inability to bear children has never been
cause for shame for any woman. Nor is her relationship with
God impaired in any way because of her lack of childbearing.
To God, the woman without children is in the same cradle of
his love as others who are without riches and pleasure:

> He raises the poor from the dust
>   and lifts the needy from the ash heap;
>   he seats them with princes,
>   with the princes of their people.
> He settles the barren woman in her home
>   as a happy mother of children
>   (Psalm 113:7-9).

Just as many believers have been honored by the gift of suffering for Christ, so too the righteous woman without offspring
is honored as a "childless mother" in God's eyes.

If shame too often has been the unfortunate and unde-
served result of barrenness, the honor attached to childbearing
is as consistent a biblical pattern for women as spiritual leadership is for men. It is difficult to escape the implication that
a wife and mother's greatest contribution lies in the gifts she
brings to that special responsibility. If men are called to be
spiritual leaders, it is nevertheless true that "the hand that
rocks the cradle rules the world."

The womb is not a woman's greatest asset, but rather the spiritual insight and personal righteousness that she instills in the precious bundles of potential we call children. As between the man and the woman, arguably hers is the greater responsibility. If the father is able to lead his children in the ways of the Lord, it likely will have been the mother who made them open to that leading. Typically, it is the mother who will have introduced the child to God, and who will have laid the foundation of godly character traits. Therefore it should come as no surprise that Paul would say of the godly mother that she "will be saved through childbirth" (1 Timothy 2:15).

Again, this is not to say that the childless woman in ancient times could not be saved. Her situation would be like the man who never married. Though he would never be in a position as spiritual leader of his own family, nevertheless he would find acceptability before God through his personal righteousness and God's grace.

What we see in the pattern of the patriarchs, however, is a division of responsibilities between the man and the woman— not one greater and one lesser, but two different responsibilities, the combination of which achieves the fullness of God's purpose in mankind.

In the remainder of the Old Testament we will find both men and women who bring disgrace to themselves for failing to conscientiously exercise their respective responsibilities. And we will see both men and women who bring honor to themselves and to God by the dedication which they bring to the distinctive roles they are called to play.

Study Questions

1. What significance, if any, should we attach to the fact that ancestry and lineage were generally traced through males rather than females?

2. Why do you suppose God chose male circumcision as the sign of his covenant with the children of Israel?

3. How would you explain the account of Rebekah covering herself with a veil when she first saw Isaac? What, if anything, did the veil represent?

4. Compare the attitude of Caleb's daughter Acsah (in asking for the springs of water) with that of Michal when she rebuked David (seemingly with God's disapproval). What might we learn about the status of women and how God views them?

5. Is it appropriate for a husband to take advice from his wife? Does it matter if the issue at hand is more spiritual than secular?

6. What lessons might we learn from the story of Lot offering his daughters to the men of Sodom and the Levite offering his concubine to the Benjamites?

7 What do you make of Jeremiah's words (31:22): "The Lord will create a new thing on earth—a woman will surround a man"?

8. How must God feel when men abuse women instead of protecting them?

9. In what way is childbearing a blessing to women?

10. Is childbearing to be viewed as woman's greatest contribution?

5 As It Is Written

Male Headship in the Laws of Moses

As a law professor I am reminded constantly how much our legal system owes to the laws of Moses. All one has to do is read the Mosaic laws of homicide together with the current homicide statutes in virtually any state to realize what little distance we have traveled from the concepts and principles that came to us from the mouth of God through Moses.

Whether it be mayhem, rape, assault, or theft—our statutes covering criminal offenses are mere reflections of laws handed down centuries before Christ. And it's not just the law of crimes; there are incredibly similar civil laws as well. There were laws pertaining to bailments and restitution for loss; laws governing contracts, torts, labor law, and succession of property through inheritance. Even the world of finance was covered by laws dealing with credit, interest, and collateral. As a theocracy, no area of basic human interaction was left uncovered by these God-given laws.

If all of that is fascinating, a closer look at the laws of Moses holds in store even more surprises and interesting twists regarding male-female roles in the social fabric and religious worship of the nation of Israel.

Custom can be dictated too easily by factors unassociated with moral or religious considerations. Therefore you can never be quite sure whether custom is a good guideline for determining human conduct. By contrast, a system of laws coming directly from God ought to get us as close as possible to his divine pattern, at least for the time during which the laws were to be in force. In the laws and in the principles which lie behind these laws would be the clearest picture of God's view of human interaction—including, for our specific purpose, the relative rights and responsibilities of men and women.

The Legal Status of Women

It's time to hold onto your hat, for the laws of Moses are filled with distinctions between male and female, and female takes a distant second. If you had never been told that the laws were given by God, you might suspect that they were the product of an all-male civic club. But throughout the laws you begin to see a more benevolent undercurrent of concern than is initially apparent on the surface. Let's take a closer look.

Ceremonial Uncleanness

Leviticus 12:1-5 provides for a woman's ceremonial uncleanness following childbirth. The woman was considered unclean for seven days if the child was a boy and 14 days if a girl. To be purified from her bleeding, she would be required to wait 33 days if the child was a boy and 66 days if a girl. Even the women must have looked forward to bearing sons!

Valuation for Dedications

Vows of dedication (Leviticus 27:1-8) called for the valuation of those who might be set apart for the Lord. Here too we find differences in both age and sex. Whatever the age bracket, the woman was always valued less than her male counterpart.

Rape Victims

The value of a rape victim was certainly at rock bottom (Deuteronomy 22:28, 29). If a man raped a virgin not pledged to be married, he was required not only to pay the girl's father 50 shekels of silver but also to marry her! Of course this type of rape was distinguished from the rape of a girl "out in the country." The idea is that, away from the city, any resistance by the girl might be futile, whereas failure to cry for help within the boundary of a city would imply some complicity on the part of the girl.

Assuming that the girl was pleased to have acquired her husband through the act of rape (obviously a highly questionable assumption), there was at least the protective requirement that the man could never divorce her as long as he lived. That would prevent any temporary sham marriage just to fulfill the requirement of law.

Freeing Slaves

In the section of laws dealing with slaves (Exodus 21:7-11), it is startling to find a provision relating to the sale of a man's daughter as a slave. Of course the sale of a man's son as a slave to another Hebrew was also a legally permissible transaction. After the shock of thinking that a man would sell his own son or daughter, we can see that the provision here is for the daughter's protection. Unlike a male servant, who would be released after seven years, a female servant (who presumably was considered as a concubine) was not to be set out on the doorstep with nowhere to go and nothing to take with her. Freedom for her would have meant economic disaster. Nor could she be sold to a foreigner. And if the master gave the woman to his son as a concubine, then the master was to treat her as his own daughter.

It may be weak consolation from our current viewpoint, but this particular provision points to an important consideration we should not overlook. Compared with contemporary soci-

eties around them, the people of Israel were given a revolutionary system of legal rights and privileges. In pagan cultures
none of these protections for women existed at all! In a way
the laws of Moses became for Israel the Bill of Rights and the
Equal Rights Amendment of its day.

Ratification of Vows

In the rules regarding vows we begin to see a clearer picture of male headship in the home. The financial headship
over a woman, whether wife or daughter, is demonstrated in
the procedure for the man's ratification of a woman's vow
(Numbers 30:3-16). The basic law was that a woman's vow or
other obligation by pledge was not binding unless subsequently ratified by her husband or father. If the woman had
already made a vow, she would be released from it if the man
disapproved.

The most interesting aspect of this provision is found in the
closing comment: "These are the regulations the Lord gave
Moses concerning relationships between a man and his wife,
and between a father and his young daughter still living in his
house" (Numbers 30:16). Combined with the fact that there
were no rules at all regarding the vows of sons, the closing
comment appears to give emphasis to the more fundamental,
overriding headship of the man over the woman in the family, and not simply his *financial* headship. Indeed, the broad-
sweeping influence of the husband and father throughout all
the laws repeatedly bears out this principle. And where did
these laws come from? Directly from God himself.

Marriage to Captive

A number of provisions were a mixed bag, partly showing
women to be second-class citizens and partly showing how
they were given unusual protection for their day. One such
passage is Deuteronomy 21:10-14, regarding marriage to a
captive. It was common in ancient times for triumphant war-

riors to bring back women as part of the booty and spoils of war. God did not prohibit this practice for the Israelites, but placed humanitarian limitations on their otherwise-indiscriminate habits. Before the man could take the woman as his wife, he was required to wait a full month so that the woman could mourn her father and mother. He also was prohibited from ever selling her or treating her as a slave—itself a departure from the common custom of ancient culture.

If Virginity Doubted

Through a most unusual ceremony (Deuteronomy 22:13-21), the newlywed woman was protected from a charge by her husband that she was not a virgin at the time of their marriage. False charges subjected the man to a fine for having slandered his wife. On the other hand, if the woman's virginity were not proved, she was to be stoned to death for having been promiscuous while still in her father's house.

Divorce

Although scholars have long debated whether the laws of Moses permitted divorce for virtually any cause, unlike in neighboring nations the Israelites were at least taught the seriousness and finality of a dissolved marriage (Deuteronomy 24:1-4). The law forbade a man from remarrying a wife to whom he had given a certificate of divorce if in the meantime she had been married to another man who had either divorced her or died.

You get the idea that, prior to the laws of Moses, the men played musical wives, swapping them around from one to another and back again. At least the laws put a stop to that.

Test for Adultery

Still another unusual procedure was set up to test the validity of a husband's charge that his wife had committed adultery (Numbers 5:11-31). As with the test for virginity, it can be seen either as a male-oriented double standard or else a protection for a woman when her husband wishes to accuse her falsely. This "law of jealousy" may well have been the woman's first line of defense against male dominance.

Inheritance to Daughters

One of the most fascinating and revealing legal cases ever recorded arose out of a request by five daughters that they be allowed to inherit property from their father, who had died without leaving any sons to inherit the property. It is surprising from the very first that "they approached the entrance to the Tent of Meeting and stood before Moses, Eleazar the priest, the leaders and the whole assembly," to plead their case (Numbers 27:1,2). There is no indication that it was in any way offensive that these women should raise a legal issue so openly and directly. They apparently felt no need to rely on a close relative who was male to speak on their behalf.

The outcome of this case in an inheritance-by-males-only society is even more surprising.

> So Moses brought their case before the Lord and the Lord said to him, "What Zelophehad's daughters are saying is right. You must certainly give them property as an inheritance among their father's relatives and turn their father's inheritance over to them" (Numbers 27:5-7).

The initiative and courage of these five women resulted in a landmark decision which set precedent for all future cases where the father died without a son to take the inheritance. If there were a surviving daughter, she would inherit the same as her brother would have (Numbers 27:8-11). In a follow-up case (Numbers 36:1-13), the daughters of Zelophehad were required to marry only within their own tribe in order to keep their inheritance as part of the clan's property. This the five women agreed to do.

Distinctive Clothing

Even in their clothing men and women were to be distinctive. Deuteronomy 22:5 laid down the law against transvestite fashions: "A woman must not wear men's clothing, nor a man wear women's clothing, for the Lord your God detests anyone who does this." What must God think of today's unisex styles?

One thing, however, does seem to be clear from this provision: the distinct difference to be maintained between men and women. God created male and female in the garden, and he did not change his mind about wanting it to stay that way even in the desert.

Offensive But Instructive

There can be no question about it: The laws of Moses were male-oriented—so much so that modern sensitivities are sometimes offended. Yet what we are to make of that offensiveness is less than clear. Many people of both sexes are also offended at the death penalty which was such a major part of the laws of Moses—and the strict dietary laws, and the sacrifice of thousands of animals each year, not to mention the provisions for slaves and for the perpetuation of warfare.

To us, very little of this seems to fit our notions of human rights or animal rights. But the laws of Moses are really the laws of God. *God* gave them to Moses. And if in the intervening centuries God has also taken away the specific provisions of the law, he has not repudiated completely their significance. We still have to consider seriously what Jesus meant when he said:

Do not think that I have come to abolish the Law or the Prophets; I have not come to abolish them but to fulfill them. I tell you the truth, until heaven and earth disappear, not the smallest letter, not the least stroke of a pen, will by any means disappear from the Law until everything is accomplished (Matthew 5:17, 18).

Moreover the commandments "Love the Lord your God with all your heart and with all your soul and with all your strength" and "Love your neighbor as yourself" did not originate with Jesus. They were part of this "offensive" law (Deuteronomy 6:5; Leviticus 19:18).

If there are offensive aspects to the specific regulations of the law, we must look beyond them to the principles which they taught to a morally unsophisticated people. If animal sacrifices are repulsive to us, so should be the blood sacrifice of Jesus Christ on the cross. Yet if limited atonement for sins was the result of animal sacrifices, then praise God even more for the sacrifice of his Son that we might have complete atonement through his blood!

Likewise, if the status of women under the law is offensive to us as we look through what we consider morally sophisticated glasses, then so should be legislation today which is aimed at the oppression of women. But if the law's distinctions between men and women actually served to foster a divine principle ultimately designed for the protection of women's dignity, then let us praise God for that principle!

Male Leadership in Worship

The legal status of women under the laws of Moses is helpful in determining the relative relationships between men and women in Old Testament times. However, the real key to the principle of male spiritual leadership is found in the roles played by men and women in the nation's worship. Officially and functionally, leadership in public worship was exclusively male.

Priests and Levites

Moses, Aaron, and the 70 elders of Israel were in charge of religious matters at the time the law came into being. Thereafter, God appointed Aaron and his descendants as priests to serve in the tabernacle and later in the temple. Great pomp and circumstance accompanied the ordination of the men of the priesthood, including their anointment with special oil. "Anoint Aaron and his sons and consecrate them so they may serve me as priests," God had said (Exodus 30:30).

To assist Aaron and his sons in the service of the tabernacle, the men of the tribe of Levi were specially appointed to take the place of the firstborn from each family, who until that time had shouldered the responsibility for that duty (Numbers 3:5-10).

Though the men were given the responsibility of performing the public roles in national worship, the women worked alongside the men in support of that worship. We see a good example of this in the construction of the tabernacle. "All who were willing, men and women alike, came and brought gold jewelry of all kinds: brooches, earrings, rings and ornaments. They all presented their gold as a wave offering to the Lord." And, "Every skilled woman spun with her hands and brought what she had spun . . . ." And again, "All the women who were willing and had the skill spun the goat hair." "All the Israelite men and women who were willing brought to the Lord freewill offerings for all the work the Lord through Moses had commanded them to do" (Exodus 35:20-29).

Priest's Daughters

Included among the rules pertaining to priests is a law punishing by death any daughter of a priest who turns to prostitution. "If a priest's daughter defiles herself by becoming a prostitute, she disgraces her father; she must be burned in the fire" (Leviticus 21:9). Again, there is no comparable provision for a priest's *son* who might sleep with a prostitute (although Eli's sons, who had sexual relations with women at the entrance to the tabernacle, were put to death—1 Samuel 2:22-25).

What is more intriguing is that there is no comparable provision for the daughters of men who were not priests. The more-damaging effect which the priest's daughter would have on his ability to be a spiritual leader seems to be the reason for the distinction. Here we can hardly avoid the parallel with New Testament concern for church leaders having demonstrated spiritual success with their own children.

Offerings

When the people of Israel brought offerings to God, they were used to support the families of the priests. Those offerings which were "most holy offerings" were to be eaten by the priests: "Eat it as something most holy; every male shall eat it" (Numbers 18:10). The lesser "wave offerings" were to be given to both sons *and* daughters as the priests' regular share.

This distinction between what the males would eat and what the females would eat takes us directly to the offerings that were central to the worship—the grain, guilt, and sin offerings. When the offering was given in *support* of the worship, then all the priest's children, male and female, ate from that which was offered. When the offering was part of *the worship itself*, then only the sons of the priest were permitted to partake (Leviticus 10:12-15). Why the difference? Male spiritual leadership.

This point is emphasized in the rules regarding the cereal offering. "Like the sin offering and the guilt offering, it is most holy. Any male descendant of Aaron may eat it" (Leviticus 6:17, 18). The clear implication is, "No female may do so." Only males were allowed contact with that which was considered holy because it was part of the official worship, which was man's exclusive domain.

Feasts

Why was spiritual leadership male? Why was official worship reserved exclusively for male oversight? Are we to believe that women could not have done the job as well? Were women any less spiritual, or, to the contrary, were they not spiritually superior in many ways? Why, over and over again, do we run into the same hard fact of male headship?

God never tells us in just so many words, but he has not left us without clues. One of them is found in the *requirement* that the men attend the three main Jewish feasts. "Three times a year all your men must appear before the Lord your God at the place he will choose: at the Feast of Unleavened Bread, the Feast of Weeks and the Feast of Tabernacles" (Deuteronomy 16:16). As we might have suspected, there was no similar requirement of women. But that in itself may be a significant clue. We are not talking here about a *privilege* extended only to men, but a *requirement* imposed only on men!

It is possible, of course, that this command does no more than reflect the contemporary division of responsibility. Women ran the domestic estate, and men ran the family's affairs away from the estate. Yet the significance of the *requirement* for male participation may tell us something significant indeed. Absent the *requirement* of participation, far fewer men might have participated in the feasts. In fact, if modern church statistics were true in ancient times, *far more women than men* would have attended!

It is in this male-oriented requirement that we quite possibly come to the heart of the matter of functional male leadership. I could be wrong about this, but I suggest that it is not at all a recognition of men as being spiritually superior to women, but just the opposite. Were it not for artificially being thrust into the work of the temple, many men might never have been there at all.

Even today, if it were not for being called to a spiritual headship role in the family, many men never would have the slightest concern for personal spiritual development. (As we go along, we will develop this idea further and answer the obvious question: If men are in some way spiritually *weaker* than women, why are they put in positions of spiritual head-ship?)

Male spiritual leadership—a privilege or a responsibility? Recognition or requirement? Honor or duty? Perhaps best stat-ed, male spiritual leadership means *responsibility* with certain privileges attached, *requirement* having recognition for spiri-tual service well performed, and *duty* with honor for the con-scientious man of God.

God-Ordained Male Leadership

There is simply no question about it—under the laws of Moses, functional spiritual leadership was male. In terms of formal worship and appointive positions, it was *exclusively* male. If godly women under the law were "spiritual leaders" in their service to others and their influence for good—and they were—they were not given the responsibility for head-ship in the home or recognized leadership in the congregation of Israel.

The Mosaic system of worship would span 1400 years and still be in place at the appearance of the Messiah. Within that system, male-oriented leadership was *God's* idea, not some-thing dreamed up by Moses or by Aaron and his sons. Nor was it simply a reflection of traditional, patriarchal Mideastern custom and culture. Even though it *became* custom, it was nevertheless God-ordained from the beginning.

At his pleasure, of course, God had the prerogative to alter the role of women at any future time. Just as we know that God set aside animal sacrifices by the once-for-all sacrifice of his Son, God also could have set aside male headship. Just as God changed the pattern of worship by eliminating the tem-ple as the *place*, he also could have called women to positions of leadership and authority within the church. That he did *not* do so, as we will see, discloses God's intention that man con-tinue to bear the responsibility of spiritual headship.

Male spiritual leadership in the garden. Male spiritual leadership among the patriarchs. Male spiritual leadership in the laws of Moses. Despite perversion, abuse, and neglect, the principle runs deep and long. It is God's pattern. It is God's way.

Study Questions

1. Who is the ultimate source of the Laws of Moses? Why is that question important?
2. Would it be correct to think of the Laws of Moses as merely a codification of ancient Semitic culture?
3. In what ways did the Laws of Moses appear to favor men over women?
4. In what ways did the Laws of Moses act to protect women against abuses by men? (Consider, especially, the bill of divorce.)
5. What lessons might we learn from the case of Zelophehad's daughters (Numbers 27:5-7)?
6. Does the rule regarding distinctive clothing (in Deuteronomy 22:5) tell us anything about differences in gender roles?
7. Does the fact that men were exclusively chosen to lead the congregation of Israel in worship speak in any way to how Christian worship ought to be conducted today?
8. Is male spiritual leadership an honor or a responsibility?
9. Why do you suppose that it was only men who were required to attend the religious festivals?
10. If the principle of male spiritual leadership was reflected in the Laws of Moses, does that mean the principle has been done away with in Christ?

6 Of Prophets, Prophetesses, and Prophecy

Chosen Instruments Through Whom God Spoke

The most spiritually exhilarating period of my life came when I spent six weeks in the chalet-dotted ski resort of Davos, Switzerland, in concentrated work on *The Narrated Bible*. The entire project was a highlight of my life, but this particular period of time was unmatched by any other. The Alps had often formed the backdrop for my work and given me Alplike heights of inspiration and productivity. But this six weeks far surpassed any other because I was living, breathing, and *feeling* the lives and writings of the Old Testament prophets.

For some reason we hardly ever read the prophets. Maybe it is because they seem so historically distant. Maybe it is because the traditional arrangement of their writings in the Bible actually leads us away from the rich fabric of social, political, and religious conflict against which their prophetic messages played such a vital part. But when placed in proper context, they breathe life into the history of the kings and battles of the divided kingdom.

But it was more than a fresh perspective that caught my attention. It was the prophets themselves. Not the false prophets, of which there were many, but those great men of

God who called the people away from idolatry back to the Creator-God of the universe. These were the often-reluctant warriors of faith who denounced the people's entanglement in materialistic goals and superficial, institutionalized religion. These were the conscience-challenging spokesmen who cut through religiosity and demanded that religion move from the pious remoteness of the altar to the dusty streets of pain, poverty, and social injustice.

Where the priests had sold out to the mediocre maintenance of a caretaker ritual, the prophets called for fire in one's bones! Where moral indifference had become the order of the day, the prophets pointed to the high road of holiness and purity. And they spoke with *passion!* No three-point sermons with catchy titles for them! It was just God's message coming through like a heat-seeking missile headed straight into the inner courts of the temple.

For me, the prophets ripped away the outer trappings of my own religious exercise. They called out to me deep within my conscience. They exposed me, shamed me, and condemned me! But they also picked me up, gave me new direction, and told me what I *could* be with God's help. They showed me courage in the face of persecution, strength from the pitfalls of weakness.

But most of all the prophets brought me close to God. Because they themselves were so close to God, to know them intimately was to know God himself. Praise God for sending us the prophets!

When I returned to the States from this rich mountaintop experience, more than one friend commented, "LaGard, you've changed." Indeed I had. Nor will I ever forget the most personally rewarding teaching experience of my life: sharing my love for the prophets in a series of Wednesday-evening Bible classes at the University Church on the campus where I work and live. For several weeks we immersed ourselves in the great themes from the prophets. We learned from them, were confronted by them, and were greatly uplifted by them!

Just writing about them has stirred the memory all over again. If it has been a while since you shook hands with the men of old, I highly recommend that you blow the dust off the Old Testament and listen carefully to their message. They will usher you to the very threshold of God!

The Role of the Prophetesses

But what about the Old Testament *prophetesses?* Did they not also stir a spiritually lethargic nation to greater faithfulness? The only prophetic writings which have been preserved for us in the Bible were prophecies written by male prophets. Therefore it is easy to forget that there were also prophetesses. Even if there is no record of their preaching scathing sermons or bringing godly tirades against wickedness and empty religious charade, they nevertheless became God's instruments through which he often spoke to his people. Let's take a closer look at these special women of God.

Miriam

Retracing our steps to the period just prior to the giving of the Law we find the account of the first recorded prophetess, Miriam, the sister of Moses and of Aaron the high priest. It was Miriam who led the women of Israel in the joyous celebration following the destruction of the Egyptians in the Red Sea as the Israelites made their exodus from bondage.

> When Pharaoh's horses, chariots and horsemen went into the sea, the Lord brought the waters of the sea back over them, but the Israelites walked through the sea on dry ground. Then Miriam the prophetess, Aaron's sister, took a tambourine in her hand, and all the women followed her, with tambourines and dancing. Miriam sang to them:

"Sing to the Lord,
    for he is highly exalted.
The horse and its rider
    he has hurled into the sea"
(Exodus 15:19-21).

Miriam's role as a prophetess is not well-defined at this point, but she obviously was an influential woman from an influential family. The prophet Micah would later refer to Miriam as being God-sent, along with her two brothers: "I sent Moses to lead you, also Aaron and Miriam" (Micah 6:4). It is not surprising that, as a leader among her people, she was followed in the song of deliverance by the women of Israel. It must have been a wonderful sight watching their celebration of praise to God!

Unfortunately, there is a later incident which mars the picture we have of Miriam. For reasons not disclosed, Miriam and Aaron felt that Moses' marriage to a Cushite woman was not the will of God. "Has the Lord spoken only through Moses?" they asked him rebukingly. "Hasn't he also spoken through us?" (Numbers 12:2). When God heard this, he quickly called Miriam and Aaron on the carpet!

Listen to my words:
When a prophet of the Lord is among you,
    I reveal myself to him in visions,
    I speak to you in dreams.
But this is not true of my servant Moses;
    he is faithful in all my house.
With him I speak face to face,
    clearly and not in riddles;
    he sees the form of the Lord.
Why then were you not afraid
    to speak against my servant Moses?

(Numbers 12:6-8).

When God's presence lifted from the tent, Miriam stood leprous, like snow. Both Moses and Aaron pleaded for God to remove the leprosy, but God's reply was stern:

> "If her father had spit in her face, would she not have been in disgrace for seven days? Confine her outside the camp for seven days; after that she can be brought back." So Miriam was confined outside the camp for seven days, and the people did not move on till she was brought back (Numbers 12:14, 15).

This passage is simply packed with mind-stretching questions! Why did God not punish Aaron along with Miriam? What distinction did he see in their sins? Did it have anything to do with Miriam's being a woman, or is there more to the story that we are not told—some detail that would call for Miriam's greater punishment?

Indeed, could it possibly have meant that—prophetess or no prophetess—Miriam had challenged God's chosen leader in a way unbefitting a woman, even if the man was her brother? It does appear similar to the situation we have already seen where Michal rebuked her husband, King David. If this is the correct explanation, then it would also explain why Aaron did not receive the same punishment: One male spiritual leader could challenge another male spiritual leader, even if he were wrong in his criticism; but such a challenge would not be an option for a woman, as it would threaten the greater principle of male spiritual leadership.

An analysis of Paul's later instruction to the Corinthian Christians forbidding the woman from challenging one who has prophesied (1 Corinthians 14:34, 35) may express a similar concern.

Another curiosity is God's reference to a father disgracing his daughter by spitting in her face. Are we to take that as a common practice of the times? If so, did God approve of the practice, or was he simply making a statement about the comparative seriousness of Miriam's sin in view of their own sense of outrage at far less serious breaches? Whatever else it may mean, it does suggest a tie between an insolent daughter and a woman of God who has overstepped the bounds of spiritual leadership.

If there is anything good to salvage from this incident, it is the great respect in which Miriam apparently was held by the people. They did not move on until she was restored to her health and brought back into the camp. Not even the men were rushing to leave her behind, arrogantly proclaiming (as they might have) that "the woman had it coming to her!" Proof that God himself honored this great woman, despite her sin, is suggested in the fact that he restored her to her former position. Also, her death was recorded in the same way that men of great honor were remembered (Numbers 20:1).

One important thing we learn from this passage is something of the role of a prophet or prophetess. God spoke through them in dreams and visions to deliver messages to his people. And in whatever way he did that, he did it through Miriam as well as through her brothers Moses and Aaron.

Deborah

One of the most admired women in the Bible is the prophetess Deborah. Her role as a judge over Israel came closer to the actual meaning of the word "judge" than was typical of the other "judges" of Israel during her time, who were primarily military leaders. However, because of the cowardice of Barak, who would not go out to fight Israel's enemy (Sisera) unless Deborah went with him, Deborah was instrumental in winning a major victory for the nation.

Deborah, a prophetess, the wife of Lappidoth, was leading Israel at that time. She held court under the

Palm of Deborah between Ramah and Bethel in the hill country of Ephraim, and the Israelites came to her to have their disputes decided. She sent for Barak son of Abinoam from Kedesh in Naphtali and said to him, "The Lord, the God of Israel, commands you: 'Go, take with you ten thousand men of Naphtali and Zebulun and lead the way to Mount Tabor. I will lure Sisera, the commander of Jabin's army, with his chariots and his troops to the Kishon River and give him into your hands.'"

Barak said to her, "If you go with me, I will go; but if you don't go with me, I won't go."

"Very well," Deborah said, "I will go with you. But because of the way you are going about this, the honor will not be yours, for the Lord will hand Sisera over to a woman." So Deborah went with Barak to Kedesh, where he summoned Zebulun and Naphtali. Ten thousand men followed him, and Deborah also went with him (Judges 4:4-10).

What was a woman doing holding court and deciding disputes among the people of Israel? Such a role was uncharacteristic of women during that time—especially in the male-oriented society of Israel. What's more, Deborah was a wife and mother, not some unattached or widowed woman who might have been considered an exception to the norm. The answer is that Deborah was a prophetess, a person through whom God spoke in order to meet the needs of his people. She was not a religious leader within the priesthood of Israel. Nevertheless, as a prophetess of God she exercised political and judicial leadership—and even spiritual leadership—by bringing God's revealed judgment to bear on the cases presented to her.

It was through Deborah in her role as a prophetess that God instructed Barak to do battle with Sisera. It was not Deborah's idea, but God's command. Nevertheless Barak feared going into battle without this great woman of God. Perhaps he did not trust a woman to have brought him such a message from God. Perhaps, quite to the contrary, he saw Deborah as God's spokesperson and feared going into battle without having God's personal representative close by in his corner.

Deborah herself reminded Barak (and us) of how very extraordinary it was for a woman to be in such a focal position. The honor which was normally given to a man who was victorious in battle would not go to Barak on this occasion, but "to a woman," because he needed a woman's help to win. (Whether that is a reference to Deborah's help is less than certain. As we will see, another woman would be more directly involved in Sisera's death.) Instead of assuming an unnatural role for a woman and taking the actual lead, Deborah agreed to accompany Barak but shamed his fear of taking the leadership role which was his responsibility.

At the scene of the battle, once again God spoke to Barak through Deborah: "Go! This is the day the Lord has given Sisera into your hands. Has not the Lord gone ahead of you?" (Judges 4:14). Barak and his army then went out and God gave them the victory. Sisera himself fled but was killed by a courageous woman named Jael.

Many Christians today see Deborah as inspiration for a wider leadership role for women. Yet, in the story of Deborah, the message is clear: Great shame attached to the men of Israel for failing to assume their responsibility as leaders and protectors. Not only had they refused to exercise their role as spiritual protectors (evident from the nation's moral bankruptcy), but they were even refusing to protect the nation militarily! Deborah's leadership, and her need to push men into battle, is a graphic reminder of how far the men had sunk in the neglect of their responsibilities.

The song of Deborah and Barak following the nation's victory underscores that message. The real victory was not in defeating Sisera but in restoring a courageous, vibrant sense of leadership among the men of Israel.

> When the princes in Israel take the lead,
>> when the people willingly offer
>> themselves—praise the Lord!
>
> In the days of Shamgar son of Anath,
>> in the days of Jael, the roads were
>> abandoned;
>> travelers took to winding paths.
>
> Village life [or warriors] in Israel ceased,
>> ceased until I, Deborah, arose,
>> arose a mother in Israel.
>
> When they chose new gods,
>> war came to the city gates,
>> and not a shield or spear
>> was seen among forty thousand
>> in Israel.
>
> My heart is with Israel's princes,
>> with the willing volunteers among
>> the people.
>> Praise the Lord! (Judges 5:2, 6-9).

What a forceful statement about fallen spiritual leaders and the impact they have on an entire nation! When the men failed to exercise conscientious spiritual leadership, crime became so rampant that even ordinary travel was unsafe. And when they allowed idolatry to replace the Creator-God of heaven, the nation's enemies found them ripe for the picking. In the end, the nation's spiritual degeneration had led to such debilitation of their moral courage that they lost their will to fight for the protection of their own families.

The men in Israel during the time of Deborah were what Derek Prince calls "renegade males." They were *renegades* because they had *reneged* on their spiritual responsibilities. Are twentieth-century Christian men equally "renegade males"?

The good news is that, through Deborah, God had instilled a new spirit of leadership among the nation's princes. They found within themselves not only the will to fight but also to return to God and give him his rightful place in their hearts and lives. The postscript to the story reads simply: "Then the land had peace forty years" (Judges 5:31).

It might be urged today that we need modem "Deborahs" to bring spiritually weak men back to accountability. That would be a noble proposition, but it is not the motivation cited in today's liberationist literature. The call today is for leadership equality *per se*—that there should be no functional leadership distinctions whatever. To the contrary, Deborah's call was for a return to strong *male* leadership.

God did not use Deborah—a strong leader of her people—as a signal for either her generation or ours that he had changed his mind about male spiritual headship. To the contrary, the story of Deborah ought to be the strongest possible warning to men of every generation about the danger of abandoning the responsibility which God has given them as protectors of society's moral and spiritual strength—whether through leadership in worship or leadership in the home. If we are to regard Deborah as an example of a God-ordained female spiritual leader, then we must follow her leadership where it leads—directly and unequivocally to God's call for *male* spiritual leadership.

It is not a matter of saying to *women* that they *can't* lead. It is a matter of saying to *men* that women shouldn't *have to* lead.

Huldah

When King Josiah of Judah ordered that the temple be restored after years of idolatry, among the rubble of the neglected temple the priest found the Book of the Law. (What a sad commentary on the priesthood that, until that time, the priest did not even know where the Book of the Law was kept!) A reading of the laws of God greatly humbled King Josiah—so much so that he sent his attendants to "inquire of the Lord" what was to happen to the nation because of their neglect of the law.

In order to "inquire of the Lord," the attendants went to a woman—Huldah the prophetess.

> Hilkiah the priest . . . [and those the king had sent with him] went to speak to the prophetess Huldah, who was the wife of Shallum son of Tikvah, the son of Harhas, keeper of the wardrobe. She lived in Jerusalem, in the Second District.
>
> She said to them, "This is what the Lord, the God of Israel, says . . . ." (2 Kings 22:14, 15).

Then Huldah informed Josiah of what would happen to the nation and to himself.

In this brief reference we see another woman serving as the instrument through which God sends his message. One has to stop and ask how the king's attendants even knew about Huldah and the likelihood that God would speak through her. The obvious answer is that Huldah had spoken previously on God's behalf. There seems to be nothing remarkable or surprising to them that she should play that role. And the implication is that there were other women who also were prophetesses during this time. No great stir is made of the fact that a message from God happens to come through a woman.

Was Huldah a spiritual *leader?* Not in the sense that she was called to the priesthood or would be perpetuated in her function by yet another "Hulda." But, like other prophetesses, she was a woman of God through whom he spoke to his people.

Throughout the Old Testament, God spoke through women as well as men. But prophetesses held no continuing, established function of spiritual leadership. Nor did the prophets. On the whole, Old Testament prophets and prophetesses played only an ad hoc role as God's instruments of revelation. In service and influence they were certainly leaders, but they were never a regular part of the religious superstructure. If, like Deborah, they exercised moral leadership, they were never priests or priestesses. They were never "in charge of the worship." Honored, yes—greatly honored—but never given the responsibility for headship either in the family or in the congregation of Israel's corporate worship to God.

This is not to say that God always worked his will through the religious establishment. God often worked completely outside that establishment, and in fact later destroyed the establishment altogether under Christ. What it does say is that God's own exceptions did not detract from his consistent call for male headship within that establishment for as long as he intended the establishment to exist.

The key word is *headship*—not the active participation in which godly women have always shared, nor the kind of leadership which prophetesses exercised as special instruments of God's revelations.

Where we can point to a dozen women in the Old Testament who played particularly significant roles in the life of the nation, we must not forget that day in and day out, year in and year out, century in and century out, it was the *men* of Israel—numbering in the thousands—who were chosen by God to serve as heads of their families and to perform the priestly duties. *Men* performed the duties corresponding most closely to those of our own functional leadership ministry which the church today is being urged to expand to women.

If reversal of the principle of male spiritual leadership were to be made under Christ, then the evidence for such a radical change would have to be substantial indeed, because the precedent of God's dealing with the human race up to the point of Christ's appearance is unquestionably that of male headship. Trying to use the Old Testament prophetesses as a foundation for equality in leadership roles is flying in the face of the obvious. We are seeing wishful trees and ignoring factual forests.

Let us praise the Old Testament prophetesses for their loyal and courageous service to God and his people, but let us not misuse them to build a case for something they never were—established leaders of God's people exercising ongoing religious headship.

The challenge for us in the modern church is to recognize the many ways in which we have denigrated the spiritual expression of Christian women in the name of male leadership. The challenge is to explore the avenues through which we can be blessed by the special gifts which women can contribute apart from those functional leadership roles which are specifically designated for men.

Joel's Prophecy Brings Anticipation

We could not end a discussion of the prophets and prophetesses without noting the exciting anticipation which came from the writing of one of the great prophets, Joel. Coming as it did in the context of looking forward with hope for Israel's restoration, God's message through Joel is a prophetic double-entendre also envisioning the exciting, revolutionary Christian age.

And afterward,
    I will pour out my Spirit on all people.

Your sons and your daughters will prophesy,
    your old men will dream dreams,
    your young men will see visions.

Even on my servants, both men and women,
    I will pour out my Spirit in those days
    (Joel 2:28, 29).

It is little wonder that the next time we see this passage quoted is in Acts chapter 2 when Peter joyously proclaims the fulfillment of Joel's prophecy on the occasion of the formal establishment of Christ's church. On that first Pentecost after Christ's resurrection the Holy Spirit was indeed poured out—and with power!

Was that occasion to herald a new role for women in the church? There will be more to consider before we are able to answer that question with greater certainty. But in light of what we have learned in this chapter about the role of prophetesses in the Old Testament, something else must be contemplated by Joel's prophecy than the fact that both men and women would prophesy. Since women had already been prophesying for centuries, that in itself would be unremarkable.

So what else might be the cause for such jubilation? Forget the dreams, visions, and prophecies. Those have been scattered across the pages of the Old Testament from the beginning of time. Keep your eyes on the twice-repeated phrase "I will pour out my Spirit." That is the key: "I will pour out my Spirit."

For all of God's intimate contact with men and women in the centuries before Christ, and for all the miraculous feats he had performed, not one man or one woman had received the Holy Spirit within, in the same sense that baptized believers have received it from Pentecost onward. And if that is Joel's message, then cause for jubilation is an understatement. Imagine it—God *within* us! Within both men and women, male and female!

Study Questions

1. In what way has God used prophets and prophetesses?
2. Were either of them ever given responsibility for leading the congregation of Israel in worship?
3. Given that the church today believes the role of prophecy has come to an end, does anything we know about prophets and prophetesses in biblical times stand as precedent for men and women who no longer fulfill that office?
4. Is there any current equivalent to the gift of prophecy which might suggest anything at all about spiritual leadership roles?
5. In what way was Miriam a spiritual leader?
6. In what way was Deborah a spiritual leader?
7. Why did Barak refuse to go into battle without Deborah?
8. What does it say about the men of Israel that Deborah speaks of a nation where it wasn't safe to travel, and where men were not willing to fight in defense of their country?
9. Is the life of Deborah a call for a greater spiritual leadership role for women, or a rebuke to men for being irresponsible as spiritual leaders?
10. Can women be spiritual leaders without assuming headship?

7 *Gurus, Goddesses, and Gender*

The Lure of Female-Oriented Paganism

For several years I spent a substantial part of my time writing and speaking against the New Age movement, the fastest-growing belief system in the Western world. It is an eclectic blend of Hinduism, Buddhism, psychic phenomena, me-generation selfism, reincarnation, and—incredibly enough—Christianity! Despite its many "Christian" trappings, the New Age movement is nothing short of neopaganism, in which the highest form of idolatry is the worship of self as God.

The most alarming aspect of the New Age movement is that it is being accepted, supposedly with biblical support, by bright, well-educated people in America's upper middle class. The message has a pernicious progression from "You are God" to "Therefore your truth is as valid as everyone else's truth" to "Hence there is no right and there is no wrong!"

My first involvement in opposition to this new belief system came in the writing of a response to actress Shirley MacLaine, whose best-selling book, *Out on a Limb,* has influenced millions of people to join the movement. My response, *Out on a Broken Limb,* has drawn me ever closer to what the movement is all about. Two things have stood out noticeably.

The first is that women far outnumber men in the New Age movement. In one respect this should not be surprising, because the spiritual nature of the movement would appeal very naturally to women. However, the surprise is the high percentage of women who are involved. It is a far higher percentage than one would find in traditional churches, where women also outnumber men.

When I attended the first of Shirley MacLaine's "Connecting With Your Higher Self Seminars," for example, of the 800 people who had paid 300 dollars each to attend, from 80 to 90 percent were women. The same was true when I went undercover to investigate Ms. MacLaine's psychic channeler, Kevin Ryerson. The private home where we met to watch him "go into a trance and communicate with entities from the astral plane" was filled from wall to wall—mostly with women.

Because of the great numbers of people attracted to New Age thinking, even the lesser percentage of male devotees means that thousands of men are also buying into the sophisticated cult of our time. Many are New Age musicians, artists, and channelers. But it is chiefly women who are attracted by the female-oriented message of the movement, which says that male left-brain rational thought must give way to female right-brain intuitive thought, so that "If it feels good, believe it." Even a cursory reading of New Age books will confirm this message.

It is no coincidence that the goddess of the New Age movement is female actress Shirley MacLaine or that most of the spirit channelers who have appeared on the New Age scene are also women. For the most part, women have become the popular high priestesses of this neopaganism of our time. And while there are plenty of men caught up in the movement—both as gurus and as devotees—most of the guru groupies are women.

Far from being *new,* the New Age movement has taken us back to the ancient witch of Endor. In fact, Shirley MacLaine calls herself "the good witch." A fascination with crystals has replaced actual crystal balls, and witches have been replaced by psychic mediums who entertain at spiritual "Tupperware" parties. But what has not changed is the overwhelming predominance of women in cultic practices. It is women who flood the New Age bookstores, women who load themselves down with the supposedly medicinal crystals, and women who seek the guidance of palmists, mystics, and spirit channelers.

This phenomenon has not escaped the attention of *Los Angeles Times* Religion Editor Russell Chandler. In his comprehensive review of the New Age movement, *Understanding the New Age,* Chandler dedicates an entire chapter to "Goddesses and Neopagans." Of shamanist Lynn Andrews he says:

> Her brand of urban shamanism is a vital link to the ancient, mystical knowledge of female consciousness, a link that ties in well with the growing feminist or goddess element of the New Age Movement.
>
> "Power is female. That's always the first lesson of shamanistic training," tutors warrioress Andrews, adding that the obligation of all women is the education of men (p. 118).

The irony of New Age fascination with feminism, of course, is that Eastern religions, from which New Agers draw so prolifically, are notoriously repressive of women. One need only look to the status of women in India to confirm that sad fact.

The second thing about the movement that has caught my attention is the association between modern pagan beliefs and either gender-neutral deities or female goddesses. New Age literature normally refers to God as a nonpersonal, gender-neutral "God Force," consistent with the monistic belief that "all is one." The belief in the oneness of the universe serves both to elevate us to godhood (since *we* are one and *God* is one, then we are God!) and to eliminate any idea of the maleness of God.

In fact, through the movement's belief in reincarnation, virtually all gender significance is unceremoniously thrown out the window. After all, we are told, over many past lives each one of us has been both male and female, and sometimes even androgynous.

Beyond references to an impersonal, gender-neutral "God Force," you hear frequent references to "God, she . . ." and extra play on the concept of Mother Earth. Frequent references are also made to Greek and Egyptian goddesses as progenitors of New Age enlightenment. In all, the paganism of the New Age movement is female-oriented and female-attractive. Is it just coincidence that current calls for wider involvement of women in the church should come at a time when female-oriented paganism is sweeping through society?

Pagan Prophetesses in Israel

We have seen the noble work of several women prophetesses, but there is another side to the story—a darker side, and a side to be avoided at all cost.

In a revelation to the prophet Ezekiel (Ezekiel 13:17), God refers to "the daughters of your people who prophesy," as if to indicate a large number of women in Israel active in that role. Unfortunately, the particular reference in Ezekiel is to the many *false* prophetesses who, along with the many false prophets, were to be rebuked by Ezekiel. The male prophets (Ezekiel 13:1-16) and the female prophetesses (Ezekiel 13:17-23) both are warned against prophesying out of their own imaginations.

Something intriguing emerges from a comparison of the first set of rebukes given to the prophets and the second set of rebukes given to the prophetesses. The prophetesses apparently were engaged in more identifiable occult practices than were their male counterparts.

> This is what the Sovereign Lord says: Woe to the women who sew magic charms on all their wrists and make veils of various lengths for their heads in order to ensnare people.
>
> Therefore this is what the Sovereign Lord says: I am against your magic charms with which you ensnare people like birds and I will tear them from your arms; I will set free the people that you ensnare like birds. I will tear off your veils and save my people from your hands, and they will no longer fall prey to your power (Ezekiel 13:18, 20, 21).

It would not be particularly noteworthy if this were the only suggestion in Scripture of a tie between women and pagan practices, but the disturbing pattern keeps recurring. When we read methodically through the Bible, looking at every reference to women in the work and worship of ancient society, there are enough such passages to constitute a separate category all their own.

The Appeal of Paganism

Several passages indicate that women often *led* men into idolatry. One example is found in the experience which the men of Israel had with the Moabite and Midianite women.

> While Israel was staying in Shittim, the men began to indulge in sexual immorality with Moabite women, who invited them to the sacrifices to their gods. The people ate and bowed down before these gods. So Israel joined in worshiping the Baal of Peor. And the Lord's anger burned against them.

> The Lord said to Moses, "Take all the leaders of these
> people, kill them and expose them in broad daylight
> before the Lord, so that the Lord's fierce anger may turn
> away from Israel."
>
> So Moses said to Israel's judges, "Each of you must
> put to death those of your men who have joined in
> worshiping the Baal of Peor" (Numbers 25:1-5).

The double seduction of the men of Israel had been pre-
meditated by the Midianite women. They knew that through
sexual involvement the men could be turned easily to pagan
worship. The degree of success which they had in their mission is seen in the aftermath of a battle that God had specifically ordered against the Midianites. Instead of killing the
women along with the men—which would have been expected under these circumstances in ancient times—the men of
Israel spared the women. Moses was furious!

> "Have you allowed all the women to live?" he asked
> them. "They were the ones who followed Balaam's
> advice and were the means of turning the Israelites
> away from the Lord in what happened at Peor, so that
> a plague struck the Lord's people" (Numbers 31:15, 16).

Even after the plague and God's judgment calling for the
deaths of the leaders who had permitted the idolatrous worship, the men of Israel were still "soft on paganism" because
of the Midianite women. They failed to see what a threat the
pagan women were to their faith. Experiences like this
demonstrated the wisdom of warnings against marriages with
foreign women—women whose pagan influence would lead
spiritually weaker men away from the true God.

Not even the wise King Solomon was exempt from spiritual seduction by his wives. As if anticipating that Solomon's
many wives would turn him toward pagan practices, God had

included a warning in the laws of Moses even before there were any kings. The king, said God, "must not take many wives, or his heart will be led astray" (Deuteronomy 17:17).

Interestingly, the command did not focus on *foreign* wives or *pagan* wives, but simply *many* wives. If women naturally tend to be spiritually inclined—perhaps even more so than men—then a balance can be struck between one woman and one man by calling the man to exercise responsibility through spiritual headship. But the odds of even a spiritually strong man maintaining independent leadership over many spiritually inclined women would be great—more than most men could handle.

The problem is intensified if the spiritually inclined women happen to be inclined toward paganism, as Solomon discovered.

> King Solomon, however, loved many foreign women besides Pharaoh's daughter—Moabites, Ammonites, Edomites, Sidonians and Hittites. They were from nations about which the Lord had told the Israelites, "You must not intermarry with them, because they will surely turn your hearts after their gods." Nevertheless, Solomon held fast to them in love. He had seven hundred wives of royal birth and three hundred concubines, and his wives led him astray.
>
> As Solomon grew old, his wives turned his heart after other gods, and his heart was not fully devoted to the Lord his God, as the heart of David his father had been. He followed Ashtoreth the goddess of the Sidonians, and Molech the detestable god of the Ammonites. So Solomon did evil in the eyes of the Lord; he did not follow the Lord completely, as David his father had done.
>
> On a hill east of Jerusalem, Solomon built a high place for Chemosh the detestable god of Moab, and for Molech the detestable god of the Ammonites. He did

the same for all his foreign wives, who burned incense and offered sacrifices to their gods (1 Kings 11:1-8).

Solomon's wives were not the only women involved in paganism. When Asa, king of Judah, instituted his religious reforms, he began with his own household. "King Asa also deposed his grandmother Maacah from her position as queen mother, because she had made a repulsive Asherah pole. Asa cut the pole down, broke it up and burned it in the Kidron Valley" (2 Chronicles 15:16).

The Lure of Female Deities

As with the New Age movement today, not only were women easily attracted to pagan practices, but it was to female deities that they sometimes were drawn. Although the male god, Baal, got most of the attention by idolatrous Israelites, the prophet Jeremiah warned against those who worshiped the goddess known as the Queen of Heaven.

Do you not see what they are doing in the towns of Judah and in the streets of Jerusalem? The children gather wood, the fathers light the fire, and the women knead the dough and make cakes of bread for the Queen of Heaven" (Jeremiah 7:17, 18).

This pagan association with female deities presents us with a far more serious problem than mere gender change. Because God presents himself as a male deity, the gratuitous change in gender actually becomes a form of idolatry. Clearly the Queen of Heaven is not the Father God of all creation!

C. S. Lewis points to yet another danger of female-oriented deities:

Goddesses have, of course, been worshipped: many religions have had priestesses. But they are religions quite different from Christianity . . . a child who had been taught to pray to a mother in heaven would have a religious life radically different from that of a Christian child (Collins, *God in the Dock*).

When Israel fell as a result of turning toward pagan worship, the most surprising thing is that even after the destruction of Jerusalem there were many people who had not learned their lesson. A remnant of those who were not taken away into Babylonian captivity arrogantly defied a direct command of God that they not move to Egypt and even had the further audacity to force Jeremiah to go with them! It is no secret why God had warned them not to "pitch their tents toward Sodom," as it were. God was well aware that Egypt was a fertile ground for pagan practices, including the worship of female goddesses.

The tie between the women and their favorite female goddess becomes crystal clear in an unusually venomous defense of their pagan practices by the women involved. The same heated verbal exchange with Jeremiah also gives us one of the best insights into the relationship between the women and their spiritually weak husbands.

Then all the men who knew that their wives were burning incense to other gods, along with all the women who were present—a large assembly—and all the people living in Lower and Upper Egypt, said to Jeremiah, "We will not listen to the message you have spoken to us in the name of the Lord! We will certainly do everything we said we would: We will burn incense to the Queen of Heaven and will pour out drink offerings to her just as we and our fathers, our kings and our officials did in the towns of Judah and in the streets of Jerusalem. At that time we had plenty of food and were well off and suffered no harm. But ever since we stopped burning incense to the Queen of Heaven and pouring out drink offerings to her, we have had nothing and have been perishing by sword and famine."

The women added, "When we burned incense to the Queen of Heaven and poured out drink offerings to her, did not our husbands know that we were making cakes like her image and pouring out drink offerings to her?" (Jeremiah 44:15-19).

It is difficult to escape the progression of events, which the women themselves so readily acknowledged:

The women were fascinated by the female Queen of Heaven and began to worship her; their husbands knew what the women were doing and did nothing to stop it; and soon even the men were involved in pagan worship, from the kings and highest officials on down the line! Can you imagine a more graphic illustration of male leadership gone amok?

But I suggest that the progression really started two steps earlier, when the men of Israel reneged in their spiritual responsibilities, thereby creating a spiritual vacuum. Women, like men, can choose to rebel against God under any circumstances. But I suspect that, for some women of Israel, it was only in the context of such a vacuum that they would have considered turning to anything other than the one true God.

If women have the gift of breathing life into religious practice, men have a responsibility to help ensure that it is the *right* religious practice. Nor are wives excluded from the reciprocal concern of helping to keep their husbands on the right track. Faithfulness is a cord of three strands: husband, wife, and God.

Intermarriage and Paganism

When you look at how many times the men of Israel got into trouble by marrying foreign wives, you begin to wonder about chickens and eggs. Which came first—foreign women who made spiritually weak men of their husbands, or spiritually weak men who married foreign women? I suspect it is the latter. If the men had been faithful to the law, which warned against intermarriage with foreign women (Deuteronomy 7:3), they would never have gotten themselves into marital relationships which had the potential for destroying their faith.

It is not, of course, the women's *foreignness* that put men at risk, but their *paganness*. God is not warning against marriage between those of different races or cultures, but between believers and nonbelievers.

Yet even during the period of exile the men remaining in Palestine had resorted to intermarriage, ushering in paganism and bringing destruction to the nation. When Ezra led the second return to Jerusalem from captivity, he could not believe what he discovered: Even the priests and Levites had married foreign women! To their credit, all the men who had taken foreign wives made the extraordinary decision to put them away (Ezra chapter 10).

If only that could have been the happy ending. But no—within 30 years Nehemiah found the same condition! His record of that discovery is unusually frank. He got so angry that he actually—well, see for yourself.

> In those days I saw men of Judah who had married women from Ashdod, Ammon and Moab. Half of their children spoke the language of Ashdod or the language of one of the other peoples, and did not know how to speak the language of Judah. I rebuked them and called curses down on them. I beat some of the men and pulled out their hair. I made them take an oath in God's name and said: "You are not to give your daughters in marriage to their sons, nor are you to take their daughters in marriage for your sons or for yourselves. Was it not because of marriages like these that Solomon

king of Israel sinned? Among the many nations there
was no king like him. He was loved by his God, and
God made him king over all Israel, but even he was led
into sin by foreign women. Must we hear now that you
too are doing all this terrible wickedness and are being
unfaithful to our God by marrying foreign women?"
(Nehemiah 13:23-27).

Nehemiah was upset, and well he should have been!
Generation after generation of Israel's men had failed to
appreciate how easily their wives could influence their spiritual allegiance. Male spiritual leadership was God's way to
keep men spiritually strong, but their intermarriage with pagan
women sapped their moral strength and left them vulnerable.

Male Headship As a Safeguard

Who would have guessed that the spiritual influence of a
man's wife could be his Achilles heel? The potential for a wife
to have an adverse spiritual influence over her husband arises
out of what is normally a good trait of marriage partners: They
want to please each other. Paul reminds us in his first
Corinthian letter that "a married man is concerned about the
affairs of this world—how he can please his wife . . ." and also
that "a married woman is concerned about the affairs of this
world—how she can please her husband" (1 Corinthians 7:33,
34).

If the wife has strong feelings about her religious beliefs, it
is likely that a spiritually weaker husband will yield to her personal beliefs and perhaps even begin to follow them himself.
When pagan beliefs are involved, that pattern becomes particularly disastrous.

The counter possibility is that when the husband has strong
religious beliefs, his wife likely will yield to those beliefs and
follow in his footsteps—all the more reason for Christian men
to be spiritually strong. They have responsibility, not only for

themselves, but also for their wives and children, who look to them for strength and direction.

In many cases our greatest strength is also our greatest weakness. In what may be woman's greatest strength— an openness to spirituality—there is the potential for misdirection. This may explain, for example, why female interest in paganism is so often related to female deities and goddesses.

For many women, the often-prominent female character of paganism *seems* right. For example, if a woman's father or husband was spiritually weak, her own spiritual strength might seem better reflected in a female deity. In such a case, perhaps, the woman could relate better to a goddess than to a god.

And a woman who has experienced only misguided, oppressive male headship quite understandably may run in the direction of what appears to be more sympathetic, female-oriented spiritual leadership.

Finally, a prideful woman, intent on rejecting properly exercised male spiritual leadership, may latch onto female-oriented paganism as her way out of what she feels to be unjust male domination. It is this third possibility which seems to manifest itself most clearly in the female-oriented New Age movement. With some women, God's "maleness" is less a gender problem than a submission problem.

Looking ahead to issues of submission which would be raised concerning women in New Testament times, the predominantly pagan cultural backdrop undoubtedly figures significantly in setting the scene. In Corinth, for example, the cult of Isis gave women the same power as men. And in Ephesus the god Artemis was known for loving women and helping them to capture men in war. It is not surprising, then, that Christian women in Corinth and Ephesus should have been influenced by such female-liberating paganism, causing them to question traditional male headship at home and in the church.

Paul's teaching on the subject (which we will review in greater detail) could hardly be more relevant to a twenty-first century society heading into neopaganism in the New Age of gender-free, if not female-oriented, "enlightenment." If what Paul wrote was simply cultural, it is also *our* culture. If what he wrote was to deal with special circumstances, they are *our* circumstances.

In truth, the same culture and circumstances have been repeated often throughout history. More than once, female-oriented paganism has filled the void left by the absence of spiritually strong men of God. So too have Christian women felt obligated to fill the empty shoes of men who have abandoned conscientious leadership in the church. To most of us that would seem the right thing to do—in fact, necessary. In the case of Deborah it was even God's idea. But when it justifies a permanent major shift in divine order, it is not God's way. It is the way of lesser gods and goddesses.

Study Questions

1. Is there any substantive difference between the idea of "Father God" as opposed to "Mother God?"

2. Why do you suppose pagan religions and occult worshipers have female goddesses and priestesses?

3. What is one to conclude from the fact that women gurus seem to dominate the New Age movement? Is it any more telling than that women tend to be more active in all religions?

4. Is there any way in which women have a greater capacity to influence men spiritually than men have to influence women spiritually?

5. Was C. S. Lewis right when he opined that "a child who had been taught to pray to a mother in heaven would have a religious life radically different from that of a Christian child [presumably taught to believe in Father God]?"

6. What was the real danger in the men of Israel marrying foreign wives? Is there any lesson which we today should draw from Israel's experience?

7. In what way might male spiritual leadership be compromised by what Paul said in 1 Corinthians 7:33: "a married man is concerned about the affairs of this world—how he can please his wife . . ."?

8. Would it be fair to say that, for good or for ill, a woman typically has more of a tendency to gravitate to extremes in her spirituality than does a man?

9. Would it be fair to say that, for good or for ill, a man typically is confined in his spirituality by a more rational approach to faith?

10. How do gender roles in our culture compare with gender roles in the pagan culture of Paul's day?

8 So Much for Barefoot and Pregnant

Broken Stereotypes of Old Testament Women

In my many wanderings around the globe I have witnessed an amazing phenomenon: The men of the world sit around in village centers drinking tea, smoking who knows what, and discussing the great affairs of state, while the women of the world break their backs taking care of the men.

There is a colorful collage of such scenes in my memory: The corner tea shop in Istanbul crowded with men talking for hour upon hour. A dark-skinned woman of Ethiopia bent beneath the burden of a load of wood that I could not even have picked up. The graceful swaying of young women in South Africa as they carry along on their heads gallons of water in metal tubs. The beautiful women of Thailand washing clothes in the same river where family members bathe, relieve themselves of bodily wastes, and draw their drinking water. Customs men in the Bombay airport moving at slower than snail's pace while frail women scurry around cleaning up after them.

Worldwide conditions in other cultures, mostly dominated by non-Christian religions, are a reminder of how liberating Christianity has already been for women, despite its theology of male spiritual leadership (or possibly *because* of a theology of male spiritual leadership?).

I suspect that, if you are a woman, you may have said to yourself, "Maybe what happens in Turkey, Africa, India, and the Far East is different by degree, but not in principle. I still slave away at home while my husband is out with his friends or business associates, doing whatever men do—even though I *also* have a job away from home." When American women entered the work force, they didn't get severance pay from their responsibilities on the home front. Instead of *exchanging* jobs, they acquired a *second* job.

For all the trendy talk about dual parenting and "house husbands," the fact is that most marriages remain fairly one-sided. I have a lot of liberal-talking male friends, but I keep noticing that their wives most often have to take out the trash!

On the positive side of the ledger is the feeling shared by most women that they can handle anything thrown their way, whether at home or on the job. Whether changing diapers or chairing a committee meeting at the office, today's woman is comfortable within herself (if also sometimes frazzled beyond repair when her "he man" does not contribute his part to child-rearing and housekeeping). If there have been times in recent history when women did not feel secure unless they were barefoot and pregnant in the kitchen, that traditional image has never been supported by Scripture, not even in the patriarchal system of ancient Israel.

What we see in the Old Testament is a cross-section of women, some bad and many more good. For every wicked Jezebel there are hundreds of righteous Deborahs. For every manipulative Delilah there are scores of loyal Ruths. For every woman who, lacking faith, "looked back" like Lot's wife, there were many more who, strong in their faith, stood up courageously like Esther.

In the same way, a narrow reading of Scripture can tempt us to see only one side of women in a male-oriented society.

If we are not careful, we can be led to think that the women of Israel were mindless creatures, hardly more valuable than property, who knew nothing more than babies and basket-weaving. But that is not at all an accurate picture.

Even when women were cast in the worst possible light, they came off looking far more active and influential than we normally assume. For example, the adulteress castigated in Proverbs chapters 5-7 is seen to be an independent woman able to wrap an unwise man around her finger through seductive persuasion worthy of the most seductive man. It is not an admirable trait in either sex, but if a woman can influence a man for evil, she can influence a man for good as well.

In a scathing rebuke, Isaiah paints an unflattering picture of women who are anything but meek little homebodies nervously awaiting their husband's permission before they take the next breath. If you have never read this passage, hang on for a stinging indictment!

The Lord says,

"The women of Zion are haughty,
walking along with outstretched necks,
    flirting with their eyes,
tripping along with mincing steps,
    with ornaments jingling on
    their ankles.
Therefore the Lord will bring sores on the
    heads of the women of Zion;
the Lord will make their scalps bald."

In that day the Lord will snatch away their finery: the bangles and headbands and crescent necklaces, the earrings and bracelets and veils, the headdresses and ankle chains and sashes, the perfume bottles and charms, the signet rings and nose rings, the fine robes

and the capes and cloaks, the purses and mirrors, and
the linen garments and tiaras and shawls.

Instead of fragrance there will be a stench;
    instead of a sash, a rope;
instead of well-dressed hair, baldness;
    instead of fine clothing, sackcloth;
    instead of beauty, branding.

Your men will fall by the sword,
    your warriors in battle.

The gates of Zion will lament and mourn;
    destitute she will sit on the ground.

In that day seven women
    will take hold of one man
and say, "We will eat our own food
    and provide our own clothes;
only let us be called by your name.
    Take away our disgrace!"

You women who are so complacent,
    rise up and listen to me;
you daughters who feel secure,
    hear what I have to say!

In little more than a year
    you who feel secure will tremble;
the grape harvest will fail,
    and the harvest of fruit will not come.

Tremble, you complacent women;
    shudder, you daughters who
    feel secure!

Strip off your clothes,
    put sackcloth around your waists
    (Isaiah 3:16—4:1; 32:9-11).

Do these haughty women look like oppressed, second-class citizens groveling for crumbs of attention and respect from brutal male patriarchal overlords? Granted, they undoubtedly represented a small minority of women in the upper class— more in the league of finely dressed Western women of today than their poorer, Third World sisters. Nevertheless, the point is clear: Not all women chafed insufferably under male domination. Nor were they rumpled and haggard mothers with runny-nosed children at each breast. Quite the contrary, women of ancient times could be as sophisticated as women of modern times.

From what we see of the haughty women of Israel and their trendy designer fashions, we should not be surprised that Paul later would draw a connection between the Christian woman's modest manner of dress and her call to submission (1 Timothy 2:9-15).

If the women of Isaiah's day were complacent in their luxury, they were anything but passive in exerting their influence. In fact it was the *male* spiritual leaders who had become so passive that they were being controlled by the most unlikely oppressors. Ironically, Isaiah's bitter attack against the haughty women of Jerusalem was immediately preceded by condemnation of Israel's elders and leaders:

> Youths oppress my people,
> women rule over them.
>
> O my people, your guides lead you astray;
> they turn you from the path.
>
> The Lord takes his place in court;
> he rises to judge the people.
>
> The Lord enters into judgment
> against the elders and leaders of his
> people . . . (Isaiah 3:12-14).

If the women were out of place in their prideful display of independence and materialistic success, the men were also out of place in failing to *fill* their "place" responsibly. God found them guilty of being AWOL and sentenced them to unfamiliar submission to others. Whether their submission was to "youths" and "women," as most translations indicate, or to "tax gatherers" and "extortioners," as rendered in the Septuagint, it is clear that the men had not set the proper spiritual tone either for themselves or for the women of Israel.

A Star-Studded Women's Hall of Fame

The common stereotype of a typical woman during the centuries before Christ is overworn, outplayed, and often simply wrong. Just as now, godly women in ancient times were gentle in demeanor but strong in character; submissive but not subservient; domestic but not confined to the kitchen or bedroom; if less formally educated, by no means lacking in intellectual prowess. In fact we repeatedly find biblical accounts of women who outclassed the men in strength, courage, intelligence, moral fortitude, spirituality, and honor.

Their stories confirm that differences in assigned spiritual roles say nothing about relative worth. Their gifts and talents also confirm that "secondary" is far from the appropriate word to describe the special dimension which women bring to God's work on earth. With that in mind, let's take a look at some of God's special women in biblical times.

Abigail

When we think of King David's wives, it is usually Bathsheba who first comes to mind, probably because of her association with David in their great sin of adultery. Or perhaps we remember the disgraced Michal, daughter of Saul, who condemned her husband for his joyous dancing upon returning the ark of the Lord to its place. But my candidate for a wonderful wife is the lesser known Abigail.

When David first met her, Abigail was married to a brutish man named Nabal. It is said that "she was an intelligent and beautiful woman, but her husband, a Calebite, was surly and mean in his dealings" (1 Samuel 25:3). While passing through Nabal's vicinity, David sent messengers requesting Nabal's hospitality, reminding him of the protection that David's men had previously given Nabal's shepherds. Nabal sent back an impudent response that infuriated David and caused him to vow that every man belonging to Nabal would be killed by the next day.

A servant told Abigail of Nabal's insults toward David and of the impending disaster. The biblical record says that 'Abigail lost no time." She took bread, wine, meat, cakes, and figs and went out to meet David. "But she did not tell her husband Nabal," we learn. When Abigail saw David she explained that her husband was "just like his name—his name is Fool, and folly goes with him."

Then Abigail made a remarkable observation to discourage David from fulfilling his vow to kill Nabal and his servants:

> "When the Lord has done for my master every good thing he promised concerning him and has appointed him leader over Israel, my master will not have on his conscience the staggering burden of needless bloodshed or of having avenged himself . . . ."
>
> David said to Abigail, "Praise be to the Lord, the God of Israel, who has sent you today to meet me. May you be blessed for your good judgment and for keeping me from bloodshed this day and from avenging myself with my own hands" (1 Samuel 25:30-33).

Here was a woman, both beautiful and intelligent, who knew her husband was a wicked fool, and who acted independently and courageously to do the right thing. Abigail further distinguished herself by sharing her rich spiritual insight with David. It might have been expected that she would apologize to David on behalf of her husband, but who would expect her to speak to David's heart about his own spiritual welfare? She not only showed David a better way to avenge himself, but she also showed that a godly woman could have better judgment than her husband and the future king of Israel put together!

Once again there is reason to believe that God has not called men to spiritual leadership because men are spiritually superior to women. As we have suggested, it may be for exactly the opposite reason: that women come by spiritual concern and faithfulness rather naturally, whereas men may need an extra shove!

The end of the story is true storybook stuff. Within two weeks God struck Nabal dead, David asked Abigail to marry him, and the two of them (along with David's many other wives) lived happily ever after (with the exception of a couple of serious moral failures for David along the way). What a special woman, Abigail!

Wise Woman of Abel Beth Maacah

We are not given her name; she was just "a wise woman." *Just* a wise woman? What a great honor for any woman—or man—to be remembered for being wise! The story takes place in a city called Abel Beth Maacah. King David's general, Joab, had cornered David's enemy, Sheba, in the city and was about to destroy the city to get at him. From that point forward the rarely-told story deserves full details!

> While they were battering the wall to bring it down, a wise woman called from the city, "Listen! Listen! Tell Joab to come here so I can speak to him." He went toward her, and she asked, "Are you Joab?"
>
> "I am," he answered.
>
> She said, "Listen to what your servant has to say."

"I'm listening," he said.

She continued, "Long ago they used to say, 'Get your answer at Abel,' and that settled it.

We are the peaceful and faithful in Israel. You are trying to destroy a city that is a mother in Israel. Why do you want to swallow up the Lord's inheritance?"

"Far be it from me!" Joab replied, "Far be it from me to swallow up or destroy! That is not the case. A man named Sheba son of Bicri, from the hill country of Ephraim, has lifted up his hand against the king, against David. Hand over this one man, and I'll withdraw from the city."

The woman said to Joab, "His head will be thrown to you from the wall."

Then the woman went to all the people with her wise advice, and they cut off the head of Sheba son of Bicri and threw it to Joab. So he sounded the trumpet, and his men dispersed from the city, each returning to his home (2 Samuel 20:15-22).

It was a reasonable tactic, really, and a man could have thought it up as easily as a woman. But a man *didn't*. It was a woman, a *wise* woman, who went to the people with her wise advice. And "all the people" (apparently both men and women) acted on that advice and saved their city from destruction—all because of one unnamed wise woman.

Thank God for all the unnamed and unknown wise women of the world! Women are not always acting from the intuitive side of their brains; their rationality often puts the men to shame. Left to his own "masculine rationality," Joab would have destroyed a whole city just to kill one man. Not one but *two* men lost their heads that day.

And what did this wise woman say? "You are trying to destroy a city that is a *mother* in Israel." Why a "mother"? Because it had a reputation that you could "get your answer at Abel." The city was like a mother in that it was a reliable source of truth and insight. No wonder the woman was so wise! She was her "mother's" daughter— another quite special daughter of Israel. Was she a leader? Not officially. But, oh, how she led!

The Queen of Sheba

There was one *very* official woman leader in the Old Testament who even got honorable mention by Jesus. She was the Queen of Sheba, or the Queen of the South, as Jesus referred to her. It was the Queen of Sheba who made the long pilgrimage to Jerusalem in search of the wisdom of Solomon. Referring to Solomon's wisdom and wealth, it was she who said, "The half has not been told."

Her quest for wisdom instead of mere entertainment or the normal tourist attractions says much about the spiritual nature of this woman. We know nothing about her religious beliefs, but we do know that she came as a sincere searcher. In fact the record says that she tested Solomon "with hard questions." Convinced by what she heard, she praised the God of Israel. Although we are not told explicitly whether she worshiped the one God of Israel when she returned to her palace, Jesus' later reference to her suggests that she did.

The brief reference came in a conversation that Jesus was having with skeptical Pharisees who were demanding to see a miraculous sign to prove Jesus' claim of being the Son of God. Jesus refused to humor them but intimated that his resurrection would be the proof they were looking for. Rebuking them further, he said that the penitent men of Nineveh would testify against them at the judgment, as would the Queen of Sheba: "The Queen of the South will rise at the judgment with this generation and condemn it; for she came from the ends of the earth to listen to Solomon's wisdom, and now one greater than Solomon is here" (Matthew 12:42).

Here Jesus refers to a woman as an example of sincere spiritual searching in the process of rebuking male spiritual leaders who had lost all sense of what it meant to be spiritual seekers. They had the position, the headship, and—in their day of institutionalized Judaism—even the power which attached to their role. But they didn't have a clue about true spirituality. Role and essence should go together, but in their case it didn't.

Although the Queen of Sheba was not a political leader in God's chosen nation of Israel, she managed in her spiritual quest to put the men to shame. Unlike the Pharisees, she had none of the *role* with its empty trappings, but she had the *essence*. Of the many gifts she brought to Solomon, the most precious was her openness to truth.

That same quest for spiritual understanding often characterizes godly women. You may disagree, but I sense that it is *women* who most frequently read their Bibles; *women,* apparently, who most often commune with God in prayer, and *women* who often ask the hardest questions—even about the proper role of women in the church.

If a man and a woman were to pick up their Bibles at the same time, it would not be surprising to find them doing two different things with the book they hold in their hands. From my experience, men tend to *study* the Bible (often in preparation for some doctrinal discussion), whereas women tend to *read* the Bible—just *read* it—to see what it has to say to them.

To the extent that these general observations are accurate, there is good news and bad news in each approach. The more methodical study of Scripture which is characteristic of most men gives them a more consistent overview of the Word, but in their effort to determine doctrine, personal edification often eludes them. On the other hand, the ready openness to the Word which is characteristic of most women gives them a rich insight into spiritual truths, but their typically lesser concern about doctrine can impair their understanding of God's will in the bigger picture.

If you wonder whether I'm merely guessing here about typical male-female reading habits, stand in a Christian bookstore and watch where the customers go. Concordances, Greek lexicons, and biblical commentaries in the reference section attract the men like baseball on a Saturday afternoon. Women head straight for the racks containing inspirational books, personal testimonies, and Christian responses to human hurts.

In fact you don't even have to watch where the customers go once they are in the store. Just watch the front door for who is coming in. Whatever type of books they may be after, you can easily confirm the surveys which tell us that 80 percent of the customers will be women and only 20 percent will be men. Often the women drive long distances over crowded freeways bearing bundles of children—all in search of God's will for their lives. They are twentieth-century "Queens of Sheba," if you will.

No official roles in the church. No honor of spiritual headship in the home. No titles, no positions; no clerical collars, robes, or special privileges. Nothing but a willingness to learn from God and a desire to share spiritual wisdom with their children—and sometimes with husbands who would never think of accompanying them in that noble quest.

Solomon had all the knowledge one would ever want, and official leadership to boot, yet he ended up falling away into idolatry. The Queen of Sheba had only hard questions to ask, but at the judgment the Lord will call her as a witness against learned, positioned men who fail to see the message in her mission. God will also call the men of Nineveh to testify against the men of America if we fail to repent and to assume the spiritual responsibility which God has given us.

Wouldn't you love to know more about the Queen of Sheba? I suspect "the half has not been told"!

Reflections on Wives

With over 700 wives and 300 concubines, Solomon must have known something about women. In his many proverbs, he shares both good and bad, honorable and dishonorable. On the more negative side—

Like a gold ring in a pig's snout
> is a beautiful woman who shows
> no discretion (Proverbs 11:22).

A foolish son is his father's ruin,
> and a quarrelsome wife is like a constant
> dripping (Proverbs 19:13).

Better to live on a corner of the roof
> than share a house with a
> quarrelsome wife (Proverbs 21:9; 25:24).

Better to live in a desert
> than with a quarrelsome and ill-tempered
> wife (Proverbs 21:19).

A quarrelsome wife is like
> a constant dripping on a rainy day;
> restraining her is like restraining the
> wind or grasping oil with the hand
> (Proverbs 27:15, 16).

And what about quarrelsome *husbands?* Surely remote deserts and quiet corners of roofs sometimes start to look pretty good to wives as well!

For some proverbs that cut both ways—

A wife of noble character is her husband's
> crown, but a disgraceful wife is like decay
> in his bones (Proverbs 12:4).

The wise woman builds her house,
>   but with her own hands the foolish one
>   tears hers down (Proverbs 14:1).

In terms of spiritual leadership the husband is the head of the wife, but if Solomon is right about it, the crown of glory the man wears on his own head is a godly woman! Interesting, isn't it? The woman's own character may contribute to the way in which she is "led" by her husband; and no matter what "headship" he may exercise in the family, the man's own spirituality may be enhanced even more by the woman God has given him.

And for proverbs that give the godly wife full honors—

He who finds a wife finds what is good
>   and receives favor from the Lord
>   (Proverbs 18:22).

Houses and wealth are inherited from parents,
>   but a prudent wife is from the Lord
>   (Proverbs 19:14).

Too often godly wives (and godly husbands) are taken for granted. But Solomon reminds us that, as it was in the beginning, the righteous wife is that "perfect match" for her husband, that "suitable helper" to strengthen his own spiritual consciousness. If man is in the driver's seat, it is likely that a woman knows the way as well as, or better than, he does. Thank God for spiritual navigators who can read God's heart to us while we concentrate on the mechanics of doctrine and the dangers which may lurk around the next corner!

The Worthy Woman of Proverbs

Few passages in the Bible are more loved than Proverbs chapter 31 with its description of "the worthy woman," "the wife of noble character," or "the strong and powerful woman," depending on which translation you prefer. Of course we tend to think that Solomon wrote all of the Proverbs, but this passage seems to be attributed to King Lemuel, about which little is known other than this masterful testimony to a very special woman of God.

If indeed all of Proverbs chapter 31 is King Lemuel's oracle, then two details take on great significance. The first is that it was an oracle "his mother taught him" (Proverbs 31:1). Right away we see the "power behind the throne" to be a godly woman. No, not as the chief of staff in a position of political authority, like the Queen of Sheba or Deborah, but as a mother still concerned about her grown-up son who had gained prominence. This was not the first time she had given him spiritual wisdom. It must have seemed to her like only yesterday that she was reading "Bible story books" to her young son, teaching him songs about Noah and the ark, and instilling in him a sense of spiritual responsibility that one day would nurture his position as a leader among his people.

The second detail is what she had to say about women who were not quite as noble as the "noble woman."

> O my son, O son of my womb
> O son of my vows,
> do not spend your strength on women,
> your vigor on those who ruin kings
> (Proverbs 31:2, 3).

What a remarkable contrast is given to us in this one chapter—all the way from the kind of a woman who could ruin a king to the kind of a woman whose husband would rise up and call blessed!

So who is this woman we all know as the perfect wife and mother? She obviously was not King Lemuel's wife, although she certainly was worthy of being queen. The "worthy woman" may be no one in particular but only a montage of desirable qualities in a woman—the kind of qualities a mother might desire for her son's wife, though pity the daughter-in-law who has to live up to such high expectations!

We have read this passage so many times before, but a book of this nature would be incomplete without including it in full. Besides, it has much to tell us about the relationship between the husband and the wife, about the nature of women in ancient times, and about roles, attitudes, and spiritual strength.

A wife of noble character who can find?
   She is worth far more than rubies.
Her husband has full confidence in her
   and lacks nothing of value.
She brings him good, not harm,
   all the days of her life.
She selects wool and flax
   and works with eager hands.
She is like the merchant ships,
   bringing her food from afar.
She gets up while it is still dark;
   she provides food for her family
   and portions for her servant girls.
She considers a field and buys it;
   out of her earnings she plants a vineyard.
She sets about her work vigorously;
   her arms are strong for her tasks.
She sees that her trading is profitable,
   and her lamp does not go out at night.
In her hand she holds the distaff
   and grasps the spindle with her fingers.
She opens her arms to the poor
   and extends her hands to the needy.

When it snows, she has no fear for her
  household; for all of them are clothed in
  scarlet.
She makes coverings for her bed;
  she is clothed in fine linen and purple.
Her husband is respected at the city gate,
  where he takes his seat among the elders
  of the land.
She makes linen garments and sells them,
  and supplies the merchants with sashes.
She is clothed with strength and dignity;
  she can laugh at the days to come.
She speaks with wisdom,
  and faithful instruction is on her tongue.
She watches over the affairs of her household
  and does not eat the bread of idleness.
Her children arise and call her blessed;
  her husband also, and he praises her:
"Many women do noble things,
  but you surpass them all."
Charm is deceptive, and beauty is fleeting;
  but a woman who fears the Lord is to be
  praised.
Give her the reward she has earned,
  and let her works bring her praise at the
  city gate (Proverbs 31:10-31).

I don't know about you, but I'm exhausted just reading about everything this woman accomplished in one 24-hour period!

As I reckon it, once and for all this ought to explode the myth of godly women sitting around the house barefoot and pregnant. She was an industrious self-starter and a good manager, businesswoman, and financier—an entrepreneur extraordinaire. "Clothed with strength and dignity"—what a tribute!

A wise teacher. And one of my favorite qualities in a woman—she was lighthearted.

It is hard to know where to begin in analyzing this wonderful picture of a woman, but it is important to note that her personal strength and economic skills were centered around her domestic responsibilities, even if the definition of "domestic" has shrunk greatly from her time to ours. She was not out to compete with her husband (or with any other man, for that matter). She competed only with herself, being both internally and externally motivated.

What she did even in her business enterprises was consistent with what other women in her economic position did during that time. Because the normal "household" consisted of a large extended family, including other relatives and servants, the "woman of the house" was a business manager over everything that related to the running of the household. Nor was her husband pulling all the strings around the house. He didn't have to; he had "full confidence in her."

Her many skills and talents lent dignity to the whole idea of domestic responsibilities. For example, it's hard to imagine ever hearing her say, with a slight hint of embarrassment, "Oh, I'm just a housewife." She seems to have made "watching over the affairs of her household" an art form! Women today worry a lot about "wasting" their talents. Somehow I can't imagine the "worthy woman" of Proverbs having enough leisure time even to consider whether her talents were being wasted.

And her childbearing role found its greatest fulfillment, not in the womb itself, which doesn't even get passing mention, but in the "wisdom and faithful instruction" she gave to her children, who saw in her a woman of God and praised her for it. Truly her greatest beauty was her godly character.

But despite her noble character and wisdom, her faithful instruction, and her fear of the Lord, God's wonderful woman was not called to be a spiritual leader in the way that we are being urged to recognize women today. She would never have been eligible to be a priest, or an elder along with her husband.

Is that because she lacked talent? Obviously not. Is it because she was not as spiritual as her husband? Not a chance. Is it because she wasn't wise enough to handle the responsibility? Not on your life. Is it because she wasn't a "worthy" woman? What is this passage all about but her inestimable worth as a woman of God!

The answer is simple: She wasn't eligible because it wasn't God's desire to call her to that particular responsibility. He had another, possibly greater, work for her to do; another, arguably greater, responsibility; another, surprisingly greater, role to play.

Was the "worthy woman" a leader? Yes! Was she a *spiritual* leader? Again the answer is yes. To this day, millions of women have patterned their lives after her. But she was a leader in a different way and in a different realm altogether from her husband. His was the responsibility of headship in their marriage and of designated leadership among the congregation of God's people. Hers was the responsibility of a faith-filled wife and mother—an intelligent, industrious, and strong woman of God. In fact, she was singled out for praise for the very reason that she led so wonderfully in the way that God called her to lead.

Study Questions

1. Does the principle of male spiritual leadership ever imply that women are inferior to men?
2. If Isaiah's rebuke (in 3:16—4:1; 32:9-11) of Israel's haughty women is stinging, what does it say positively about the independence and strength of women?
3. What does it say about the men of Israel when Isaiah says (in 3:12-14) that "Youths oppress my people, women rule over them?"
4. What were some of Abigail's finest qualities?
5. What lessons can we learn from the "wise woman" of Abel Beth Maacah?
6. In what ways may men and women profit from listening to each other—especially *as men* and *as women?*
7 How does the Queen of Sheba represent the finest aspects of a woman's spirituality?
8. What does the wisdom of the proverbs teach us—good or bad—about women?
9. Is the woman of Proverbs 31 overly idealized? Is she still a role model for today's woman?
10. How can a man be a spiritual leader when his wife is stronger emotionally, intellectually, or spiritually?

9 Overturning Tables of Abuse

Jesus, A Respecter of Women

By the time of Christ's appearance on this earth, male spiritual leadership had been brutally robbed of its centerpiece—spirituality—and left with a void quickly filled by disdain and cruelty. Spousal abuse is not an invention of our time. Its prevalence today, sometimes even among Christians, is shocking but not new.

I'll never forget the faces of one emotionally scarred woman after another who sought refuge in my office when I was a criminal prosecutor. Nor can I forget the extent to which one abused wife found it necessary to defend herself.

I came home exhausted from a long day in court trying a murder case. A typical barroom brawl that got uglier by the minute, it was a saga of bar girls, drunks, and "no goods" hanging around waiting for trouble to happen until it finally did. And someone died.

Just as I was going to bed, a call from the City Police told me of yet another shooting incident. Another man had been killed, and his body had been taken to the morgue. The morgue was in the basement of the local hospital, which happened to be within a block of my small apartment. So I put on my clothes and a grim face and walked over.

With all the excitement of investigating and trying homicide cases, I never got used to the creepy feeling of the morgue. Death hung over it like a cold midwinter fog, just waiting to envelop you. But I was in for more of a shock than I anticipated. When the sheet was drawn back to reveal the man's cold face, I recognized him instantly. He was one of my star witnesses in the murder trial! The man—we'll call him Paul Peterson—owned the tavern where the shooting had taken place and was a vital link in proving my case. For a moment I was less upset by Peterson's own death than about the possibility of losing the trial.

There was no mystery about who shot Peterson; it was his estranged wife, whom we'll call Norma. Norma admitted the shooting, but claimed self-defense. Her story was that Peterson had come to her house drunk and abusive. That's what had led to their separation in the first place—his abuse. But on this occasion she felt her life was being threatened, so she shot him with a handgun she had bought just two days before. "Just two days before?" I thought to myself. "Was she *wanting* an excuse to kill him? Maybe she bought the gun, called him to the house, got him drunk, and blew him away."

It was one of those cases where you had to look into the depths of a person's soul to know the answer. Norma did not have the look of a woman who could premeditate a killing. Despite his respectability in the community, Peterson apparently had been guilty of spousal abuse over a long period of time. It wouldn't have justified Norma's killing him, but it certainly could shed a different light on what may have happened that night.

I later decided not to try Norma for Peterson's death. Instead, I held a coroner's inquest. Whether from the ambivalent facts themselves or whether out of sympathy for the abuse she had suffered at the hands of Peterson, the jury found no criminal activity on Norma's part. I had to agree—for both reasons. I figured that, if we were wrong about it, Norma would still be having to live with her conscience long after we had forgotten about her case. Unfortunately, even if we were right, it would be years before Norma could block out of her memory the horror of that night.

Norma is just one of millions of women abused daily by men. Somewhere along the line, men have perverted the call to headship. For them, headship is a ticket for brutish behavior. The abuse they dish out may be physical, sexual, or psychological. It may be manifested in anger or sullenness. It may be the daily demeaning that robs a women of her dignity or that takes away her feeling of self-worth.

Night after night, year after year, Paul Peterson had smothered the spirit of a good woman who had loved him, probably even while he was abusing her. He had abused her until she couldn't take it anymore. He had led her to do the inconceivable—something which never would have occurred to her on her wedding day about the eventual meaning of those words "Till death do us part." How was she to know that marriage would be turned into a license for cruelty?

A Good Idea Gone Bad

From Creation, male spiritual leadership has been God's idea. It didn't originate with the less-than-50-percent of the population that is male. But a sad thing happened on the way to the kingdom—men dropped the word "spiritual" altogether, then changed the meaning of "leader" to "autocrat," and ended up thinking that women were objects for their capricious whims, even cruel and violent whims. It is not to be supposed that men were never the victims of a woman's cruelty; it undoubtedly happens more than we know and can bring a good man to ruin. But for a variety of reasons, men are more often the abusers.

Even if it never reached the extreme of abuse with most men, the honor and respect given to the "worthy woman" of Proverbs had deteriorated under institutional Judaism until, by the time of Christ, Jewish men were thanking God in their morning prayers that they were not born a Gentile, a slave, or . . . a *woman!* (In light of that traditional Jewish man's prayer, Paul's statement in Galatians that in Christ we are no longer Jew nor Gentile, slave nor free, male nor female, starts to take on added significance.)

Of course the Jewish men were probably right in thanking God for not being born a woman. Considering the disrespectful way they treated women, who could blame them for not wanting to be a victim of their own harshness!

Into this cultural context came another man. Quite a different man. The Son of Man. And what he did for women was revolutionary for his time: He restored their dignity. Where women were ignored, he paid attention; where they were seen as objects, he saw them as persons of intelligence and sensitivity; where they were abused, he brought love.

Did Jesus renounce the principle of male spiritual leadership? No. In fact he perpetuated it in his own ministry. But what he *did* do was to put the word "spiritual" back into the principle and to personally demonstrate servant leadership as a kind of leadership which the Jewish men of his generation had never understood.

Women of Honor at Jesus' Birth

The events surrounding Jesus' birth bring special honor to women. God could have chosen to appear on earth in some angelic form, but he chose to be incarnated into the flesh of humanity. He was to be the Son of Man, born of a woman, a champion of women, to be praised by women.

Of course Mary, the mother of Jesus, heads the list. Have you ever wondered why God chose Mary from among the thousands of Jewish women who were living at that time? What special qualities did she have that would make her the perfect choice? She was not a prominent woman of her day soon to marry a rich husband, or the wife-to-be of an influential leader in the synagogue. Were it not for her role as the mother of the promised Messiah, she likely would have been just an unnamed, unknown housewife and mother in Palestine.

But God knew something about Mary that made her the right woman to bear the son who would become the world's Savior. Perhaps it was the humility with which she would accept this unusual role. We take it for granted that the Holy Spirit came upon this virgin woman and she became pregnant. But can we imagine what Mary must have thought? One day she is not pregnant and the next day she is—without having had sexual relations with a man! Sure, somebody told her it would happen that way, but who would have believed him? Would *we?*

Nor were illegitimate pregnancies the order of the day when B.C. became A.D. Can we appreciate how embarrassing it would have been for Mary—and Joseph as well—when the "church folk" in town started wagging self-righteous fingers at them? It was not all singing shepherds, idyllic manger scenes, and gifts of gold, frankincense, and myrrh. No, it required a very special woman to take this kind of shame in stride. God knew that Mary would be that very special woman.

> The angel went to her and said, "Greetings, you who are highly favored! The Lord is with you."
>
> Mary was greatly troubled at his words and wondered what kind of greeting this might be. But the angel said to her, "Do not be afraid, Mary, you have found favor with God. You will be with child and give birth to a son, and you are to give him the name Jesus . . . ."
>
> "How will this be," Mary asked the angel, "since I am a virgin?"
>
> The angel answered, "The Holy Spirit will come upon you, and the power of the Most High will over-shadow you . . . ."

"I am the Lord's servant," Mary answered. "May it be to me as you have said" (Luke 1:28-38).

Mary was not the sinless woman, immaculately conceived, that Roman Catholicism officially pronounced her to be (only as recently as 1854) in order to eliminate an obvious problem with the doctrine of original sin. But she was "highly favored" and had "found favor with God" as a uniquely worthy woman! Nothing in Scripture indicates that Mary is to be venerated as deity, or to be the intermediary or object of our prayers, but we should hold her in the highest regard, as God did.

In fact Mary had no idea how very accurate her song of praise to God would turn out to be:

My soul glorifies the Lord
    and my spirit rejoices in God my Savior,
for he has been mindful
    of the humble state of his servant.
From now on all generations will call me
    blessed, for the Mighty One has done
    great things for me—
    holy is his name
(Luke 1:46-49).

Indeed we recognize Mary as especially blessed for the gift of God's Son in her womb—just as each of us is blessed with the birth of that same Son in our own hearts!

Anna

We know little about her, but the aging prophetess Anna was privileged to witness the young Jesus before her death, and she praised God for that special honor.

There was also a prophetess, Anna, the daughter of Phanuel, of the tribe of Asher. She was very old; she had lived with her husband seven years after her marriage, and then was a widow until she was eighty-four. She never left the temple but worshiped night and day, fasting and praying. Coming up to them at that very moment, she gave thanks to God and spoke about the child to all who were looking forward to the redemption of Jerusalem (Luke 2:36-38).

Imagine a woman who would spend her whole lifetime in the temple, praying and fasting. In fact, imagine a *man* who would spend *his* whole lifetime in praying and fasting! Those of us who hold, or would seek, leadership positions ought to consider very carefully how the fervent, dedicated lives of even those who have no official leadership roles put our feeble efforts to shame! Praise God for the wonderful life of Anna the prophetess, and for all women of God who tell people seeking redemption about the child whom God gave Anna the privilege to see.

Jesus' Great Tribute to Mary

The most interesting relationship that Jesus must have shared with a woman was with his own mother, Mary. Wouldn't you love to have been a butterfly on the windowsill in the home of Joseph and Mary, to hear and see everything that went on during Jesus' childhood? Son of God though he was, surely the baby Jesus cried and had to have his diapers changed!

It must have come as quite a shock to Mary when Jesus, at the age of 12, spoke to her with what appeared to be rebuke. You remember the story. Jesus had gone with his parents to Jerusalem for the Feast of the Passover. On the way home Joseph and Mary discovered that Jesus was not among their family and friends as they had supposed, and hurried back to Jerusalem to find him. They found him in the temple discussing the fine points of the law with the learned Jewish teachers. Note the exchange which then took place:

> His mother said to him, "Son, why have you treated us like this? Your father and I have been anxiously searching for you."
>
> "Why were you searching for me?" he asked. "Didn't you know I had to be in my Father's house?" But they did not understand what he was saying to them (Luke 2:48-50).

Was Jesus, the boy of 12, asserting his own authority over his parents? Verse 51 gives us interesting insight into both son and mother: "Then he went down to Nazareth with them and was obedient to them. But his mother treasured all these things in her heart."

I must admit that my curiosity runs rampant at this point. I can't help wondering if Joseph's unrecorded later disappearance from the scene (presumably through death) wasn't a statement about the importance of Mary, and perhaps beyond her the importance of women generally. If Joseph had been living during Jesus' ministry, we might never have had the benefit of some of the conversations between Jesus and Mary to which we have become privy.

For example, there is that intriguing conversation on the occasion of Jesus' first miracle, the turning of the water to wine at the wedding feast at Cana:

> A wedding took place at Cana in Galilee. Jesus' mother was there, and Jesus and his disciples had also been invited to the wedding.
>
> When the wine was gone, Jesus' mother said to him, "They have no more wine."
>
> "Dear woman, why do you involve me?" Jesus replied, "My time has not yet come."

His mother said to the servants, "Do whatever he tells you" (John 2:1-5).

Jesus tells the servants what to do, turning the water they draw for him into the best wine at the feast. Remarkable! We have come a long way from a 12-year-old boy saying, "Don't you know that I have to be in my Father's house?" to a 30-year-old man accommodating his mother. If his time truly had not yet come, why did Jesus let his mother influence that God-ordained timetable? After all, *he* was God, and she was not.

I think we may have discovered one of the highest tributes ever paid to Mary: The Son of God even changed his timetable out of respect for her!

At 30, Jesus had reached the Jewish age of formal spiritual leadership—the age at which priestly service began. Yet Jesus' mother intervenes in his life and moves things in a direction he was not prepared to go. I must admit that in my mid-fifties I often find myself in the same position. There must be an unwritten prerogative which allows mothers to forget that their sons and daughters ever grew up. Perhaps it is a right of motherhood as compensation for having to put up with us through so many trying times!

We men often pervert the better-known adage to say: "Behind every good man there is a woman . . . *pushing!*" But there may be more truth than humor in that version of the adage. Let's face it—many men *need* to be encouraged if they are ever to get anywhere! Encouragement may be the very "help suitable" that some men need. But—mother or no mother—you never get the idea that Mary tried to assume spiritual leadership over Jesus. Nor for all his respect did Jesus elevate Mary in spiritual prominence within his ministry or kingdom.

As if to make this point clear, Luke—the Gospel writer giving greater recognition to women than any other—records a telling conversation between Jesus and a woman in the crowd listening to his teaching:

As Jesus was saying these things, a woman in the crowd called out, "Blessed is the mother who gave you birth and nursed you."

He replied, "Blessed rather are those who hear the word of God and obey it" (Luke 11:27, 28).

And Matthew provides further insight:

While Jesus was still talking to the crowd, his mother and brothers stood outside, wanting to speak to him. Someone told him, "Your mother and brothers are standing outside, wanting to speak to you."

He replied to him, "Who is my mother, and who are my brothers?" Pointing to his disciples, he said, "Here are my mother and my brothers. For whoever does the will of my Father in heaven is my brother and sister and mother" (Matthew 12:46-50).

Was Mary a very special woman in the eyes of God? Yes. Was she given a public role of spiritual leadership commensurate with that honor? No. Are other mothers special women in God's eyes? Again, yes. Are they given designated roles of spiritual headship among his people? Again, no. Just because someone is "special"—whether male or female—doesn't mean that he or she is called to be a functional leader.

Honor is tied to the specific responsibilities one is given to exercise. Mary's special honor came through her role as the ultimate childbearer and not as priest, preacher, apostle, or— worse yet—the humanly deified object of veneration. Mary had been faithful within the scope of her responsibility; why should God have burdened her with further responsibilities?

How Jesus Responded to Rejected Women

The Samaritan Woman

In the beginning of his ministry Jesus went into the region of the Samaritans, who were despised by the Jews because they were a mixed people, racially and religiously. Nothing could have served better to emphasize the universal nature of Christ's kingdom. Nothing, that is, but taking his kingdom to *women* as well as to men—in fact to a particular woman who would have been on the very bottom rung of society's ladder. A woman who had been loved and left by no fewer than five husbands, and currently kept by one who had not even bothered to marry her.

When Jesus met this woman at Jacob's well, near Sychar, he surprised her by asking for a drink of water.

> The Samaritan woman said to him, "You are a Jew and I am a Samaritan woman. How can you ask me for a drink?" (For Jews do not associate with Samaritans.) (John 4:9).

At a time when women were segregated in both the temple and the synagogue and when Jewish rabbis did not deign to teach Jewish women, it is all the more remarkable that Jesus should speak about spiritual matters with a woman of Samaria. This conversation was not merely passing of time with small talk. Even though the Samaritan woman was a social outcast, she was far from ignorant about spiritual matters. It was her hard questions that led to the well-known teaching of Jesus that we are to worship God in spirit and in truth.

As if to underscore the unusual nature of such a conversation with a woman, John tells us the reaction of Jesus' disciples:

Just then his disciples returned and were surprised to find him talking with a woman.

But no one asked, "What do you want?" or "Why are you talking with her?" (John 4:27).

Because Jesus talked with many women without any eyebrows being raised, the emphasis reverts first of all to the fact that she was a *Samaritan* woman, but also to the *nature* of their discussion. What's different is that it was a serious discussion about a theological question concerning which she normally would not be expected to express an opinion.

Jesus transforms this nonstatused Samaritan woman into an exclamation point for the message he was trying to get across to institutionalized Jewish men: Worship is not a matter of tradition but comes from within the heart—a message so simple that even a rejected woman from Samaria could appreciate it more than the politically entrenched Jewish leaders!

Was the Samaritan woman a recognized spiritual leader? No. Was she nevertheless a spiritual leader? Just look at the ending to the story:

Many of the Samaritans from that town believed in him because of the woman's testimony, "He told me everything I ever did . . . ." And because of his words many more became believers.

They said to the woman, "We no longer believe just because of what you said; now we have heard for ourselves, and we know that this man really is the Savior of the world" (John 4:39, 41 ,42).

Through the faith of one rejected woman whom Jesus had treated as spiritually significant, many people were led to believe. Was she a spiritual leader? Just ask her neighbors who found Christ because of her! No one needs an official position to bring others to Christ—only a strong personal faith and a willingness to share it with others. If one door of leadership is officially closed, there are many more standing wide open.

The Canaanite Woman

Many people find it difficult to reconcile with his loving character a conversation that Jesus had with another despised woman—the Canaanite woman from the region of Tyre and Sidon. Upon first reading, it appears that Jesus is putting her down for being a non-Jewish woman. You will remember that she came to Jesus asking that he heal her demon-possessed daughter. Jesus first ignores her outright, then says he was sent only to the lost sheep of Israel. But when she pleads further, we are given this exchange:

> He replied, "It is not right to take the children's bread and toss it to their dogs."
>
> "Yes, Lord," she said, "but even the dogs eat the crumbs that fall from their masters' table."
>
> Then Jesus answered, "Woman, you have great faith! Your request is granted." And her daughter was healed from that very hour (Matthew 15:26-28).

To make sense of this passage we need to factor in the attitude of Jesus' disciples, who had said to Jesus, "Send her away, for she keeps crying out after us" (Matthew 15:23). I suspect it was for his disciples that Jesus compared children and dogs, because they thought *they* were the honored children and the Canaanites were as dogs. Through the great faith and rich insight of an outcast woman, Jesus was able to turn that around. In his kingdom no one is to be treated like dogs. All are honored guests at the table, whether Jew or Gentile, slave or free, male or female.

The Adulterous Woman

I never tire of reading the Scriptures, even though I've read them repeatedly over the years. One reason is that there are so many interesting details which I discover over and again like hidden treasures unearthed. The story of the woman caught in adultery is a good example (John 7:53—8:11). I always remember Jesus writing something in the dirt with his finger, but I sometimes forget that he did it *twice*.

Obviously we do not know what Jesus wrote, because we simply are not told. But the context suggests a couple of strong possibilities. The first writing on the ground followed the initial confrontation, when the Pharisees brought the woman to Jesus, accusing her of adultery and asking him about the law's command that she be stoned to death. What did Jesus write? I suspect it may have been: "And the *man?*" (meaning, "Where is the man who committed adultery with her? What kind of double standard is going on here?").

Then he said to them, "If any one of you is without sin, let him be the first to throw a stone at her," and once again he wrote on the ground. If we could have peeked over his shoulder, we might have seen the words "They call themselves *spiritual* leaders?" (meaning, "Will they never learn to lead from the heart instead of from law books alone? Have centuries of spiritual responsibility eluded them altogether?").

Jesus did not disagree with the law forbidding adultery, nor did he condone the woman's involvement in the illicit relationship. But he knew that an even larger issue was at stake: Men were abusing women in the process of justifying their own guardianship of the law. Jesus was not fooled. He was the guardian of an even higher law, the law of love.

The Sinful Woman

We see the law of love in operation once again when Jesus shows compassion on "a sinful woman" who wets Jesus' feet with her tears at a feast in Jesus' honor (Luke 7:36-50). This "sinful woman" apparently was a prostitute who stunned the other guests as she walked in and anointed Jesus. But the intriguing question is, Why had she singled out Jesus for this act of adoration? Could it be that Jesus had already talked to her somewhere else, not as an object of pleasure for a price, but as a woman of spiritual value, and told her that her sins were forgiven? If so, it would not be surprising if Jesus' emphasis was one of reassurance: "Your sins *are* forgiven"—just as I have already told you. You can believe it!

In Jesus' own words, the punch line of the story is: "He who has been forgiven little loves little" (Luke 7:47)—the implication being that she who had been forgiven much loved much. This disenfranchised woman at the bottom of the social ladder was a highly appropriate object lesson for the men at the top. They may have been less sinful, but they had not appreciated Jesus to the same extent.

There is another, more likely, interpretation: These leaders were just as sinful as she was (perhaps being the very ones who had used her sexually), but they weren't willing to recognize their own sin.

Whether man or woman, recognized leader or social reject, Christ reaches down to all of us to lift us higher. He makes no distinctions. In the category of sinners to which we all belong, there *are* no distinctions.

Women of Honor in Jesus' Ministry

Women Who Followed Jesus
Whether it was intended as a purposeful comparison of women's status during Jesus' ministry or not, Luke's placement of the story of "the sinful woman" is followed immediately by a reference to the many godly women who supported Jesus and his disciples as they traveled about spreading the word.

> After this, Jesus traveled about from one town and village to another, proclaiming the good news of the kingdom of God. The Twelve were with him, and also some women who had been cured of evil spirits and diseases:
>
> Mary (called Magdalene) from whom seven demons had come out; Joanna the wife of Cuza, the manager of Herod's household; Susanna; and many others. These women were helping to support them out of their own means (Luke 8:1-3).

Far from being at the bottom of the social ladder, some of these women were right at the top—for example, Joanna, the wife of Herod's household manager. These women had generous resources at their command in order to provide the financial underpinning of Jesus' ministry. Sometimes "help suitable," even outside the marriage relationship, comes in the form of financial generosity.

Were these women taking an officially recognized leadership role in publicly preaching the Gospel? We have no record of it. But their role of holding up the hands of those who did preach was equally important. Different, but equal.

Martha and Mary

Having said all this, we must also note that the valuable support which women often supply behind the scenes—cooking and cleaning, as we too often discount it—can get in the way of their own spiritual growth. Jesus never meant a supportive role to be a substitute for the pursuit of spiritual knowledge. The incident with Martha and Mary is our best example:

> As Jesus and his disciples were on their way, he came to a village where a woman named Martha opened her home to him. She had a sister called Mary,

who sat at the Lord's feet listening to what he said. But Martha was distracted by all the preparations that had to be made. She came to him and asked, "Lord, don't you care that my sister has left me to do the work by myself? Tell her to help me!"

"Martha, Martha," the Lord answered, "you are worried and upset about many things, but only one thing is needed. Mary has chosen what is better, and it will not be taken away from her" (Luke 10:38-42).

Martha may have been jealous of Mary and reverted to playing the martyr. Or perhaps Martha had let her "support role" distract her from the quest for spiritual understanding, and Jesus did not intend for that to happen. If the woman's principal responsibility is on the home-front, it is not to be construed as her exclusive interest. The kind of interest shown by Mary in spiritual matters is the higher calling. Martha had failed to prioritize correctly.

Of course this is a trap in which men can be caught as well. If their principal responsibility is spiritual headship, it is not to be construed as their exclusive interest. Sometimes "Martha" really does need help in the kitchen—or with the children, or just sharing precious moments together. No role or responsibility ought to be used as an excuse for failing to see greater needs at hand.

I would go out on a limb to say that most women are better at integrating their "home-front responsibilities" with a quest for spiritual understanding than most men are at integrating their "headship responsibilities" with the same spiritual quest. For the married woman with children, her principal responsibilities may cry out to her from the crib and playroom. And her inclination toward spirituality would suggest two sisters in one— call her "Mary Martha."

By contrast, the man's principal responsibilities on the spiritual front can easily be forgotten and misconstrued under the more nebulous label of "headship." He can convince himself that since he is the designated spiritual leader, by this fact alone he is automatically spiritually-minded; and that since he is exercising family headship, no matter how autocratically, his headship is of a spiritual nature. Naturally, neither of these conclusions is automatically correct. Both men and women have much to learn from Martha and Mary.

Whether these sisters are the same Martha and Mary who were the sisters of Lazarus is unclear. If not, what an interesting similarity we find in the story of Lazarus' sister Mary anointing Jesus with the expensive perfume! At a dinner being given in Jesus' honor:

> Martha served, while Lazarus was among those reclining at the table with him. Then Mary took about a pint of pure nard, an expensive perfume; she poured it on Jesus' feet and wiped his feet with her hair (John 12:2, 3).

When Judas hypocritically complained that the money-would have been better spent on the poor (probably meaning himself when he would filch it from the money-bag), Jesus commended Mary for making the spiritually superior choice. "I tell you the truth," said Jesus, "wherever the gospel is preached throughout the world, what she has done will also be told, in memory of her" (Mark 14:9).

In giving honor to whom honor is due, more than once Jesus singled out godly women for special praise. And even now we have proved the accuracy of Jesus' prediction by remembering again Mary's sacrifice of love. Her honor did not lie in a position of authority or recognized spiritual leadership. She held no clergylike office among the believers and played no public role in proclamation of the Gospel.

Nor did Mary's honor come strictly from a role she might have played as a childbearer—honorable as that role might have been. Her award came for nothing less than spiritual excellence. That's what really matters, regardless of one's principal role or responsibility: spiritual excellence!

Women at the Resurrection

If there were any doubt that Jesus loved women and women loved Jesus, such doubt would dissipate in the final events surrounding Jesus' life. As Jesus was being led away to crucifixion, Luke tells us that "a large number of people followed him, including women who mourned and wailed for him" (Luke 23:27). This surely must have been an emotion-packed tribute to Jesus for the respect and honor he had shown toward a generation of women who often experienced nothing but neglect and abuse!

Nor did the women shun the horrible scene of the cross. Mark and Luke record that the women stood by Jesus up to the bitter end.

> Some women were watching from a distance. Among them were Mary Magdalene, Mary the mother of James the younger and of Joses, and Salome. In Galilee these women had followed him and cared for his needs. Many other women who had come up with him to Jerusalem were also there (Mark 15:40, 41).

And,

> When all the people who had gathered to witness this sight saw what took place, they beat their breasts and went away. But all those who knew him, including the women who had followed him from Galilee, stood at a distance, watching these things (Luke 23:48, 49).

There is always special notice of the faithful women—faithful to the very end.

But it was not to be the end! When the Sabbath was over and the women came to the tomb to anoint Jesus' body with the burial spices, they discovered the amazing fact of Jesus' resurrection. The tomb was empty! And to whom did Jesus first reveal himself? To women—faithful women who had stood by him. He appeared first to Mary Magdalene (Mark 16:9) and then to the other women who were hurrying away from the tomb (Matthew 28:8-10). But when the women told the disciples what they had seen, the men didn't believe them, "because their words seemed to them like nonsense" (Luke 24:11).

It would happen again through the Christian centuries— women being the first to see the good news and telling men about it. And to many men it would seem like nonsense. But because of believing women, many other men have been encouraged to "run to the open tomb" of faith and to put their trust in Christ.

Christ's Legacy Regarding Leadership

Does the ability to lead another person to Christ give a woman the mandate to take a leadership role either in the family or in the church? Did Jesus usher in a new era of spiritual leadership? Did he "change the rules" regarding the respective responsibilities of men and women of God? I see article after article and book after book in which the author answers all those questions in the affirmative, saying, "Look how respectfully and honorably Jesus looked upon women." But where is the hard evidence for any revolutionary change in spiritual roles?

Certainly it does not come from Jesus' lips. He never directly addressed the issue, one way or the other. In reaching out to the rejected women of his day, Jesus never put them in a position of spiritual headship either in their own marriages or among his disciples. In honoring the women who supported him with their money, labor, and tears, Jesus never told them to assume the mantle of spiritual leadership—not even over men who had demonstrated themselves to be spiritually inferior. And in appearing first to women after his resurrection, Jesus never suggested that he was reversing the principle of male spiritual leadership established when God first created man and woman.

Regarding women, Jesus came to turn abuse into respect, high-handedness into servant leadership. Instead of being spiritual *protectors,* men had become spiritual *threats* to women. Jesus came to show men what the principle of male leadership was all about—to correct centuries of misunderstanding about the responsibiities given to men. Far from coming to let men off the hook, Jesus came to rebuke them. And how he shamed them—taking rejected women with superior spiritual insights as illustrations to make his point!

This obvious difference—between elevating women in respect and honor on one hand and elevating them in position and responsibility on the other—is almost universally ignored in today's push for dramatic role changes for women in the church. And when anyone dares to suggest such a fundamental distinction, some respond, "But Jesus obviously did not want to offend," or "Elevating women 'officially' would not have sat well with the people in Jesus' time."

In what other situation was Jesus ever concerned about "offending" people with the truth! When do we see him shrinking back from revolutionary teaching just because it would not have "sat well" with the establishment? Even Jesus' enemies gave him more credit than that!

> "Teacher," they said, "we know you are a man of integrity and that you teach the way of God in accordance with the truth. You aren't swayed by men, because you pay no attention to who they are" (Matthew 22:16).

If Jesus had intended to overthrow the principle of male spiritual leadership, he would have done it—pointedly, openly, clearly, boldly, and unashamedly!

And what great opportunities Jesus had for making such a revolutionary statement about women! One clear statement, of course, would have been in his choice of apostles. If he had chosen six men and six women, we wouldn't be left to wonder. Even if the ascended Christ had reached down after the establishment of the church on Pentecost and specially chosen a woman as an apostle—as he did with Paul—again, the conclusion would have been undeniable. But neither of those obvious choices was made by Christ.

When sending out the 72, two by two (Luke 10:1-16), Jesus easily could have included some of the women from Galilee who followed him as a support group. Yet there is no indication that any but men were sent. If women followed Jesus in certain ways, they apparently did not follow Jesus in other ways. Despite the fact that both men and women ate the Passover meal, only the Twelve—all men—were part of the upper-room experience. We know that the women in Jesus' support group were in Jerusalem at the time, but the Last Supper was an all-male affair—as was the procession to the Garden of Gethsemane, and the glorious view of the ascension.

Are we to believe that Jesus would have overlooked so great an opportunity to demonstrate a radical new concept in spiritual leadership? When he chose to be born in a manger, the son of penny-poor parents, he was making a powerful statement about the revolutionary nature of his kingdom. When he chose to take his ministry to the Gentiles as well as to the Jews, he made yet another grand statement about the universality of his kingdom. What he did through his actions while on earth always spoke volumes.

So when Jesus chose 12 people having no recognized status whatever among the religious establishment, he was making a telling statement about traditional religious hierarchy and the abuse of scriptural scholarship. And when in the face of every opportunity otherwise he chose 12 *men* as his foundation for the church, he was making an even stronger statement about the principle of male spiritual leadership: It was still to be the order of the day under Christianity—more enlightened, perhaps, and more responsible, but still the guiding principle for families and the church.

Naturally, we must be cautious about those whom Jesus did *not* appoint, for neither did he appoint blacks or Gentiles, both of whom later appear to have been included in leadership positions within the church (See Mark 15:21 and Acts 16:1). The point is that we must look somewhere beyond Jesus' own actions if we are to find a dramatic shift in the principle of male headship. Jesus himself maintained the status quo.

Of course, the strongest possible statement from Jesus would not have been merely a symbolic act, such as choosing women apostles, but giving us explicit teaching on the subject: some forthright message that male headship had served its purpose but was no longer the pattern; some word of expectation that, in his church, women would exercise the same leadership roles as men, and that they would be called to responsibilities of leadership which for centuries had been given to men. But there is only silence from Jesus. Resounding silence.

Many people today are telling us that Jesus *said* this thing or *did* that thing which implies a changing role for women in the church. But when we go back to the Gospels and find nothing in support of the claims being made, it is difficult to escape the conclusion that they are proceeding precariously on the strength of selective and self-serving memories of Jesus' ministry.

Male spiritual leadership. As it was in the beginning, so it was at the end of Jesus' ministry. Neither in word nor in deed did Jesus ever renounce it. Instead of misinterpreting what

Jesus did in restoring dignity to women, let us follow his lead by honoring godly women of our own day. Let us not call them to a responsibility to which Jesus never called them, but let us honor their unique contributions even as he did.

Study Questions

1. What happens when men drop the word "spiritual" from the principle of male spiritual leadership?
2. How did Jewish men treat women at the time of Christ?
3. How did Jesus treat the women with whom he came into contact?
4. Did Jesus have a problem with the idea of women disciples? Did he value their contributions to his ministry?
5. Why do you suppose Jesus chose only men to be part of the Twelve?
6. If Jesus had wanted to make a statement overturning the principle of male spiritual leadership would the patriarchical culture of his day have made him hesitate?
7. In what ways did Jesus pay special tribute to women?
8. Does honoring women mean that men are relieved of their responsibility for male spiritual leadership?
9. Does calling men to spiritual leadership responsibility necessarily dishonor women?
10. Is there anything at all in Jesus' ministry that would suggest his rejection of the principle of male spiritual leadership?

10 Broken Barriers in the Early Church

Women Among the First Christians

Have you ever thought you were close to your destination only to discover that you were much farther away than you thought? Some years ago I was visiting with my sister and her family in Pietermaritzburg, South Africa, where Sandra and her husband, Paddy, work to spread the Gospel among the blacks and Indians in the townships and villages around their home in the province of Natal. I arrived in time to join them for their vacation. Along with another family, we drove through the territory of the timeless Zulu people, seeing them in traditional dress and their centuries-old simple way of life.

As we left the grassy lowlands of the Zulus, we headed our cars up into the breathtaking Drakensberg mountains. Rugged and majestic with jagged peaks and sweeping vistas, the Drakensbergs stretch for miles, barely touched by the human intrusions inevitable to such grandeur.

Our campsite was primitive by American standards, but once the tents were up and the aroma of the cooking potjiekos wafted across the camp, we were enveloped in a comfortable feeling of hearth and home. As evening fell around our campfire and the darkened sky brought the resplendent display of stars found only in the Southern hemisphere, to my amazement I heard joyous songs of praise to God being sung by young people in the adjacent camp. In a nation of often-superstitious religions, we had managed to camp next to others of like faith! On this wondrous night, one sensed that the portals of heaven were but a step away!

The beauty of the night gave way to sleep and then the glorious dawn calling us to life again. The plan for the day was a four-hour walk through the mountains. Our friends, Les and Linda, assured us it was an easy half-day walk even for the children. So off we went like merry troupers, lightly packed for such a short outing.

Crossing an ice-cold mountain-fed stream, we headed for some low marshlands, wet with morning dew. I led the way to clear a path for the little ones in our party. After an hour we started climbing onto more rocky terrain, glad to be out of the wet grasses which had soaked our clothes. By now the children were tiring of this "fun adventure," and we began carrying the younger two. It was rough going during the next hour as we walked up precarious trails past secluded waterfalls and quiet pools.

It soon became clear that we long since should have reached the halfway point, but it was nowhere in sight. We pressed on, thinking we would discover it just over the next ridge. Or was it the *next* ridge? With each ridge we fell into exhausted heaps—tired, hungry, and discouraged. By now the water bottle was almost empty and the little food we had brought was gone. Manufactured humor kept our spirits alive along the way, but secretly everyone knew we had grossly miscalculated the distance of our journey. Not so secret was Sandra's hurting knee, which began to slow us down significantly, and the exhaustion of the children, which meant the almost full-time burden of carrying them.

Gloria, the three-year-old, fell asleep while I was carrying her, like a sack of potatoes, on my back. At one point I looked down a 300-foot drop within a foot of the trail and winced at the thought of what would happen if I were to slip even the slightest. Once again I looked up ahead to the bend in the path, thinking it might be the last of the *day—hoping* it would be the end of the trail. But, no—bend after bend and ridge after ridge eluded the hoped-for conclusion to our outing.

What started out as a leisurely four-hour walk turned out to be a harrowing nine-hour experience. It didn't matter that the walk would have been a piece of cake for more conditioned hikers, or even easily manageable had the children not been with us. As we dragged ourselves back into camp at the end of a day of unexpected struggle, thankful for a safe return, we knew we had suffered greatly from our miscalculation. What we had been so sure of at the outset had turned out to be anything but what we first thought it would be. In fact, it never was the four-hour walk we expected to find.

False Hope from Joel's Prophecy

I see in our experience that day yet another picture—a scene of disappointed expectations for those who seize upon one passage after another in the hope that it will lead to their hoped-for conclusions about a significant role change for women in the church. When crossing the vast terrain of Scripture, one expects a leisurely stroll through the known territory of the Old Testament. It records for us a patriarchical period in which male spiritual leadership was so obvious that no one could question it.

But just when we expect to head in a different direction in the New Testament, with Jesus leading the way, we are in for a shock: Jesus doesn't lead in a different direction at all! Rather, he blocks off the dangerous sidetrails which had caused so many to stumble and fall (abuse and disdain), and leads us back to the original path of male spiritual leadership.

It is then that we assume Jesus was just preparing us for what would happen further up the trail. We think we can see a ridge of hope ahead, and we trudge forward into Luke's

account of the Acts of the Apostles. We tell ourselves that, with
the coming of the Holy Spirit to the fledgling church, the complete picture will be revealed to the apostles. And as we reach
the top of the ridge it looks like we were right! There it is in
Acts chapter 2, with the events accompanying the dramatic
establishment of the church on Pentecost.

As Peter stands up to explain how the apostles are able to
speak miraculously in the languages of all the people represented, he quotes the prophecy of Joel which points to the
pouring out of God's Spirit:

> In the last days, God says,
>> I will pour out my Spirit on all people.
>
> Your sons and daughters will prophesy,
>> your young men will see visions,
>> your old men will dream dreams.
>
> Even on my servants, both men and women,
>> I will pour out my Spirit in those days,
>> and they will prophesy.
>
> I will show wonders in the heaven above
>> and signs on the earth below,
>> blood and fire and billows of smoke.
>
> The sun will be turned to darkness
>> and the moon to blood
>> before the coming of the great and glorious
>> day of the Lord.
>
> And everyone who calls
>> on the name of the Lord will be saved
>> (Acts 2:17-21).

As we stand on the mountaintop of Acts chapter 2, two
seemingly-significant changes appear to lead where many
Christians seek to go: 1) that at last God's Spirit was to be

poured out on both men *and* women, and 2) that women would prophesy in the same way that men would prophesy. What many think they see from this vantage point is the end of the trail—the Holy Spirit's significant alteration of the principle of male leadership.

But there are others standing on the same mountaintop who quickly point out that time and again during our easy stroll through the Old Testament we came across women who were prophesying the same way men were. There would be nothing new about women prophesying in the early church. Since Old Testament prophetesses exercised their gift of prophecy during centuries of normative male headship, Peter's reference to Joel's prophecy represents no radical change in that regard.

Still another problem exists for those so intent on reaching a particular conclusion that they look around bends in the trail for what they want to see: Stretching the gift of prophecy to imply approval for women preaching and holding other functional positions of leadership within the church is as short-sighted as equating prophetesses with priests in the Old Testament. Prophetesses never were priests. Spiritual roles are not identical commodities that are interchangeable at will.

Even if the gift of prophecy were something radically new for Christian women in the first century, it would have said nothing regarding the principle of male spiritual leadership. In fact, as we look ahead to another ridge of hope for many people today—Paul's letter to the Corinthians—we discover that certain limitations put on prophetesses were imposed for the purpose of preserving male spiritual leadership during the public exercise of the women's prophetic gift.

The Good News of Joel's Prophecy

Whatever Joel was referring to would be revolutionary! It would be as if the sun were turned to darkness and the moon to blood! If the principle of male spiritual leadership was not changed by the coming of the Holy Spirit, what was? The first thing we notice is how many more people are soon to be on the path to heaven, for God says through Joel, "I will pour out my Spirit on *all* people"—not just the chosen race of Israel, but Gentiles too. In Christ there is neither Jew nor Gentile!

Not even Peter fully realizes the dramatic breakthrough envisioned by God in these words. It will not be until after further demonstrations of the Spirit's power in the home of Cornelius (Acts chapter 10) that Peter understands that the Gospel is also for the Gentiles. But that is clearly Joel's message. And what a glorious message!

The second thing we notice is that identity with God is no longer to be vicarious. Each person carries his or her own weight on the journey toward the spiritual home. Under the old covenant, women were identified with God through men, for it was only men who were circumcised as an outward sign of the covenant. But speaking through Joel, God promised that "even on my servants, both men and women, I will pour out my Spirit in those days." The revolutionary change was that God's covenant extended directly to women as well as to men. In Christ there is neither male nor female!

Where only men were circumcised under the old covenant, both men and women were to be baptized under the new covenant. It was their entrance by faith into a relationship whereby God would pour out not only the gift of tongues on this inaugural occasion but indeed *his very Spirit* upon them! We see that promise in the conclusion to Peter's sermon:

> When the people heard this, they were cut to the heart and said to Peter and the other apostles, "Brothers, what shall we do?"
>
> Peter replied, "Repent and be baptized, every one of you, in the name of Jesus Christ for the forgiveness of your sins. And you will receive the gift of the Holy Spirit. The promise is for you and your children and for all who are far off—for all whom the Lord our God will

call" (Acts 2:37-39).

And what was the promise associated with repentance and baptism? Nothing less than the presence of the Holy Spirit in the lives of God's people! As wonderful as the *gifts* of the Holy Spirit would be in confirming the Gospel to a disbelieving ancient world, those miraculous gifts would not begin to compare with the *gift* of the Holy Spirit himself!

To say that Joel was referring to the spiritual gift of prophecy for both men and women greatly minimizes the significance of this unprecedented occasion. Again, the gift of prophecy—whether for men or for women—was not unusual. It was not something which was ushered in either by Jesus or by the appearance of the Holy Spirit on Pentecost. It was nothing to jump up and down about. What *was* worth jumping up and down about was the good news that God would live within us—all of us, whether Jew or Gentile, slave or free, male or female!

Under the old covenant there were barriers on the road to being identified as God's chosen people—race barriers, economic barriers, even sex barriers. In Christ there were to be no barriers—not even the barrier of our own humanity, because God would cross that barrier in filling our lives with his Spirit. Not all Christians, whether male or female, would have the gift of prophecy, but all would have the gift of the Spirit. Not all Christians would have the gift of tongues, but all would have the gift of the Spirit. Not all Christians would have the gifts of interpretation, or healing, or administration—but all would have the Spirit himself as a gift.

Nor would all Christians be given the responsibility of spiritual leadership in the church, but all would have the gift of the Holy Spirit in their lives—whether faithful Christian men or godly Christian women. *That* was the good news prophesied by Joel. *That* was the Gospel message preached by Peter. And *that* is the revolutionary appeal of Christ's kingdom!

Proof of the Pudding

Nowhere in Luke's account of the first-century church do we find a hint of "shared spiritual leadership" between men and women in the church. Nowhere in the book of Acts do we find any references to women publicly proclaiming the Gospel to gender-mixed audiences, or becoming apostles, or being appointed elders or deacons, or filling any other functional leadership role within the church. But what we do find is worthy of heavenly anthems!

In one passage after another we find confirmation of the personal relationship which women found with God through their Lord and Savior, Jesus Christ. When men approached God through faith and faith-responsive baptism, so did women. Men were not baptized for entire families, as Jewish men had been circumcised to consecrate their households. We see both men *and* women being baptized, with women becoming Christians on their own without their unbelieving husbands joining in their commitment. Both unknown, unnamed women in the lower echelons of society and women of great prominence in Jewish or Greek society personally put their faith in Christ and were baptized.

It must have been a marvelous feeling of spiritual liberation! If women in Scripture were not "counted" among the leaders of God's people, as we noted earlier, they certainly "count" when it comes to their personal relationship with God through Christ. And not only do they count, but they are of equal value in every way.

Look at Luke's many accounts of women becoming Christians in the days of the apostles. Luke dramatizes the revolutionary nature of the broken sex barrier by repeatedly calling attention to the conversions of both men *and women.*

Within the first few days after Pentecost:

And all the believers used to meet together in Solomon's Colonnade. No one else dared join them, even though they were highly regarded by the people. Nevertheless, more and more men *and women* believed in the Lord and were added to their number (Acts 5:12-14).

In Samaria, where Philip was preaching:

But when they believed Philip as he preached the good news of the kingdom of God and the name of Jesus Christ, they were baptized, both men *and women* (Acts 8:12).

With Paul and Silas in Thessalonica:

Some of the Jews were persuaded and joined Paul and Silas, as did a large number of God-fearing Greeks *and not a few prominent women* (Acts 17:4).

With Paul in Berea:

Many of the Jews believed, *as did also a number of prominent Greek women* and many Greek men (Acts 17:12).

And with Paul in Athens:

A few men became followers of Paul and believed. Among them was Dionysius, a member of the Areopagus, *also a woman* named Damaris, and a number of others (Acts 17:34).

Were these women breaking ground by becoming functional leaders in the church? No. They were breaking even more important ground: They were approaching God without the intervention of any man but the Son of Man, Jesus Christ himself! *That* was novel; *that* was revolutionary; *that* was the good news for godly women both then and now!

What Happened to Male Leadership?

Did the spiritual liberation of women mean that godly men were relieved of responsibility for being spiritual leaders? Luke gives no grounds for that assumption. In fact, when the need arose for a special administrative task to be done among the first Christians, it fell to the men to do it. You may recall the appointment of the seven men to help with the daily food distributions:

> In those days when the number of disciples was increasing, the Grecian Jews among them complained against the Hebraic Jews because their widows were being overlooked in the daily distribution of food. So the Twelve gathered all the disciples together and said, "It would not be right for us to neglect the ministry of the word of God in order to wait on tables. Brothers, choose seven men from among you who are known to be full of the Spirit and wisdom. We will turn this responsibility over to them and will give our attention to prayer and the ministry of the word" (Acts 6:1- 4).

Many people today concede that women can or should be excluded from the pulpit and from such spiritual headship positions as being elders in a local congregation, so long as women are not excluded from other positions of service within the church. For them, a comfortable line of demarcation seems to be public proclamation of the Word or perhaps only ultimate responsibility for the spiritual needs of the congregation. This is why one often hears appeals for women to be deaconesses, but less so for their being elders or bishops, as that position of leadership is described in Scripture.

Yet in the matter of caring for the needy widows in the burgeoning post-Pentecost Jerusalem church, responsibility for prayer and for the ministry of the Word were divorced from the work of the chosen Seven, almost as if to emphasize the irrelevance of such a distinction when it comes to the principle of male spiritual leadership. From Luke's examples of church leadership, both in this instance and elsewhere, the more certain line of distinction seems to have been whether the task was either public or corporate. When it was public or corporate within the church, only men were given the responsibility.

Are we to believe that none of the women who were being converted could have performed the task as admirably as the men? Would not such a responsibility have been consistent with women's traditional household-management skills? And should we assume that the Christian women lacked the spirit and wisdom of godly men? A close look at the women in Luke's account of the early Christians shows that skill, ability, talent, and basic spirituality were not the controlling factors in the principle of male spiritual leadership.

Dorcas

A perfect example of someone qualified by temperament and spirituality to perform such a task would have been Dorcas, of whom it was said: "In Joppa there was a disciple named Tabitha (which, when translated, is Dorcas), who was always doing good and helping the poor" (Acts 9:36). But no "Dorcases" were given the official responsibility of doing what Dorcas did quite naturally in her everyday service to God. In her work among the needy, was Dorcas a deacon? Yes, in the sense that the word "deacon" means servant; no, in the sense that in certain contexts "deacon" is applied to an officially recognized position within the body of believers.

Even in the appointment of the Seven, you get a sense of "officially recognized servanthood" when the apostles set out qualifications for appointment to this particular task and limited the appointment to men. In Paul's epistles, even more specific and formal qualifications are laid down for those who would serve as elders and deacons, quite apart from those who might serve informally in much the same way, doing what would be done by others more "officially recognized."

Lydia

The conversion of Lydia provides us another example of a woman whose apparent business skills would have equipped her well for an "officially recognized position" of leadership within the church:

> On the Sabbath we went outside the city gate to the river, where we expected to find a place of prayer. We sat down and began to speak to the women who had gathered there. One of those listening was a woman named Lydia, a dealer in purple cloth from the city of Thyatira, who was a worshiper of God. The Lord opened her heart to respond to Paul's message. When she and the members of her household were baptized, she invited us to her home. "If you consider me a believer in the Lord," she said, "come and stay at my house." And she persuaded us (Acts 16:13-15).

When Paul and Silas were subsequently arrested and jailed, then miraculously released, it was to Lydia's house that they went to join their brothers. Both in talent and in spiritual devotion, Lydia and other prominent women like her may have been well-suited for positions of spiritual headship in the church. But nothing in Luke's account ever suggests that such appointments ever occurred. Nevertheless, we can only assume that Lydia's life of faith led others to Christ. In that sense—as a woman of God—she was a spiritual leader in the finest sense. And to that kind of leadership we are all called, both men and women.

Philip's Four Daughters

If what we are looking for in Luke's account is a reference to women playing a significant role in the early church, we might note a brief passage about the daughters of Philip the evangelist. It takes place near the end of Paul's third missionary journey, where Luke recalls, "We reached Caesarea and stayed at the house of Philip the evangelist, one of the Seven. He had four unmarried daughters who prophesied" (Acts 21:8,9).

But we have been down this trail before—many times. And it has always led to the same conclusion: God's use of women as prophetesses was never equated with more than ad hoc leadership. It was not ongoing female leadership or "shared spiritual leadership" in the open-ended sense that many Christians today hope to find it.

The irony of this brief reference is that the father of these four special women of God was one of the chosen Seven whose male-only status began this part of our discussion. Even though his daughters served God through the gift of prophecy, they were not asked to serve God through the gift of administration. We recognize that having one godly gift does not entitle a person to yet another gift. Similarly, a woman is not called to exercise a role to which men alone have been called.

Priscilla

If ever there was a godly woman capable of spiritual leadership, surely it must have been Aquila's wife, Priscilla. Laboring together as a godly couple in the work of the Lord, Priscilla and Aquila seemed to show up wherever the need arose. We have this account from Luke of their influence on the evangelist Apollos:

> A Jew named Apollos, a native of Alexandria, came to Ephesus. He was a learned man, with a thorough knowledge of the Scriptures. He had been instructed in the way of the Lord, and he spoke with great fervor and taught about Jesus accurately, though he knew only the baptism of John. He began to speak boldly in the synagogue. When Priscilla and Aquila heard him, they invited him to their home and explained to him the way of God more adequately (Acts 18:24-26).

Sometimes we get the idea that if a woman cannot be "an official spiritual leader" she has no value at all. Not so in the case of Priscilla, whose name is even listed here before her husband's! At other times we get the idea that male spiritual leadership means that women are not to be educated in Scripture, or that, if they are, they should keep it to themselves. Neither of these ideas fits the example provided by Priscilla. More than once she was recognized as an important part of the work of the first-century church. In fact, Paul refers to Priscilla and Aquila as "fellow workers in Christ Jesus" who had "risked their lives" for him (Romans 16:3, 4).

Yet one must not assume more than we are told about Priscilla. Everywhere I turn I see liberation advocates using Priscilla as an example of "shared spiritual leadership." If that means functional headship within either the church or the home, then it is an assumption quite beyond the available evidence. Far from taking a public role in the church in the kind of open way that is being urged for Christian women today, the Scripture's primary reference to Priscilla finds her joining together with her husband to take Apollos aside *privately* and share her understanding with him.

As far as we are told, Priscilla held no official position within the church. Nothing indicates that she was an elder or deacon in a local congregation or that she was regarded as a public evangelist. As a matter of fact, we get the idea that she would not have needed any of those outer trappings to do what she did for the cause of Christ. As Paul put it, Priscilla and Aquila were *workers*. With so much work to be done, they didn't need to be designated leaders. They led through lives of service.

False Hopes and Wondrous Heights

With the availability of such prominent and capable women as Dorcas, Lydia, Philip's daughters, and Priscilla, it is all the more remarkable that the book of Acts is devoid of any reference to women exercising functional leadership roles within the church. For anyone wishing to establish biblical precedent for appointive positions for women within the church today, female headship is conspicuous by its absence. So too is "shared leadership." What we discover as we walk the trail of Luke's account of the acts of the apostles are more ridges of promise on the horizon of hope, each giving way to disappointment for those who want to find a radically different role for today's women.

What I didn't tell you before about our day of challenge in the Drakensbergs was that, despite the frustration resulting from our miscalculation, we saw scenes of incomparable beauty along the way. Between times of frustration, there were majestic views from the mountain peaks we crossed that day. And that is equally true of Luke's historical record of the early church. We do not find what many hope to find—equality at all levels of leadership. But what we *do* discover in the coming of the Holy Spirit on Pentecost must not be understated.

With the appearance of the Holy Spirit, the trail in Acts leads to majestic new heights of spiritual recognition for women in the sight of God. Never again would women be dependent upon men for their own spiritual identification. Never again would a man's beliefs dictate the faith of his wife or children. Never again would a covenant symbol be the exclusive possession of men. In Christ, each person—male or female—comes to God through his or her own faith. Each one is baptized pursuant to his or her own choice. Each is accepted as an individual of equal spiritual worth. The barriers are broken, the path is open to all, and women walk with the same dignity as men. Praise God for leading all of us home together—whether men of strength or women of God!

Study Questions

1. On Pentecost, when Peter quoted from Joel's prophecy about God pouring out his Spirit on both men and women, was there anything groundbreaking about women prophesying? If not, what *was* revolutionary for women in the new Christian era?

2. Even assuming that Christian women prophesied in the early church, is there any evidence from Luke's account of the acts of the apostles that women assumed spiritual leadership roles in the gathered work and worship of the church?

3. Did women receive other special gifts of the Holy Spirit at the dawn of the Christian age? If so, did that lead to the exercise of spiritual leadership responsibility?

4. Were there women in the early church who would have been qualified by ability or training to serve as leaders in the church? Cite any examples of those who might have been so qualified.

5. Do you think Dorcas might have felt slighted that, as a woman, she was not called to a position of spiritual leadership?

6. When there were women like Dorcas who were willing and able to serve the needs of others, does it make sense in human terms that seven *men* were appointed to serve the Grecian widows? What accounts for that if not for the principle of male spiritual leadership?

7. In what way does Priscilla provide a good example of a woman who leads a man into a better understanding of God's will?

8. What does it say about Priscilla taking Apollos aside privately before teaching him the way of the Lord more perfectly?

9. Must either men or women have an official "title" in order to serve?

10. Is there any evidence in the book of Acts of women taking leadership positions in the gathered worship of the church?

11 Neither Male nor Female?

Overlooking the Obvious

Sometimes we get so caught up in proving what we want to believe that we overlook the obvious. I was reminded of that in a case where my opponent, the defense attorney, ended up being hoisted on his own petard. He was having a field day cross-examining my witness to a brutal beating which had resulted in the death of a woman who had been living with her killer for several months.

Along with several other farm laborers who lived in shanties surrounding a common grassy area, Tom Willis had watched the defendant beat his helpless girlfriend with an oak shovel handle, splintering it into pieces with each blow. Willis testified to having seen the defendant hit the woman but said he did not realize how serious the beating was at the time. In fact, no one had gone to her rescue.

The following cross-examination was aimed at discrediting Willis' testimony. For a while I thought Willis might succumb to the withering barrage of questions, carefully crafted to take advantage of his simplemindedness and lack of education.

Counsel: Now, Tom, you say you saw Robertson hit the victim with a shovel handle, is that right?

Willis: Yes, sir, that's what I saw.

Counsel: Well, now, what time of night did this take place?

Willis: I'd say 'bout 10 or 11.

Counsel: Was it dark at that time?

Willis: Yeah, sure was.

Counsel: In fact it was *real* dark, wasn't it?

Willis: Yes, sir, I guess it was.

Counsel: Well, Tom, were there any lights on in the yard?

Willis: No, sir, weren't no lights out there.

Counsel: But you're telling the jury you could see well enough to recognize my client holding an oak shovel handle, is that right?

Willis: Yes, sir, I could see it good.

Counsel: But you admit it was really dark at that time.

Willis: Yes, sir, shore was.

At that point the defense counsel thought he had Willis where he wanted him and moved in for the kill.

Counsel: Now, Tom, you say it was dark out there that night, and that no lights were on anywhere around the yard, yet you claim you clearly saw Robertson hitting the victim with a shovel handle. Just how far can you see at night anyway, Tom?

"How far can I see at night?" Tom mused momentarily. "Well, sir," he said, "just how far is the *moon?*"

The judge smiled, the jurors laughed, and I wanted to stand up and cheer! Even the defense counsel seemed amused by his own undoing. By concentrating on the answer he expected to get, he overlooked the possibility that he might get a different answer.

Overlooking the Obvious

In the case being made for a significantly different role for women in the church, several biblical passages are being lifted out of their contexts to support propositions which they do not address. We have already seen Peter's Pentecost reference to Joel's prophecy stretched beyond its intended meaning, and we will examine other references as well. But no passage has been abused more blatantly than Galatians 3:28, perhaps because it provides the most dramatic, if simplistic, slogan for the cause: "Neither Male Nor Female."

The complete passage is as follows:

> You are all sons of God through faith in Christ Jesus, for all of you who were baptized into Christ have clothed yourselves with Christ. There is neither Jew nor Greek, slave nor free, male nor female, for you are all one in Christ Jesus. If you belong to Christ, then you are Abraham's seed, and heirs according to the promise (Galatians 3:26-29).

Today this passage is being hailed as the Magna Carta for women in the church, the Christian woman's Declaration of Independence and Emancipation Proclamation. Because of Galatians 3:28, prior patriarchal distinctions in religious matters are said to be out the window. Sex barriers in the church are said to be broken and distinctions of spiritual leadership abandoned.

The most surprising aspect of this interpretation is the fact that the letter to the Galatians was written by the same apostle Paul whose writings in Corinthians, Timothy, and Titus have been viewed as restrictive to Christian women. If Paul intended Galatians 3:28 to overturn the centuries-old principle of male spiritual leadership and to usher in a new era of shared spiritual responsibility, it is ironic that he would pen *later* letters imposing restrictions on Christian women and perpetuating the headship of men in both the home and the church!

In fact, Paul's guidelines for women in public worship may have been necessitated by the same misinterpretation of Galatians 3:28 which we are seeing today. Even in the first century there were apparently those who read into Paul's letter a radical message which, judging from his other letters, he never intended.

It should not be surprising that Paul would need to clarify statements in his later letters. Similar misunderstandings about freedom in Christ prompted his responses regarding marriage and divorce (1 Corinthians 7) and meat sacrificed to idols (1 Corinthians 8). And Paul's second Thessalonian letter was an answer to those who misinterpreted his first Thessalonian letter and anticipated an immediate second coming.

To keep a proper balance, Paul always seems to deliver a one-two punch: free, but not without responsibility to the weak; soon, but not immediate. With regard to Christian men and women the message is: one in Christ, but different in responsibility.

Context—Always Context

The most important thing about the phrase "neither male nor female" being used in the current gender struggle is that it occurs in a letter having nothing to do with roles in the church. Neither the principle of male leadership nor "shared leadership" is under consideration. In fact, leadership is not Paul's concern at all. He is not addressing the husband-wife relationship or what women may or may not do in church worship.

Anyone who has used Galatians 3:28 in support of a wider role for women in the church, or has heard it used that way, owes it to himself or herself to reread the entire letter. It will take only a few minutes. As you read, ask yourself what Paul is talking about. Does he address the issues we have been discussing in this book?

If you do reread the Galatian letter, you will note that Paul begins his letter by expressing concern about a popular doctrine which saw Christianity as an afterthought tacked onto Judaism. According to that view, circumcision was still required of male believers. The truth of the matter is that these advocates of "Jewish Christianity" were attempting to impose the entire Jewish law on Gentile converts. In a nutshell, this is how Paul approached the problem:

> I am astonished that you are so quickly deserting the one who called you by the grace of Christ and are turning to a different gospel—which is really no gospel at all. Evidently some people are throwing you into confusion and are trying to pervert the gospel of Christ (1:6, 7).

> We who are Jews by birth and not "Gentile sinners" know that a man is not justified by observing the law, but by faith in Jesus Christ . . . (2:15, 16).

> The Scripture foresaw that God would justify the Gentiles by faith, and announced the gospel in advance to Abraham: "All nations will be blessed through you." So those who have faith are blessed along with Abraham, the man of faith (3:8, 9).

> Clearly no one is justified before God by the law, because, "The righteous will live by faith . . ." (3:11).

> Before this faith came, we were held prisoners by the law, locked up until faith should be revealed. So the law was put in charge to lead us to Christ that we might be justified by faith. Now that faith has come, we are no longer under the supervision of the law.

> You are all sons of God through faith in Christ Jesus, for all of you who were baptized into Christ have clothed yourselves with Christ. There is neither Jew nor Greek, slave nor free, male nor female, for you are all one in Christ Jesus. If you belong to Christ, then you are Abraham's seed, and heirs according to the promise (3:23-29).

> I, Paul, tell you that if you let yourselves be circumcised, Christ will be of no value to you at all (5:2).

> For in Christ Jesus neither circumcision nor uncircumcision has any value. The only thing that counts is faith expressing itself through love (5:6).

It is the continued requirement of circumcision for male believers (in addition to Christian baptism) that Paul is concerned about, not the role of women in the church. It is the imposition of the old law that prompts this letter, not the patriarchal principle of male spiritual leadership which was instituted in the Garden of Eden long before the law was given to Moses. Paul's letter is about *our faith relationship with God,* not *relationships with each other as we worship God.* Naturally, our relationship with God will affect all our other relationships, including those between men and women, but that is not Paul's focus here.

When Paul writes here about our faith relationship with God, he tells us there are no distinctions. When he later writes about our relationships with each other, he tells us there are indeed distinctions between what Christian men and Christian women are called to do. In the same way that Christians are given different spiritual gifts, men and women are sometimes called to exercise their individual gifts in different arenas.

The message of Paul's combined writings is analogous to a familiar concept from the sports scene. Paul himself liked to use sports analogies. As individuals, we are all on God's team—equal in importance, equal in access to God. But being a team member with equal team status doesn't mean we all play the same position.

Before considering what positions we are called to play, Paul must first establish the fact that we are on the team. And in the Galatian letter he is pointing out that team membership is determined in a radically different way from that of any time prior to Christ—as a matter of personal choice and not by inheritance or (worse yet) vicarious identity through someone of another sex.

Coming One by One

In the past, many have interpreted Galatians 3:28 as simply a statement that in Christ everyone can be saved, including Gentiles, slaves, and women. Of course that traditional interpretation overlooks the fact that Gentiles, slaves, and women were able to have a relationship with God even before the coming of Christ. What's new in Christ is what we have mentioned before: Each person comes to God through *personal* faith, not on the coattails of any other person. Women in particular would no longer have their identity with God predicated upon male-oriented lineage and the exclusively-male symbol of circumcision.

The sentence preceding the mention of "neither male nor female" tells us what Paul meant by that phrase:

"You are all sons of God by faith in Christ Jesus." Under the old law, one's relationship with God was in a sense established by heredity (or ownership, in the case of slaves). From the standpoint of the heart, of course, it was personal faith that bridged a person to God. But to be a "son of God" one had to be a "son" of Abraham. Jewish women, therefore, found salvation under the spiritual umbrella of Jewish men—fathers, brothers, and husbands. In Christ, however, all obedient believers become "sons"—whether Jews or Gentiles, slaves or free, male or female.

The significance of "sonship" lay in the ability to *inherit*, for only the sons inherited by natural right. In telling us the good news that Christian women now come to God on their own faith, apart from any man, Paul tells us that the woman of God inherits spiritual blessings in her own right. In fact the sentence which follows our key phrase confirms it: "If you belong to Christ, then you are Abraham's seed, and heirs according to the promise."

In Christ both men and women are *natural* heirs, as if they were sons under the old law. *That* is the good news! *That* is the Gospel. *That* is the message of Galatians.

And how do we become "sons" of inheritance? Paul just told us: "You are all sons of God through faith in Christ Jesus, for all of you who were baptized into Christ have clothed yourselves with Christ." It is through faith and faith-responsive baptism that each of us—whoever we may be—personally chooses a relationship with God, personally commits our will to his will, and personally answers his call to a righteous life. It is in *this* sense that "there is neither Jew nor Greek, slave nor free, male nor female."

In Galatians, Paul is not talking about who does what in congregational worship, or who might lead prayers in home fellowships, or who may be designated for a specific responsibility in the church, but about *how we get to God.* When he pointed to the elimination of artificial distinctions, Paul obviously did not mean that one ceases to be Jewish by race, a servant by position, or a woman by sex. The Holy Spirit's message through Paul is that *one's race, position, or sex is no longer a barrier to identity with God.*

"One" But Different

When Paul says that we are all one in Christ, it is easy to focus on the word "one" and assume that it means total homogeneity. Yes, in Christ we are all "sons," but not all sons were given the headship responsibility of the firstborn son. Before God we are all equal in status but different in the kinds of servanthood to which we have been called.

Not even the cheer "One for all and all for one!" suggests that everyone on the team or in the group has the same function. It does not even mean that everyone should be equally *entitled* to the various functions which might be exercised.

For example, despite the fact that as a body of citizens we are "one nation under God," we are not all entitled to fly in Air Force One, the President's personal airplane. Even though we are all citizens, if we are younger than 35 we cannot be the President who flies in Air Force One. Nor if we are younger than 18 can we vote for that President. Being "one" in relationship does not necessarily mean being one in function.

In his first letter, Peter reminds us that we Christians—male and female—are "a royal priesthood" (1 Peter 2:9). When Christ abolished the established priesthood of Israel, he appointed us as priests in their place. We are all priests, and Christ is our High Priest. As men and women before God, we are one in priesthood. (Churches concerned about the ordination of women as priests have already gone one step too far in establishing a special priesthood, whether for men or for women.) Yet our oneness does not mean that we are all called to exercise the same priestly responsibilities. That's what 1 Corinthians 12 is all about: "There are different kinds of service, but the same Lord" (1 Corinthians 12:5).

Perhaps the best illustration of this idea is found in the relationship between God and Christ. God is the head of Christ and the Father over the Son. Yet Jesus proclaimed, "I and the Father are one" (John 10:30). Oneness doesn't eliminate distinctive roles, even in the Godhead.

In terms of Paul's letter to the Galatians, being "one" in Christ means having equal access to God. It means being equally entitled to God's spiritual promises and blessings despite external differences—whether race, economic status, gender, or unique responsibilities determined by gender.

Our oneness in Christ is a reminder that none of us has a right to look down on other Christians as second-class citizens. There is no room for thinking that one is spiritually superior to another Christian or more entitled to God's blessings. If a man is an elder or a deacon, he is not spiritually superior to those who are not given that position of oversight. If a woman is not permitted to be an evangelist or an elder or deacon, she is neither spiritually inferior to those men who are such nor slighted by being called to different responsibilities.

The Futility of Other Interpretations

Any interpretation of "neither male nor female" other than the one naturally suggested by the context of Galatians is laced with problems. Our distinct physical characteristics have not been obliterated, and that is more important than we first might suppose. Because Christian women, like all other women, are the ones who give birth to babies and normally provide their newborn's physical nourishment, the woman's typical responsibility tends toward home and family. The fact that a woman is "in Christ" does not change the duties related to the physical functions of her body. (Of course, we are speaking here of normative responsibilities. The single woman and the childless wife are not excluded.)

The man's typically greater physical strength has historically dictated his role as the family's protector and provider. Even though modern social relationships and employment circumstances have greatly diminished the importance of a man's physical strength, his role as provider and protector is commensurate with his responsibility for the spiritual guidance and protection of the family. It is an obligation which he bears, not because of spiritual superiority, but because it is a God-imposed duty. Galatians 3:28 changes neither the natural distinctions between male and female nor their commensurate spiritual roles.

A more serious problem encountered in treating Galatians 3:28 as a declaration of independence for women in the church is the corresponding implication regarding women in the home. If "neither male nor female" eliminates role distinctions in the *church,* it also eliminates role distinctions in the *home* between a Christian husband and a Christian wife. The distinctions between men and women in the home are part of the same ancient order as are the distinctions in the church.

Male spiritual leadership in the church is but an extension of male spiritual leadership in the home. The principle predates the establishment of the church, the institution of the laws of Moses, and even the patriarchal covenant with Abraham. As we have seen, the principle of male spiritual leadership goes back to the very beginning, to the first man and the first woman.

Between husbands and wives, the only time there will truly be "neither male nor female" will be in heaven, for in heaven there will be "no marriage nor giving in marriage," no headship or submission. We won't need the principle of male spiritual leadership in heaven. There, all will truly be "one." But in this life we would delude ourselves if we were to think that all distinctions between husbands and wives have gone by the board.

Even if we were to believe that the principle of male spiritual leadership ought to be maintained in the home but eliminated in the church, we would encounter still other practical problems. For example, if all Christians are "one" in the sense being urged today, what justification would there be for Paul to make *any* distinctions between Christian men and women? For example, Paul's instruction to Timothy that women are to "learn in quietness and full submission" may be subject to diverse interpretation. But regardless of the interpretation. Paul is making *some* distinction between men and women.

We must not forget that Paul is the same apostle who wrote that in Christ there is "neither male nor female." Are we to suppose that Paul would have thrown out all distinctions in Galatians chapter 3 only to reinstitute distinctions in 1 Timothy chapter 2? (And if we were to suppose that Paul's letter to the Galatians *followed* his letter to Timothy, are we to suppose that either Paul or the Holy Spirit changed his mind? Would not Paul have *specifically* overruled his earlier instructions regarding women?)

The same problem exists with regard to what Paul said in 1 Corinthians chapter 11 about head coverings and male headship. Whatever we might understand to be the application of the "covering" in our worship experience today, Paul makes a strongly worded distinction between Christian men and women. As God is the head of Christ, the husband is the head of the wife, he says. The same goes for his direction in 1 Corinthians chapter 14 that the women are not to ask questions while in the assembly, but only in the privacy of their home. There is no similar prohibition for men.

In both of these instances, Paul is making distinctions which could not be made if all distinctions whatsoever between men and women were eliminated by the phrase "neither male nor female."

For those who say that *some* distinctions can be made in the church, a practical inconsistency arises. For example, if we conceded that only men can serve as elders (since most agree that this leadership role is limited to men) but that women can serve as deaconesses (since many believe the qualifications for this office are less gender-specific), then even that distinction would violate the liberation supposedly intended by the words "neither male nor female."

I often read and hear that "a woman can do anything a man can do except be a preacher or an elder." But if the purpose of Galatians 3:28 had been to eliminate role distinctions in the church, it would have eliminated *all* role distinctions. It would be wrong to limit the responsibilities of even elders or preachers to men only. In fact, on the strength of that logic, a number of denominations have appointed women as preachers and elders.

Consistency demands that our interpretation be all or nothing. If *some* distinctions can be drawn, then Galatians chapter 3 is not the all-encompassing gender eliminator it is claimed to be. It therefore remains for us to discover what distinctions God has ordained.

It also behooves us to once-and-for-all abandon use of "neither male nor female" as a magic wand to either totally eliminate role distinctions within the church or perhaps to selectively justify those roles which we want to be gender neutral. If we are going to insist that a particular service to the church is truly gender neutral, it will have to be on the basis of some passage other than Galatians chapter 3.

Paul's letter to the Galatians gives no basis whatever for abandoning the principle of male spiritual leadership as it relates to the *horizontal* relationship between Christian men and women in the affairs of the church. It is our *vertical* relationship with God, and the unity which then results horizontally, that concerned Paul in this letter.

In our *vertical* relationship there is neither black nor white, neither rich nor poor, neither old nor young, neither educated nor uneducated, neither American nor Soviet, neither Republican nor Democrat, neither management nor labor— and, praise God, neither male nor female—but through obedient faith we are all "one" in Christ Jesus!

Study Questions

1. Galatians 3:28 has been hailed as the Emancipation Proclamation for women in the church. What is the overall context of Galatians? Is Paul addressing the issue of gender roles, or something else?

2. Whether man or woman, what do we all become when we have a vertical relationship with Christ?

3. Does it necessarily follow that, because we are one in Christ, we all have been called to the same responsibility?

4. Citing "neither slave nor free" along with "neither male nor female," many would draw a parallel between liberation of women in the church and the movement for racial equality. Is that a good parallel to make? Why?

5. If Galatians was Paul's first epistle (as the evidence seems to indicate), and if it was meant to liberate women, how does one explain that, in his later letters, Paul lays down any number of guidelines calling for differences to be maintained between men and women as they respond in service to God?

6. If the intended purpose of Galatians 3:28 was to eliminate all distinctions between Christian men and women, is there any justification for Paul's teaching that the husband is the head of the wife, even as Christ is head of the church?

7. If "neither male nor female" has completely broken down the gender barrier, is it right for a woman to do any and everything *except* be an elder, deacon, or preacher?

8. What did Paul mean when he said that, in Christ, we are neither male nor female?

9. How do the physiological differences between men and women suggest that "neither male nor female" is not the whole story?

10. In what way can a biblical view of "neither male nor female" contribute in a positive way to implementing the spirit of male spiritual leadership?

12 Postscript Theology

Is the Ending of Romans a New Beginning for Women?

For many of us, letter-writing has become a lost art. Although others seem to prefer putting pen to paper, I much prefer to pick up the phone and hear a friendly voice on the other end. Nevertheless I can remember a time when I enjoyed writing letters, and one thing seemed an essential part of these youthful letters: *postscripts*. In fact, a letter without *two* postscripts seemed unfinished. If you were like me, you'll remember adding not only the P.S. but the P.P.S. It wasn't a matter of being so absentminded as to have omitted something in the main body of the letter; it was just a matter of proper form for a young kid.

It is possible for a postscript to be important regardless of what the main body of the letter contains. However, normally the postscript is not the first place one would look for matters of great significance. Never is that more true than in Paul's letters to the various individuals and churches for whom, through the inspiration of the Holy Spirit, he set forth the doctrine of Christ. Each of his inspired letters ends with miscellaneous personal greetings and last-minute instructions which we recognize to be doctrinally unimportant postscripts to doctrinally important letters.

Curiously, however, Paul's closing remarks in his letter to the Romans have recently been seized upon as providing doctrinal support for a wider role for women in the church today.

> I commend to you our sister Phoebe, a servant of the church in Cenchrea.
>
> I ask you to receive her in the Lord in a way worthy of the saints and to give her any help she may need from you, for she has been a great help to many people, including me.
>
> Greet Priscilla and Aquila, my fellow workers in Christ Jesus. They risked their lives for me. Not only I but all the churches of the Gentiles are grateful to them.
>
> Greet also the church that meets at their house. Greet my dear friend Epenetus, who was the first convert to Christ in the province of Asia.
>
> Greet Mary, who worked very hard for you. Greet Andronicus and Junias, my relatives who have been in prison with me. They are outstanding among the apostles, and they were in Christ before I was.
>
> Greet Ampliatus, whom I love in the Lord. Greet Urbanus, our fellow worker in Christ, and my dear friend Stachys.
>
> Greet Apelles, tested and approved in Christ. Greet those who belong to the household of Aristobulus.
>
> Greet Herodion, my relative. Greet those in the household of Narcissus who are in the Lord.
>
> Greet Tryphena and Tryphosa, those women who work hard in the Lord. Greet my dear friend Persis, another woman who has worked very hard in the Lord.
>
> Greet Rufus, chosen in the Lord, and his mother, who has been a mother to me, too.
>
> Greet Asyncritus, Phlegon, Hermes, Patrobas, Hermas and the brothers with them.

Greet Philologus, Julia, Nereus and his sister, and Olympas and all the saints with them.

Greet one another with a holy kiss. All the churches of Christ send greetings (Romans 16:1-16).

From Greetings to Theology

In the personal greetings in Romans 16:1-16 we find warm, laudatory references to a number of Christians in Rome. Included among them are at least nine godly women whom Paul singles out for praise: Phoebe (a servant); Priscilla (a fellow worker who, along with her husband, Aquila, had risked her life for Paul); Mary (a hard worker); Junius (who, along with her husband, Andronicus, had been imprisoned with Paul and who was "outstanding among the apostles"); Tryphena and Tryphosa (hard workers); Persis (a very hard worker); Rufus' mother (who had been like a mother to Paul); and Nereus' sister (about whom we are given no further information).

From their description as "workers," "hard workers," and "very hard workers," it is clear that Christian women in the first-century church were active and involved in the kingdom. Paul does not spell out for us what kind of work these women did, but in his letters to Timothy and Titus, Paul indicates some of the ways that first-century Christian women were called to serve.

For example, Paul's instructions to Timothy regarding the support of widows indicates that godly women not only brought up children in the home but were hospitable, service-oriented (washing the feet of the saints), helpful to those in trouble, and devoted "to all kinds of good deeds" (1 Timothy 5:9, 10).

Woman's role in the church also extended to various teaching responsibilities. We have already seen that Priscilla was a co-teacher with her husband, Aquila, in the private explanation of the Gospel to Apollos (Acts 18:24-28). And Paul told

Titus to "teach the older women to . . . train the younger women to love their husbands and children, and to be self-controlled and pure, to be busy at home, to be kind, and to be subject to their husbands . . ." (Titus 2:3-5).

Therefore it is not surprising that Paul would honor women in the church for their valuable contributions to the cause of Christ. But having said that, we are still left with women as "workers"—not women as functional spiritual leaders in appointive positions. It jumps the gun to assume that "workers" shared the same responsibilities as "leaders."

A good illustration of the distinction between workers and leaders can be found in the construction of the tabernacle, where women worked hard alongside the men to provide and assemble the various pieces of the tabernacle but were never called to the responsibilities of priesthood once the tabernacle was completed—or where women served at the entrance to the tent of meeting, but not inside (Exodus 38:8).

Was Junius an Apostle?

In the case of Junius and her husband, Andronicus, we are presented with a somewhat enigmatic reference. Paul refers to that godly couple as being "outstanding among the apostles." Andronicus seems to get lost in the shuffle, but many people today interpret Paul's passing reference to say that Junius in particular was *an outstanding apostle.*

Of course we know that she was not one of "the Twelve," as Paul referred to them (1 Corinthians 15:5), whom Jesus chose during his ministry. And we know that she was not chosen as a replacement for Judas. (In fact when that selection was made, only men were put forward as possible replacements even though godly women were among those assembled on that specific occasion). Nor is there any indication that Junius was specially chosen like "one abnormally born," as was the apostle Paul (2 Corinthians 15:8).

Therefore if Paul was referring to Junius as herself *being* an apostle, it could only have been in a generic sense, using the word "apostle" to mean a person marked by the gift of miracles (2 Corinthians 12:12), or as "one sent." It is that sense, for example, in which Barnabas was called an apostle (Acts 14:14), and Epaphroditus was referred to as "your messenger" (Philippians 2:25). As the ultimate One sent from God, Jesus himself was called an apostle (Hebrews 3:1). Because a woman could be a messenger of the Word to others without being set forward in a public leadership role—as in the case of Priscilla, and in the case of the "older women" teaching the "younger women"—no verdict can be directed for women to occupy leadership roles based on this brief reference alone.

In truth, a more likely understanding of this passage may give Junius even greater honor as a woman of God in the service of the Lord. If Paul's reference means that Junius was *recognized by the apostles* as being an outstanding godly woman, then she has great honor indeed. Her work was well-known and highly appreciated among those apostles who were specially chosen by Christ.

In the less formal sense that Junius was an "apostle," we too should be "apostles"—all of us! All of us ought to be messengers of the Word and ambassadors for Christ. But we must be careful not to confuse mission with place, or function with special responsibility. We have all been called to serve, to work, and to teach. We have not all been called to exercise headship. Spiritual leadership within the church is a responsibility which God, for his own reasons, has placed on the shoulders of godly men.

Was Phoebe a Deaconess?

We can get caught in the same trap of word usage when Paul refers to Phoebe as a "servant" (Romans 16:1). A possible rendering of the word "servant" is the word "deaconess," at least if one overlooks the fact that only the masculine form for the word "deacon" is found in Scripture. (There is no feminine form of the Greek word for deacon.) Those who accept the variant translation conclude from Paul's reference to Phoebe as a "deaconess" that there must have been deaconesses in the early church.

In the apostolic church, local spiritual leaders were elders (variously called presbyters, bishops, pastors, and shepherds) and deacons (variously called servants or ministers). Qualifications for those who would exercise these two specially designated responsibilities are given by Paul in his letters to Timothy and Titus (1 Timothy 3:1-13; Titus 1:5-9). Because these men were required to be "a husband of but one wife," and because the elders of Israel before them had always been men rather than women, most Christians agree that the elders, at least, were exclusively male.

There is less agreement regarding the role of deacons. Some believe that, in 1 Timothy 3:11, Paul provided for women to be "deaconesses" when he set out qualifications for a certain class of women to whom most translations refer as "their wives." (Interestingly, those who prefer the translation of "women" over "wives" in this passage typically insist on the opposite translation for the same Greek word—*gune*—when Paul uses it in 1 Corinthians 14 to restrict women from certain participation in worship!)

Whole sets of arguments are available on both sides regarding Paul's intended reference in this passage. However, because the passage is sandwiched between various qualifications for deacons, the most natural reference would be to the wives of those being considered for deacons. In the larger context, perhaps, Paul might also be referring to the wives of those being considered for elders. But because Paul says of deacons that they "must be the husband of but one wife" (1 Timothy 3:12), he does not appear to include women in that office.

Does this mean that there were no women serving as deacons in the church? It depends on what we mean by the word "deacon." As with the word "apostle," the word "deacon" can be used in both a formal and an informal sense. The word itself means to serve, to minister. Used in that sense, every Christian ought to be a deacon, a servant—even a minister. But when the word is used to designate a recognized position of headship within the church, to which specific qualifications attach, there is no clear reference to women being that kind of deacon in the first century.

It is not until the second or third century that we have any strong evidence of deaconesses playing a role within the church. In that time period, of course, we find other significant departures from the New Testament pattern, including recognition of priests within the established church hierarchy—itself a departure from the pattern.

Differences Without Distinctions

From time to time I have performed many of the functions which would be performed by a deacon in a local church, and sometimes even the functions of an elder. Yet I have never been appointed or recognized by a local congregation either as an elder or a deacon. I never felt slighted when, as a single man, I did not meet the qualifications of those who would be placed in such positions.

More important, my lack of a title or official position has never diminished the work that I do for the Lord. Nor do I feel disenfranchised, or discriminated against, or robbed of my talents. Each of us has more than enough work to do for the cause of Christ. Each of us has a significant contribution to make. Each of us has an important role to play.

What could be more clear from 1 Corinthians chapter 12 than that the body has many contributing parts? Not everyone can be the head, or the heart. But where would the head be if there were not hands to work and feet to walk? No eyes to see, no ears to hear? And if we think that being denied a particular leadership role makes us second-class citizens, Paul says, "On the contrary, those parts of the body that seem to be weaker are indispensable, and the parts that we think are less honorable we treat with special honor" (1 Corinthians 12:22).

Part of our problem may be that we are concentrating more on the honor attached to a recognized position within the church than we are on the work to be done, regardless of title or recognized position. A personnel director of a major company says that one of the major distinctions he looks for in hiring is whether someone wants to *do* something or instead merely *be* something.

Men who seek to maintain traditional male roles must ask some serious questions about their motivation for occupying the positions they hold. Is it in order to *be* or to *do?* One of the nagging frustrations of godly women is that there are far too many men who hold positions of spiritual responsibility without being either *spiritual* or *responsible.*

All of us, whether men or women, must remember that "the body is a unit, though it is made up of many parts, and though all its parts are many, they form one body. So it is with Christ" (1 Corinthians 12:12).

And in a statement reminiscent of Galatians 3:28, Paul tells us: "For we were all baptized by one Spirit into one body—whether Jews or Greeks, slave or free—and we were all given the one Spirit to drink" (1 Corinthians 12:13). Once again we see that we are all one in Christ, even though we are called to different responsibilities. While it is true that both men and women in the first century were given the various gifts of tongues, prophecy, interpretation, and healing, one distinction remained between men and women—spiritual leadership.

Too Much Burden for a Postscript?

There are those who suggest that we must look not only at what Paul *said* but also at how he *acted.* In Romans 16, we are told, Paul "acts" as if women in the church were spiritual leaders in the same way that men were. Yet we are hardly dealing with doctrinal teaching through apostolic example in Paul's closing remarks in Romans chapter 16, particularly when one compares this list of personal greetings to the specific and detailed instructions Paul gives in other passages relating to the comparative roles of men and women in the church.

To read a revolutionary teaching into a passage not intended to be a doctrinal statement is laying a terribly heavy burden on a part of a letter which is equivalent to a postscript. Even more disturbing is the reality that such an interpretation of Paul's "actions" flies in the face of his clear teaching in passages obviously intended as doctrinal instruction. Are we to believe that Paul wrote one way and acted another?

What Paul did in Romans chapter 16 was to give honor to whom honor was due. And in the early church, as in the church today, Christian women were due great honor—even when, as in the case of Euodia and Syntyche (Philippians 4:2,3), they were displaying a less honorable side of themselves than normal. Indeed they were workers, *fellow* workers, *hard* workers, *very* hard workers, servants, and outstanding women of the Word.

They did not shrink from the work God had given them simply because they were not called to exercise spiritual headship. They did not demand equality of position or cry "Foul" when elders and deacons were appointed from among the men. They did not insist on taking traditionally male roles within the church in order to make a statement about egalitarianism in Christ. They worked and served, and Paul honored them for their service.

We must not make more of Romans chapter 16 than Paul intended. Nor should we make less of it. Clearly women were a vital part of the early church, just as they continue to be today.

Study Questions

1. What potential danger is there in viewing Romans 16:1-16 as anything more than a theologically insignificant post-script to his theologically crucial letter?

2. In what ways has verse 16 already been taken out of context in the rather questionable pursuit of doctrinal justifications?

3. What does it say about the strength of any doctrinal proposition when one has to grab for dubious straws in unlikely contexts?

4. If ambivalent coincidental references concerning gender roles might possibly suggest interpretations which run counter to crystal clear guidelines laid down purposely in other contexts, how should we judge the more ambivalent references?

5. Thinking of Phoebe, in what two senses may the word "deacon" be used?

6. Does it readily appear that Phoebe would meet the qualifications of those who are to be specifically appointed as deacons in 1 Timothy 3:8-13?

7. As for Junius, in what two senses may the word "apostle" be used?

8. If Junius were an apostle in the same sense as the Twelve, or Matthias, or Paul, what would likely appear in the Scriptures?

9. In what way have some men viewed the importance of title and position so as to give rise to equally unbiblical attitudes on the part of some women?

10. If Paul did, in fact, take a strong position in favor of male spiritual leadership, what does his list of greetings nevertheless say about how he viewed the work of women in the church?

13 *Spiritual Headship Unveiled*

A Hierarchy of Spiritual Authority

Among my most vivid boyhood memories is a mental picture of aunts, uncles, and cousins gathered around a crowded dining table at a family reunion, bowing their heads to pray. Normally it would not have been an unusual picture. Many families honor God through prayer as they begin a meal together. But my cerebral funnybone was struck to the point of hilarity when my aunts and cousins quickly grabbed paper napkins and held them over their heads just as we all bowed for the prayer. At that point in my spiritual understanding, I didn't have a clue as to the religious significance of wearing napkins during prayer. At most, I knew it was something that only women did, not men.

Some years later my family moved to a congregation where the women of the church wore hats or veils on their heads during the worship services. It was a relatively unusual practice among those in our particular fellowship, but a well-respected preacher in that part of the country had taught two generations of women that 1 Corinthians chapter 11 demanded the wearing of some kind of covering.

Although my father did not believe a covering was required, my mother and sisters began wearing hats or veils for the sake of harmony with the other women in the congregation (1 Corinthians chapters 8—10). Ever since that time, they—like many other Christian women—have struggled with the instructions given by Paul regarding a covering for women.

The passage in question presents one of the most difficult challenges to biblical exegesis in all the New Testament. It speaks specifically of heads, hair, and coverings, and more broadly of spiritual leadership in general. Just when you think the passage refers only to local customs among first-century Christians, Paul reaches back to Creation, and even to the angels, to explain why women are called in some way to be distinct from men in the context of worship.

As the passage begins, we see once again the ancient principle that man is to be the spiritual head of the woman. What's surprising is that Paul compares this headship with the relationship between Christ and man, and even between Christ and God!

> Now I want you to realize that the head of every man is Christ, and the head of the woman is man, and the head of Christ is God (1 Corinthians 11:3).

Of the three relationships Paul mentions, the most striking is the headship of God over Christ. If that seems strange, since Christ *is* God, we must remember that God the *Father* is the spiritual head of Christ the *Son*. This relationship was perhaps best demonstrated when Jesus the Christ prayed to God the Father that the "cup" of death pass away from him, yet humbly submitted to the Father's headship in order to atone for our sins. "Not my will, but yours be done," he said (Luke 22:42).

This brief reference to God being the head of Christ speaks volumes about the headship of man over woman. Because Christ *is* God, what we discover in their relationship is a spiritual headship between equals. Better still, it is a functional headship within a united wholeness of deity. Likewise, if man is to be the head of the woman, it is a spiritual headship between spiritual equals. Better still, it is a functional headship within a united wholeness of marriage.

Almost as striking is the second relationship which Paul mentions—the headship of Christ over man. If we were to ask ourselves whether Christ is not also the head of each Christian woman, of course the answer is yes. Therefore, Paul is making an obvious point about headship when he singles out man as being in submission to the headship of Christ. He is suggesting a picture of spiritual hierarchy, from God to Christ to man to woman. If there is headship between equals as between God and Christ, there is also a hierarchy of function within the spiritual realm. And as between the husband and the wife, man is to be the spiritual head.

Veils and Headship

Having laid the theological foundation for what he is about to say, Paul turns to specific instructions regarding the use of a covering when men and women are praying or prophesying.

> Every man who prays or prophesies with his head covered dishonors his head. And every woman who prays or prophesies with her head uncovered dishonors her head—it is just as though her head were shaved. If a woman does not cover her head, she should have her hair cut off; and if it is a disgrace for a woman to have her hair cut or shaved off, she should cover her head (1 Corinthians 11:4-6).

I suspect that in our culture we will never fully appreciate the significance of what Paul was saying about covering one's head while praying or prophesying. Nevertheless we find ourselves naturally observing the essence of his instructions, sometimes in the most unexpected circumstances. For exam-

ple, you can see it in the academic exercises in which my col-
leagues and I so often participate in a university setting. For
both the invocation and benediction, the men in the audience
remove the academic mortarboards from their heads while the
women keep theirs in place. If that is mere tradition, where
did it come from? Hardly anyone would think of 1 Corinthians
chapter 11, but I suspect it is a similar practice to which Paul
is referring.

I have never been convinced that a hat—or, worse yet, a
napkin hastily held over the head—captured the significance
of a veil as a covering for a woman, especially when you think
that hats are worn for decoration rather than as a sign of
humility and submission. All you have to do is travel to the
Middle East to observe the women wearing real veils, not just
in religious worship but *all* the time. It confirms the feeling
that hats and even temporary veils are weak substitutes for the
kind of veils Paul must have been talking about.

I am aware of the debate regarding the nature of the covering for Christian women, and others have done a better job
of sifting through the issues than I can within the confines of
this book. But there is evidence that the problem in Corinth
was not in *instituting* the wearing of veils for worship, as if
something new and different were being demanded of
Christian women. Quite the contrary, both Christian and non-
Christian women of that time wore veils as part of their daily
attire, as a sign of submission to their husbands. Even today,
all we have to do is turn on the evening news and see that
millions of Middle Eastern women still dress that way.

Why then did Paul feel compelled to require the customary
veil to be worn during acts of worship? Although we are not
told directly, the most likely reason is that first-century
Christian women were doffing their veils as a statement of liberation and freedom in Christ. After all, had not Paul written
to the Galatians that in Christ there is neither male nor female?
It would have been easy for some to interpret such teaching

to mean that there were no longer any distinctions between men and women in the work and worship of the church.

Significantly, this passage follows on·the heels of Paul's discussion about freedom in Christ. Some among the Corinthians were saying, "Everything is permissible," but Paul answered by saying, "Not everything is beneficial . . . not everything is constructive" (1 Corinthians 10:23). Paul was concerned that Christians do nothing that might leave the wrong impression. Removing their veils would make what Paul knew would be the wrong statement. For all the theological freedom that Christian women had in Christ, they were still to be in submission to their husband's spiritual headship, both in the home and in worship.

For first-century Christian women, the removal of the veil during worship not only conflicted with the ancient principle of male spiritual leadership—which Paul reaffirms in this passage—but put them in the category of brazen hussies in the eyes of society. In the culture of their time, only immoral women went about unveiled. Therefore Paul is concerned about both the principle of male leadership and the statement being made by any abandonment of the veil.

If today in our culture neither a veil nor a hat conveys spiritual submission, then wearing these "coverings" during worship loses all significance in modern times. Nevertheless the principle of male spiritual leadership itself remains valid, and Paul's instruction to us today would be to maintain whatever cultural distinctions make appropriate statements about that principle.

Despite being veiled, Christian women in the first century were praying and prophesying. For many, this fact presents further difficulty in light of Paul's instructions to Timothy that women were not to teach, but to learn in quietness—a matter we will deal with in another context. Suffice it to say that, in whatever way the woman was participating in public worship, she was to be distinct from her male counterpart. Paul's words "neither male nor female" had not abolished male spiritual headship. And unlike the customary veil, which signified that distinction, the distinction itself remains intact even in our time.

Mere Custom or Divine Principle?

As if aware of our modern concerns regarding this difficult issue, Paul takes pains to separate custom from principle. He appeals to Creation itself, and to the angels, in order to distinguish the principle of male headship from mere custom:

> A man ought not to cover his head, since he is the image and glory of God; but the woman is the glory of man. For man did not come from woman, but woman from man; neither was man created for woman, but woman for man. For this reason, and because of the angels, the woman ought to have a sign of authority on her head (1 Corinthians 11:7-10).

How much more forcefully could Paul have separated the principle from mere custom than by taking the principle back to a time before the establishment of customs! Male spiritual leadership, says Paul, predated the chauvinistic Jewish tradition of intertestamental times, the male-oriented laws of Moses, and even the patriarchal social structure of Abraham and Sarah. Male spiritual leadership was a fact of Creation, a divine pattern established by the Creator.

Male spiritual leadership is tied to the principle of firstborn, which itself grew out of the "firstcreated" status of Adam. It is tied with the responsibility of spiritual protection for the woman, who was made to be the perfect match for man. Before there was a veil, before there was a worship service, before there was a culture in which customs could be established, man was the designated spiritual head of his wife—both in the marriage relationship and in their relationship to God.

Note the play on words and concepts which weaves this passage together. The issue is spiritual headship; the object of concern—whether covered or uncovered—is one's physical head. The man is *not* to cover his head because Christ is spiritual head over the church. The woman, on the other hand, *is* to cover her head as a sign of submission to the spiritual leadership of her husband. The symbolism could hardly be more pronounced. Whatever else the woman's covering implied for Christian women in the first century, Paul's primary concern was about spiritual headship. And in whatever way it might be manifested today, Christian women in the twentieth century are likewise to recognize the spiritual headship of their husbands.

There is a popular translation today of the word normally rendered as "head." The new definition for "head" is "the source" (as in "the source of a river"), the connotation of which would eliminate any idea of spiritual headship. But the problem with that translation is the obvious lack of any connection between the husband being "the source" of his wife and Paul's instructions regarding the wearing of veils. What symbolism would the veil represent relative to man's being the "source"?

Furthermore, in what way is the husband "the source" of his wife? There must be something *practical* and *relevant* to which one could point as flowing from that definition. Can any man after Adam legitimately be considered a source of a woman when, through the birth process, each man's own source is in fact a woman? Paul's obvious message is that a distinction is to be maintained between men and women in worship because the man is designated as the spiritual *head*.

Christ As the Example of Headship

In writing to the Christians in Ephesus about the nature of the church, Paul instructed them to "submit to one another out of reverence for Christ" (Ephesians 5:21). Yet just when we might think that mutual submission in the marriage relationship would exclude any headship by the husband, in the next verse Paul tells wives to "submit to your husbands as to the Lord." Why, Paul? "For the husband is the head of the wife as Christ is the head of the church, his body, of which he is the Savior. Now as the church submits to Christ, so also wives should submit to their husbands in everything" (Ephesians 5:23,24). Or, as Paul wrote in Colossians 3:18-21, "Wives, submit to your husbands, as is fitting in the Lord."

For Paul, the husband's headship over the wife is modeled after Christ's own headship of the church. This means that the husband is not the head of his wife as an *autocrat* but as a *servant,* "for even the Son of Man did not come to be served, but to serve" (Mark 10:45).

Christ is not only the *source* from whom all spiritual blessings flow but also the nurturing and protective *head of the church.* Because of this analogy, the husband's headship takes on definition:

> Husbands, love your wives, just as Christ loved the church and gave himself up for her to make her holy, cleansing her by the washing with water through the word, and to present her to himself as a radiant church, without stain or wrinkle or any other blemish, but holy and blameless. In this same way, husbands ought to love their wives as their own bodies. He who loves his wife loves himself. After all, no one ever hated his own body, but he feeds and cares for it, just as Christ does the church— for we are members of his body. For this reason a man will leave his father and mother and be united to his wife, and the two will become one flesh. This is a profound mystery—but I am talking about Christ and the church. However, each one of you also must love his wife as he loves himself, and the wife must respect her husband (Ephesians 5:25-33).

How is the husband to be the head of his wife? As Christ is the head of the church: by loving her as he loves himself, by sacrificing for her, by helping to make her holy through his own knowledge and understanding of the Word, by protecting her from the blemish of sin, and by feeding and caring for her spiritually. Are you surprised by that definition of "headship"? As you can see, it is a perfectly biblical definition.

While many women would be eager to submit to that kind of nurturing by their husbands, many others still find the thought of spiritual headship offensive. The idea, for example, that the husband has a responsibility for nurturing his wife's spirituality would cause some to say, "I am responsible for myself. I don't want someone else—even my husband—to be a 'spiritual protector.'"

Instilled in the men and women of our generation is a compulsion for economic, political, and ideological independence. Hardly anyone appreciates even benevolent paternalism. Yet if we are to follow in Christ's footsteps, we must learn to appreciate the kind of caring headship which he exercises over his own bride, the church. In Christ it is not a matter of personal rights but of sacrificial service. As in so many of Christ's teachings, kingdom principles run counter to our own instincts and the world's. Wives need to learn the blessings of submission to their husbands. Husbands need to learn the blessings of submission to God.

From the Home to the Church

Man brings glory to God in his role as head of the family. Woman brings glory both to God and to her husband in her role as wife and mother. Just as the man submits to God in exercising his designated responsibility of spiritual leadership, the woman submits to her husband in fulfilling her responsibilities within marriage and the home, as modeled in Proverbs 31.

Many people have the idea that the husband-wife relationship is somehow limited to home and family—that once outside the home in Christian worship the husband's headship of the wife ceases. But the Scriptures teach that the relationship between husband and wife in the home and between the man and woman in worship is more than merely circumstantial.

Husbands don't cease being husbands when they become "the man" at the time of worship. Wives don't cease being wives when they become "the woman" in an act of worship. Paul invariably assumes that "men" are husbands and "women" are wives. Undoubtedly in the early church, because marriage took place relatively early, there was little distinction between the two. Women were either wives or widows or daughters of men who maintained spiritual headship over them.

There is no reason to stretch Paul's instructions to mean that every man is the spiritual head of every woman, or that men in general are somehow in authority over women in general. When I was a single adult male I was not the spiritual head of any man's wife or daughter, not even during some form of public worship. Nevertheless, pursuant to apostolic teaching the principle of male spiritual headship in the home extends as well to male headship in worship.

Are we to expect a husband to be the spiritual head of his own wife at home, yet submit to the spiritual headship of other men's wives during worship? Are we to expect a wife to be submissive to her own husband in the home, yet exercise spiritual leadership over other women's husbands in the work of the church? Not even some form of "shared spiritual leadership" would avoid this confusion of roles.

If in today's deferred and broken-marriage society we have many more single women with no obvious male spiritual leader in their lives, we may encounter a special problem not faced in the first-century church. However, that problem neither demands nor permits a different interpretation of Paul's instructions, and by no means nullifies the general principle of male leadership in public worship. In the Old Testament, single women did not become eligible for leadership roles within the nation's religious structure by virtue of being unmarried. Nor is there any indication that circumstances have changed in that regard with the advent of Christianity.

Today's single women normally have the benefit of concerned pastoral counseling and sharing with those who lead the church spiritually. And where that source happens to prove fruitless—perhaps even frustrating—there are usually other men of strength to whom single Christian women may turn for such sharing—fathers, brothers, and fellow Christians who appreciate their felt needs.

As far as 1 Corinthians chapter 11 is concerned, the clincher is that Paul is referring to *public worship*—*not* to the marriage relationship within the home—when he calls for a distinction to be maintained between Christian men (whether husbands or not) and Christian women (whether wives or not).

Of Angels and Authority

Paul's reference to the angels has mystified many a student of the Word. There are almost as many interpretations as there are interpreters. At least one credible interpretation would be consistent with what we know of the rebellious angels who received God's harsh censure. Jude's letter indicates a suggested parallel: "The angels who did not keep their positions of authority but abandoned their own home—these he has kept in darkness, bound with everlasting chains for judgment on the great Day" (Jude 6). The angels had left their place in the spiritual hierarchy and God punished them. Paul here may be citing the rebellious angels as a warning against refusing to submit to spiritual headship. If this is a correct understanding of Paul's reference, then Christian women who assert themselves and seek an "equal" role in God's hierarchy of leadership run the same risk as the rebellious angels. "For this reason," Paul concludes, "the woman ought to have a sign of authority on her head."

If there is any word which might be offensive to Christian women in our day and which allows the potential for abuse by Christian men, it must be the word "authority." It is difficult enough for rights-conscious citizens of democratic nations to appreciate the word "submission," but the connotation of its counterpart—"authority"—seems to take us yet another giant step beyond "headship" or "spiritual leadership." "Authority" is a hard word. It conjures notions of arbitrary, brutal dictatorship, if for no other reason than that is how it has been exercised all too often.

There was a time when brides promised "to love, honor, and *obey.*" The word "obey" was stark recognition of the husband's "authority"—perhaps *too* stark, because we rarely ever hear it said at weddings anymore. Perhaps it is because too many grooms got the idea that they were to lord it over their wives, to make all the decisions for the family, and to act as if the wife were an object to be controlled rather than a partner to be protected. Too many got the idea that they were supposed to cover their wives, not just with veils of respected headship, but with smothering blankets of authoritarianism. They didn't understand that the call to spiritual headship was a call to cover their wives with love, understanding, and tender concern.

Whereas children are instructed to *obey* their parents, and slaves are told to *obey* their masters, women are taught to *submit* to their husbands. It's a biblical distinction with an important difference. "Obey" implies duty arising out of an unequal relationship. "Submit" implies response from one of *equal* status. When properly understood and exercised, the spiritual headship of the husband will lead the wife to naturally and willingly submit to his "authority." She will not see his spiritual headship as a threat but as a blessing.

And how will a woman show her appreciation for that kind of headship? The true sign of the wife's submission to her husband's "authority" will be "known in the gates" through her godly character, not in something on her head. After all, a woman could wear a veil every waking moment and never have a submissive spirit. Likewise, she could go about her daily activities without a hat or a veil and have the kind of character which the whole world would recognize as that of a godly, submissive woman—or, better yet, as a woman of strength in Christ whose freedom is secured by her husband's spiritual leadership and protection.

If the veil is not the "sign of authority" today, what is? Is it not the respect which is shown for the husband's headship in the home? Is it not an attitude of humility and submission? Is it not the maturity shown by Christian women in search of servanthood within the realm of service to which they have been called?

And what is the corresponding sign of spiritual leadership among Christian men? Is it dominance in the home and arbitrary control in the church, or is it servant leadership in the church and loving concern for the family's spiritual welfare? Is it a man treating his wife with cavalier disdain or honoring her as his glory?

Paul realizes the potential for abuse in the exercise of authority, even spiritual authority—or perhaps *especially* spiritual authority. Therefore he is quick to remind Christian men:

> In the Lord, however, woman is not independent of man, nor is man independent of woman. For as woman came from man, so also man is born of woman. But everything comes from God (1 Corinthians 11:11, 12).

If the Creation principle of headship from Genesis chapter 2 supports the idea (suggested in 1 Corinthians 11:7-10) of male spiritual authority in the home and in the church, then the principle of unity and interdependence from Genesis chapter 1 is a reminder (in 1 Corinthians 11:11, 12) that headship is not to be confused with dictatorship. Both man *and* woman were created in the image of God. Christian men and women are the same, yet different in responsibility; they are also different, yet the same in value and importance to God. Therefore, if man is to exercise spiritual authority, he must do so in the way that God himself exercises spiritual authority toward those created in his image: with love, respect, concern, patience, and goodwill.

Nature—Not Custom

In this perspective, Paul appeals to something other than culture and custom as the basis for his instructions:

> Judge for yourselves: Is it proper for a woman to pray to God with her head uncovered? Does not the very nature of things teach you that if a man has long hair, it is a disgrace to him, but that if a woman has long hair, it is her glory? For long hair is given to her as a covering (1 Corinthians 11:13-15).

Here Paul assumes that the spiritual distinction between men and women is as fundamental as "the nature of things." It doesn't have anything to do with custom, culture, or even veils. It goes back to long hair and short hair, or—as it were—male bodies and female bodies. It is as fundamental as the gender factor itself.

No wonder Paul's conclusion destroys any notion of cultural tradition or even personal bias on the part of Paul himself:

> If anyone wants to be contentious about this, we have no other practice—nor do the churches of God (1 Corinthians 11:16).

The word "practice," meaning "custom, habit, or usage," is not to be confused with tradition. Paul is not justifying his instruction regarding veils as something being done because "we've always done it that way," or because it is a matter of social custom. What he is saying is that neither locality, cultural expectations, nor his personal ideas are the determining factor. All the apostles in every place, regardless of local or cultural custom, taught the same. His instructions are tied to the Creation-old principle of male spiritual headship.

Paul's Teaching Corroborated

If Paul's teaching had come solely from his Jewish background, the Gentile Christians might have pointed to cultural anomalies arising from a Jewish patriarchal past. But Paul's instructions were consistent with the practice of all the churches which had been established in the first century, regardless of custom, culture, or heritage.

If it were merely a personal bias, the Christians who had been discipled by Peter or John might have taken Paul to task for his peculiar understanding of male-female roles within the church. However, we know that Peter wrote the same things to the Christians in Pontus, Galatia, Cappadocia, Asia, and Bithynia:

> Wives, in the same way be submissive to your husbands so that, if any of them do not believe the word, they may be won over without words by the behavior of their wives, when they see the purity and reverence of your lives. Your beauty should not come from outward adornment, such as braided hair and the wearing of gold jewelry and fine clothes. Instead, it should be that of your inner self, the unfading beauty of a gentle and quiet spirit, which is of great worth in God's sight. For this is the way the holy women of the past who put their hope in God used to make themselves beautiful. They were submissive to their own husbands, like Sarah, who obeyed Abraham and called him her master. You are her daughters if you do what is right and do not give way to fear (1 Peter 3:1-6).

Where Paul concentrates on the symbolism of the veil, Peter goes to the heart of true submission seen in a woman's behavior and character. It is not what a woman wears that shows true submission, Peter says, but who she is.

Peter agrees with Paul that the distinction between husband and wife is more basic than Christian worship, or even Christian marriage. I often hear Christian women say, "I *have* to be the spiritual leader in my family. My husband is not the spiritual leader he ought to be, and *somebody* has to pick up the ball!" But Peter is writing to women whose husbands are not Christians at all, much less Christian men who are shirking their leadership responsibility. Yet he tells them to be submissive with reverence, and to remember Sarah, who obeyed Abraham and called him master!

The wife of an unbeliever or a weak Christian husband finds herself with two distinct responsibilities. As a wife, she is to be submissive to her husband. As a Christian mother, she is the only spiritual leader her children have. Therefore she must become the "priest" of the family before God, offering up prayers on behalf of her children and for the salvation or spiritual strength of her husband.

Because a wife's submission is "as unto the Lord," she can submit to even an unbeliever, or a weak Christian husband, with security and assurance. For the Lord will be her "husband" and provide the protection she and her family need. God honors the wife's submission by providing his own spiritual strength.

Whether veil or no veil, whether Christian husband or unbelieving husband, whether strong Christian husband or weak Christian husband, both Paul and Peter, writing through inspiration of the Holy Spirit, take us back to "the very nature of things" because the God of nature made us to be distinct, with different roles and responsibilities to be accepted and faithfully exercised.

Nor does Peter overlook the kind of caution which Paul gave the Christian men in Corinth with regard to spiritual leadership:

Husbands, in the same way be considerate as you live with your wives, and treat them with respect as the weaker partner and as heirs with you of the gracious gift of life, so that nothing will hinder your prayers (1 Peter 3:7).

Whenever the man's headship is enjoined upon the woman, the writer immediately reminds the man of the limitations on that headship. Headship implies union with the body. Headship implies a need for the body. Neither the head nor the body is meant to function separately. Nor would the head ask of the body more than it was capable of doing, or direct it to do something harmful to it.

Unlike what we see too often in the business world or in the hierarchical structures of academia, the purpose of headship in marriage is not to dictate but to serve. Just as Christ's purpose as the spiritual Head of the church is to lead the world to God, so also the man's purpose as the spiritual head of his family is to lift up his family to God. Authoritarian rule leads to distrust, alienation, and separation. Conscientious spiritual leadership leads to trust, submission, and unity.

Men are usually quick to "come to a woman's rescue" when she is in danger. Here Peter seemingly calls for that protective instinct to be exercised on an even higher level. Spiritually, as well as physically, a Christian man is to treat his wife as if she were a weaker partner.

Women are often the stronger partner spiritually. By virtue of mutual Christian responsibility wives are called to be spiritual protectors of their husbands as well. (What wife would not come to her husband's *physical* rescue if she could possibly do so?) But in the spiritual realm, husbands are the "designated leaders." It is the men who are charged with the responsibility for nurturing and protecting those over whom they have been made the spiritual head—as *if* their wives were weaker, remembering that they are joint heirs before God.

The Veil Hides the Issue

The wearing of a veil was a matter of concern which Paul addressed to Christian women in the first century. The question was: Were they free to take it off now that they had become Christians? The answer was "no"—not because the veil itself had inherent spiritual value but because freedom in Christ had not eliminated the principle of male headship, which in their culture the veil signified.

Although the veil symbolized the husband's headship over the wife, this marital headship was as important in worship as it was in the home. Perhaps it was even more important in worship because of the statement it was making to a pagan world. Christianity had liberated women by giving them equal access to God through Christ, but it had not overthrown the principle of male spiritual leadership.

Nor was that principle—as opposed to the veil itself—simply a matter of ancient custom. The principle came from Creation and continues today to call for individual service to God within the bounds of divinely imposed role relationships. We discard those roles of "authority" and "submission" only at the risk of suffering the same punishment as the rebellious angels.

Male spiritual leadership is not simply a culturally maintained, male-oriented tradition. It is as natural as nature itself. It is not a matter of mere custom in a bygone era; it is consistent with the way God created us to be. When exercised properly, it works. When followed conscientiously, it is God's way.

Therefore we can ill afford to let the veil of an ancient culture obscure the bigger message: that the husband is the spiritual nurturer and protector of his wife and that her role of submission extends even to Christian worship in which Christian men have been given the responsibility for leadership.

Study Questions

1. What blockbuster message comes from knowing that God is the head of Christ?
2. What is the relationship between headship and hierarchy?
3. If headship does not imply superiority, what does it imply?
4. In what way is the principle of male spiritual leadership connected to the ancient custom of women wearing veils?
5. If Paul is not instructing women to put on veils, why is he telling them not to take them off?
6. How was the practice of wearing veils in the first century different from the practice of some today who put on a veil or hat during a time of gathered worship?
7. When Paul said that women needed to have a sign of authority on their head *"because of the angels,"* what do you think he had in mind?
8. What authority, if any, does a man have over a woman, or a husband over a wife?
9. If the husband is to be the head of the wife as Christ is the head of the church, what does it say about Christ's headship when a wife chooses not to be submissive to her husband?
10. If the husband is to be the head of the wife as Christ is the head of the church, what does that say about the nature of the headship that a man is to exercise in the home and in the church?

14 The Sounds of Silence

A Time to Speak and a Time Not to Speak

Each year as I was growing up, the highlight of my summer was the week of Vacation Bible School. The women of the congregation will probably never know what a profound influence they had on so many of us through their dedicated efforts in those special weeks. There were flannelboard lessons about Moses and Joshua, sandbox re-creations of Mount Sinai and the Red Sea, and gold stars for successful reciting of memory verses. There were always lots of kids my age and Bible games to play. But what I remember most vividly are the songs we sang.

Most of the songs had some kind of body action to help us remember the story line and have fun while we were singing. One of my favorites was "The Little Boy David." I think it was the clap at the end that we all liked the most! And then there was "The Lord's Army" with all the marching, flying, and shooting—and blowing out the candle in "This Little Light of Mine."

Imagine a hundred kids streaming into an auditorium after their morning classes, and you can understand why my father often led an entirely different kind of song to begin the devotional period. I can still see him take gentle control of all us noisy little ones with this quietly sung song:

The Lord is in his holy temple,
Let all the earth keep silence before him.
Keep silence! Keep silence!
Keep silence before him.

To insure the desired result, Dad always led it twice. And it always worked. A hundred squirming children would be quiet and still, as if on cue.

Not until years later would I discover the origin of that little song and appreciate the real significance of its lyrics. The words are taken from Habakkuk 2:20, where the prophet is speaking of God's wondrous power and sovereignty, especially when compared to lifeless, powerless idols carved by man. In the face of such a great and majestic God, Habakkuk warns: "But the Lord is in his holy temple; let all the earth be silent before him."

Naturally Habakkuk had something in mind quite different from a song to keep little children quiet in Vacation Bible School. The silence he is referring to has nothing to do with the absence of sound. Far from it. "Make a joyful noise unto the Lord, all you lands!" cries the psalmist. Rather, Habakkuk's words call us to reverence and awe before the God of all creation. Our "silence" is related to our position of submission before him. It is not a matter of silence in the strictest sense of the word, but of respect and deference. It has nothing to do with noise and everything to do with moral authority. Because God has spoken, let all the earth keep silent before him!

A Time for Literal Silence

There are times in the worship of God when noise can become a problem and when silence—actual silence—may be appropriate. Paul points to at least two such times, one which is gender-neutral and one which is gender-specific. Both have to do with the gift of prophecy, which characterized the first-century church. Before the written Word was complete, direct revelation from God was common. It came through the gifts of prophecy and interpretation and often was accompanied by the gift of tongues, which confirmed the authenticity of the prophecy.

In 1 Corinthians chapter 14 the apostle Paul was concerned about reports of noisy confusion when the church assembled to worship God. He instructed the Corinthians to do everything in an orderly fashion, which meant that there would be times when a spiritual gift ought not to be exercised.

> When you come together, everyone has a hymn, or a word of instruction, a revelation, a tongue or an interpretation. All of these must be done for the strengthening of the church. If anyone speaks in a tongue, two—or at the most three—should speak, one at a time, and someone must interpret. If there is no interpreter, the speaker should keep quiet in the church and speak to himself and God.
>
> Two or three prophets should speak, and the others should weigh carefully what is said. And if a revelation comes to someone who is sitting down, the first speaker should stop. For you can all prophesy in turn so that everyone may be instructed and encouraged. The spirits of prophets are subject to the control of prophets. For God is not a God of disorder but of peace (1 Corinthians 14:26-33).

The silence Paul is calling for in this situation is actual silence. If there is a time to speak, he says, there is also a time not to speak. And the issue is resolved as a matter of mere practicality. Moreover, the issue is gender-neutral, applying to both men and women who might be used as vessels for God's special revelations.

What follows immediately upon the heels of these instructions is more troublesome because it is gender-specific, for women only.

> As in all the congregations of the saints, women should remain silent in the churches. They are not allowed to speak, but must be in submission, as the Law says. If they want to inquire about something, they should ask their own husbands at home; for it is disgraceful for a woman to speak in the church (1 Corinthians 14:33-35).

There are some preliminary observations that help place these instructions in a broader context. First, Paul reassures the Corinthians that he is not singling them out for special rules which are not imposed upon Christians in other locations. Their situation is not a special circumstance that they have brought upon themselves, but is consistent with a principle honored throughout all the churches.

Second, Paul is his own best commentary on what he had written earlier to the Galatians regarding there being "neither male nor female" in Christ. Whatever Paul might be saying to the Corinthians, he is undeniably introducing a gender factor into the work and worship of the church beyond the respective roles which might be played within a marriage relationship. His instructions for Christian women are distinctly different from those for Christian men. Role distinctions within the church were not radically eliminated by Paul's teaching in Galatians 3:28, as is currently supposed.

Third, the silence Paul is referring to in this context—however narrowly defined in scope and application—is actual silence. As with the prior instructions, it is a time not to speak at all. It is more restrictive than simply an attitude of respect and submission, such as Habakkuk urges in the face of God's power and majesty. It is more akin to what my father was trying to accomplish with us noisy little ones when we sang "The Lord Is in His Holy Temple."

Hard Questions, Difficult Answers

On its face, this passage is clear and direct. A literal reading would forbid all Christian women from speaking during times when the church is assembled. But such a literal reading raises several thorny questions. The most obvious is how this passage can be read consistently with the preceding passages regarding the exercise of the gifts of prophecy, interpretation, and tongues. Were spiritual gifts only for Christian men? Certainly not. Women were expressing themselves audibly in the assembly when exercising their gifts.

In discussing 1 Corinthians chapter 11, we saw Paul instructing women to keep their veils on when praying or prophesying. The obvious assumption was that the women were praying and prophesying during the time of public worship. Although a woman may pray silently, just as a person with the gift of tongues may speak to God in silence (1 Corinthians 14:28), a woman could not exercise her gift of prophecy in silence.

Furthermore, if women are to remain silent at all times, how could a woman join in the congregational singing and "speak to one another in psalms, hymns and spiritual songs" (Ephesians 5:19)? Paul's instructions are narrowly defined, accommodating participation in certain aspects of worship while limiting participation in others.

The key to what is not permitted during public worship is seen in what *is* permitted outside of the assembly. "If they want to inquire about something," says Paul, "they should ask their own husbands at home; for it is a disgrace for a woman to speak in the church." The important word is "inquire." When a person is an instrument of God's special revelation, then his words are God's words. He speaks only as God directs him to speak. In the first century God chose to speak through women as well as men, and therefore it was appropriate for a woman to speak or bring forth a prophetic message in the public assembly. On the other hand, it would not have been appropriate for a woman to participate in the discussion among those who were discerning the prophet's message.

Is this to say that Christian women are in some way inferior to Christian men, or that they are not as spiritually insightful as their male counterparts? Paul leads us away from this denigrating inference, saying that it is because Christian women "must be in submission, as the Law says." It has nothing to do with spiritual capacity, maturity, or competence, but with the principle of male spiritual leadership. That principle was manifested in a male-oriented system of worship under the law, despite the obvious qualifications of godly women during that time.

The same God who revealed his message through Christian women in the New Testament church also called Christian men to the public discernment and propagation of his message. If such a distinction in spiritual gifts and responsibilities seems arbitrary and discriminatory, we could point to any number of divine commands which seem arbitrary, not the least of which is the wife's submission to her husband. Surely the man's spiritual headship in the home would be no less arbitrary than male leadership in the church. Sometimes God gives reasons for his commandments; sometimes he doesn't.

Why, for example, were the Israelites not to eat the meat of animals with cloven hooves? Why did only the men of Israel receive the sign of the Abrahamic covenant? Why are we today commanded to be baptized as a matter of obedience to God? It is too easy for us to say that we are exempt from God's commands when we cannot figure out *why* God has commanded them or when they seem to offend our sense of "what ought to be."

We may never fully understand why women are called to silence in the discernment and public proclamation of the written Word. But our submission to God demands our obedient response.

Grasping at Straws

Of all the recent attempts to shift Paul's message in 1 Corinthians chapter 14, the most inventive calls attention to particular styles of writing used by Paul. One style is Paul's use of rhetorical structure, in which he asks a question followed by an exclamation expressing his disapproval. A good example of his rhetorical writing style is seen in 1 Corinthians 6:1, 2:

> If any of you has a dispute with another, dare he take it before the ungodly for judgment instead of before the saints? [Absurd!] Do you not know that the saints will judge the world?

Other examples are found in 1 Corinthians 6:15 ("Shall I then take the members of Christ and unite them with a prostitute? Never!") and 1 Corinthians 11:13 ("Is it proper for a woman to pray to God with her head uncovered? [Absurd!]").

Using this same approach, we are told that the Corinthians themselves, not Paul, said, "Women should remain silent in the churches. They are not allowed to speak, but must be in submission as the [oral, traditional] law says"—and that Paul's response was, in effect, "Absurd!"

Even those who suggest this interpretation admit that what the Corinthians were supposed to have said is unusually long to be consistent with the other models of rhetorical structure. Yet the most serious flaw in this theory is that, unlike in the other suggested examples, in this instance alone there is no reason given as to *why* the teaching is absurd.

Nor does the context of this passage suggest that a rhetorical question is about to be followed by a disapproving exclamation. The passage begins with a statement of universal application throughout all the first-century churches: "As in all the congregations of the saints . . ." Does it make sense that such a statement is about to introduce a rhetorical structure to which Paul will respond negatively?

The irony is that Paul *does* use rhetorical structure in reaffirming the limitations on Christian women imposed by the principle of male spiritual leadership. His response to the men of Corinth who were all too willing to turn over their responsibility of leadership to Christian women was indeed rhetorical: "Did the word of God originate with you? [Absurd!] Or are you the only people it has reached? [Absurd!]"—"As in all the congregations of the saints, women should remain silent in the churches" (1 Corinthians 14:36, 33, 34).

Women or Wives?

A popular alternative reading of 1 Corinthians chapter 14 would say that the *wives* of male prophets should not ask their *husbands* regarding their prophecies until the two of them are in private. This interpretation would limit Paul's prohibition solely to the wives of prophets, leaving all other women free to participate in the congregation's public interaction. It is an enticing interpretation, since the original word for "women" can be permissibly translated as "wives."

Also, it would tie in naturally with the wife's submission to her husband, since Paul cites "submission" as justification for the rule and since a wife's questioning of her husband in the presence of others might be seen to be a challenge to his spiritual headship.

However, as we have suggested before, one cannot wholly divorce a public assembly from the collective marriages and families which comprise it. To limit Paul's instructions to one or two wives of those who had the gift of prophecy ignores the fact that most of the remaining women in the assembly were also married.

To permit another man's wife to enter into the discernment and public propagation of the message prophetically delivered by a man *not* her husband would permit potentially the same problem as between the prophet and his wife. In such a discussion a man and his wife might disagree on the interpretation and application of the message and end up with the wife questioning her husband's understanding. While this would not necessarily threaten her husband's spiritual headship, it has as much potential for doing so as between the prophet and his wife.

Are we to believe that any greater order would be maintained by permitting *other* men's wives to question the prophet, while denying his *own* wife that privilege—even if she were to ask the question with all submissiveness? We must remember that the prohibition is against *speaking*, not against speaking with a harsh or arrogant attitude.

Limiting Paul's instructions only to the "wives" of the prophets leaves too many discrepancies. For example, one wonders whether Paul might not have prohibited the husband of a *prophetess* from challenging her revealed message. Despite his headship as husband, such questioning might threaten the acceptance of her prophecy.

And what about a prophet's *daughters?* Would they be permitted to ask questions of their father that their own mother could not ask? When we change "women" to "wives" we risk exchanging one set of problems for another.

Even translating "women" as "wives" does not detract from a more generalized prohibition against women participating in the authoritative discernment and public proclamation of the Word. As we have seen before, Paul virtually assumes that the women *are* wives. In the first century, women were either wives, or widows who were once wives, or young daughters who were still under their father's spiritual headship. They did not have the "marriage gap" of the twenty-first century, in which men and women are often independent and single for a substantial part of their lives. Which raises yet another question . . .

If the women are to "ask their own husbands at home," what about those women who have no husbands? As suggested, that problem would not likely have arisen often in the first century, given the patriarchal family structure. Widows, divorcees, and single women would always have someone to turn to within the extended family for that kind of inquiry. A harder case might be put for the woman whose husband is not a Christian. Yet both then and now, the elders or other spiritually mature men in the church would provide an alternative for those who might need it.

In fact nothing prohibits a woman from inquiring of any godly man. Yet the availability of an opportunity to *inquire* is not the current issue. The real issue is the extent to which a woman may *participate* in the work and worship of the church. And it is in this aspect that Paul's prohibition becomes so troublesome for many people. It appears to limit the participation of Christian women at a point which many Christians today would consider to be restrictive.

Paul's response almost sounds as if he were aware of current discomfort with the limitations he imposed.

> If anybody thinks he is a prophet or spiritually gifted, let him acknowledge that what I am writing to you is the Lord's command. If he ignores this, he himself will be ignored (1 Corinthians 14:37, 38).

That's a pretty stiff warning. It behooves us to tread carefully in placing an interpretation on the passage other than the one which seems most apparent and most consistent with the principle of male spiritual leadership as it is traced throughout Scripture.

Just How Silent Is Silent?

If women in the early church could speak God's revelations as prophetesses, but were excluded from the discussion and application of prophecy, exactly what was it that they *could* or *could not* speak? Apparently there was a distinction between "prophesying" and "preaching"—between, on the one hand, passing on God's Word without addition or expansion and, on the other hand, applying it by exposition. Application invariably involves the exercise of discretion and moral authority over those who hear the message.

In the first century, the open forum of the synagogue was for men only. Their meetings were not the closely scheduled, well-organized "worship services" of today. There was coming and going, informality, and spontaneity. In our terms, the congregation talked back to the preacher. Better put, men preached to each other. It was more like a mutual ministry of the Word.

Similarly, the assemblies of the early church appear to have been characterized by discussion and dialogue on the meaning of the Old Testament Scriptures or of a prophecy given through someone (perhaps a woman) in the congregation. They had not developed a clergy-laity distinction. Therefore, just as in the synagogue, the discussion (as opposed to the exercise of spiritual gifts) apparently was for men only—all the men, *active* men, *involved* men.

In our time and culture, women freely participate in Bible class discussions or in Bible study groups. Does this violate the command or spirit of Paul's teaching to the Corinthians? Perhaps our best insight into this question comes from Paul's separate instructions to the evangelist Timothy:

> A woman should learn in quietness and full submission. I do not permit a woman to teach or to have authority over a man; she must be silent (1 Timothy 2:11, 12).

The Greek word here translated as "quietness" and "silent" is not the same word which Paul previously used to indicate silence in the assembly. But it has a similar meaning—to hold one's peace. Connected as it is with the word "submission," its meaning is perhaps closer to Habukkuk's use of the word "silence," meaning deferential submission. "Quietness" in this context is an attitude regarding one's relative position in a hierarchy of spiritual authority. Together with the word "submission," it recognizes God-given roles. It does not necessarily demand strict silence. It permits participation within the parameters of designated responsibilities.

When taken together with Paul's teaching to the Corinthians, this passage suggests that there may be two kinds of biblical discussions: one which authoritatively determines the direction a congregation of Christians ought to go (as in the synagogue and in first-century churches), and one which is more instructional or devotional in nature (as in the modern Bible class).

Because an element of leadership and authority is associated with the first category of discussions, it is inappropriate for Christian women to participate as if they shared that responsibility with Christian men. However, where the discussion is for the purpose of personal growth and spiritual development, learning with "quietness and full submission" is permitted.

As a *learner,* a submissive woman's "peace" is held within an acknowledged framework of spiritual headship, even though she participates in the learning process. But when Paul addresses women *teaching* or *exercising spiritual authority* over men, his call for silence ("holding their peace") precludes that specific type of participation altogether.

May a woman ever teach a man? Obviously, yes, as in the case of Aquila and Priscilla teaching Apollos (Acts 18). May a woman teach other women? Again, yes, as in the case of the older women who were to teach the younger women (Titus 2). But in the public proclamation of the Word to gender-mixed audiences, there is a bar to women's participation.

Does this mean that a woman can teach gender-mixed audiences if men in positions of authority *permit* her to teach? To put it differently, may a woman teach men as long as she does not exercise authority over them? Where is the "authority" within the church, except the moral authority exercised by those who teach and lead on behalf of the church? Paul says simply, "She must remain silent." Even if she could do a better job than any man in the congregation? Paul says, "She must remain silent."

Opinion, Custom, or Command?

But *why*, Paul? Are you simply maintaining the customs and traditions of your own generation? Is it anything more than your own personal idea about how things ought to be? Paul's response emphasizes that his instructions have nothing to do with culture, custom, or personal opinion. In other instances when it *was* only his opinion, he admitted it up front (for example, see 1 Corinthians 7:25, 40). Far from being the opinion of just one man, the rationale for the rule goes back to Creation itself and to the Creation principle of male spiritual leadership:

> For Adam was formed first, then Eve. And Adam was not the one deceived; it was the woman who was deceived and became a sinner. But women will be saved through childbirth—if they continue in faith, love and holiness with propriety (1 Timothy 2:13-15).

Why is a woman not to teach or to have authority over a man? Paul says it is because man, as "firstcreated," has the God-given responsibility for the spiritual leadership of his family, including his wife; because Adam failed in his responsibility toward Eve and allowed Satan to deceive her; because Christian women—"through childbearing," as Paul generically puts it—have been given their own realm of management and responsibility in the home, which if exercised responsibly will assure their salvation.

For some readers it may be tempting to draw an analogy here with what we concluded in the last chapter—that male headship is the indispensable principle and veils are the dispensable application. In this chapter, likewise, it is tempting to say that male headship is the indispensable principle and that public preaching and teaching by women is the dispensable application. But if we dispense with prohibitions against women taking leadership roles in the public proclamation of the Word, what vestige of the "indispensable principle" remains? Simply requiring male assent for women to take over or share in that responsibility?

For the "indispensable principle" to maintain any viability, lines will have to be drawn consistent with the obvious intent of the principle. The purpose of the principle is to define an unmistakable line of demarcation between the respective responsibilities given to men and women in the church. For men of strength to remain strong, women of God must approach that line with utmost caution.

Irony in the Application

I am intrigued by a certain irony which accompanies much of the current thinking about women's role in the modern church. Those who are calling for an expansion of women's role have gone to great lengths to point out the active role of women prophets in the early church. These prophetesses are held up as examples of "spiritual leadership" to be followed in the more contemporary utilization of women to "greet," usher, make announcements, read Scriptures, serve the communion, be deaconesses, teach gender-mixed audiences, and even preach.

The irony is that in most of the fellowships being ripped apart by these issues, there is no recognition whatever of either prophets or prophetesses. Although the subject of prophecy in the modern church is beyond the scope of this book, it is clear that, for most Christians today, a comparison between prophetesses and deaconesses is as useless as comparing apples and oranges. If one rejects the idea of modern-day prophecy, and therefore modern-day prophetesses, then one is hardly in a position to use either 1 Corinthians chapter 11 or 1 Corinthians chapter 14 as proof texts for greater involvement of women in the church.

Even those charismatic fellowships which are more open to tongues and prophecies have much to consider regarding Paul's limitations on women in the exercise of spiritual gifts. But they are in a better position to evaluate that particular concern (and in greater need of doing so) than noncharismatic fellowships.

Submission Through Service

If Christian women are to remain silent in the corporate discernment and public proclamation of the Word, they are not left without service before God. Theirs is the daily service of good deeds in the temple of humanity:

> I also want women to dress modestly, with decency and propriety, not with braided hair or gold or pearls or expensive clothes, but with good deeds, appropriate for women who profess to worship God (1 Timothy 2:9, 10).
>
> [She is to be] . . . well known for her good deeds, such as bringing up children, showing hospitality, washing the feet of the saints, helping those in trouble and devoting herself all kinds of good deeds (1 Timothy 5:10).

If this seems outmoded for woman at the dawn of the twenty-first century, one must ask whether God has changed his mind along with changing times. When Paul insists on tying his instructions to Creation itself, can we easily dismiss male spiritual leadership as a cultural relic of an irrelevant past?

"A woman should learn in quietness and full submission. I do not permit a woman to teach or to have authority over a man; she must be silent." "As in all the congregations of the saints, women should remain silent in the churches." Perhaps we'll never fully understand why. Perhaps we're even angered by it. But somehow in our hearts we must bring ourselves to sing the song of obedient children of God:

> The Lord is in his holy temple,
> Let all the earth keep silence before him.
> Keep silence! Keep silence!
> Keep silence before him.

Study Questions

1. If there were ever any question about whether Paul's teaching on male spiritual leadership was anything more than simply his personal opinion, what do we learn from I Corinthians 14:37-38?

2. What is the difference, if any, between "silence" and "quietness"?

3. How much precedent for today's church can safely be derived from passages which either regulated or gave freedom to first century prophets and prophetesses?

4. In view of the potential for differences in translation of the original Greek word for either "wives" or "women," how can we best understand passages in which the same word is used but is translated differently from other contexts?

5. Given centuries of consistent teaching about the principle of male spiritual leadership, how should we regard attempts to overturn that teaching on the strength of ambiguous usage of a single Greek word?

6. When Paul forbids women from teaching, does he mean under any and all circumstances or does he have in mind one or more limited situations?

7. How does the general principle of male spiritual leadership help us understand how we ought to apply more specific regulations about gender roles?

8. Can a woman preach or be an elder as long as there are male elders who give her "permission" to do so? Or, to put it another way, may Christian men delegate to women the responsibility to which they have been called?

9. What is the connection between women being saved through childbirth (1 Timothy 2:13-15) and the principle of male spiritual leadership?

10. Is there any link between the submissiveness to which women are called and the call of Scripture for them to dress modestly and clothe themselves with good deeds?

15 The Spiritual Man and Woman

Natural Female Spirituality; Imposed Male Spirituality

I wouldn't say I am a modern jazz enthusiast, but every time I hear a New Orleans-style jazz band I get goose bumps. The music has soul, and the instruments exude a spirit all their own. I like the way the performers play melodic variations against a regular percussive beat. It's as if everyone is doing his own thing, but doing it in perfect harmony and rhythm.

While the trumpet and trombone belt out an improvised tune, the clarinet sings the blues with a mournful wail. And the saxophone can make you weep. As one who has a bass voice, I particularly enjoy the deep vibrations of the stringed bass tucked away in the back corner of the stage. Together with the drums, the bass provides a steady beat to keep everyone on track, in harmony, and pulling together in structure and rhythm.

If there are instruments which soar with the player's imagination, there are other instruments which chart a steady course for the ensemble. And if the movement of the music is free, it is also restricted to the harmony and rhythm which has been set by the more percussive instruments.

The spiritual relationship between men and women, it seems to me, resembles the instruments in a jazz ensemble.

Where Christian women soar freely with the spirit and stretch beyond rationality in their understanding of God, Christian men, at least ideally, chart a steady course in the home and ensure the harmonious working of the church. That is what male spiritual leadership in the church is all about: setting a tone in which both men and women can thrive, and providing a doctrinal structure and rhythm in which each individual's improvisational relationship with God, if you will, can flourish without exceeding scriptural bounds.

The picture can also be seen in the blending of human voices in songs of praise to God. The male voices provide the tonal foundation for the higher, more melodious female voices. The male and female voices are harmonious because they are different. Sameness might give a greater sense of equality, but it would result in a monotone spirituality. As Paul wrote the Corinthians regarding complementary roles within the church:

> God has appointed first of all apostles, second prophets, third teachers, then workers of miracles, also those having gifts of healing, those able to help others, those with gifts of administration, and those speaking in different kinds of tongues. Are all apostles? Are all prophets? Are all teachers? Do all work miracles? Do all have gifts of healing? Do all speak in tongues? Do all interpret? (1 Corinthians 12:28-30).

Can you imagine how dull and unproductive the church would be if every Christian were an administrator? What if everyone spoke in tongues, but no one taught?

Nothing could be less exciting than the steady beat of the bass part plodding along by itself. But an unrestrained, unaccompanied soprano melody lacks fullness and perhaps even direction. Praise God for giving us every harmonious part in the anthem of the church!

When it comes to a diversity of gifts within the church, our first inclination is to say that the diversity is gender-neutral. After all, we know that at least some women in the early church were called as prophetesses. But diversity does not always express itself in gender-neutral roles. For example, the call of women prophetesses under the old law never transferred to a call to priesthood.

Simply because a woman appears qualified to be a functional leader in the church does not mean that she is either permitted to fill that role or that she is playing to her natural strength in doing so. Of course women *could* sing bass notes, but they would never be *true* bass singers. Likewise men *could* sing the soprano notes, but they would never be *true* sopranos. Men and women are different. It is not surprising that we would be called to exercise different roles to join strength with strength.

Nor can we evade the issue by saying that men and women *as individuals* have different strengths and weaknesses, even though that clearly is true. Certainly we know that a given man may cook better than a given woman and a given woman may be better suited to head a multi-national corporation than a given man. Likewise a given woman could preach a better sermon, or teach a better class, or pray a better prayer than a given man—or even a whole congregation of men. For that matter, many wives would be far better spiritual leaders in the home than their spiritually weaker husbands.

However, never in Scripture is the leadership principle altered by the obvious variations among individual talents and skills (as between individual men and women). Nor does the duty of submission for Christian women presuppose that men are better qualified in each individual case to assume the leadership role. The gender factor found throughout Scripture is applicable across the board without reference to the comparative spiritual strength of any individual man or woman.

Women—More Naturally Spiritual?

Despite modem culture's attempt to obliterate any distinctions between male and female, obvious natural distinctions remain. Most people, I think, would agree that women are generally more internally contemplative, emotionally expressive, and creative. According to the much-publicized "right-brain, left-brain syndrome," women are primarily right-brain-oriented (intuitive) and men are primarily left-brain-oriented (logical).

Listen to what men and women talk about with each other. Men talk about politics, business, sports, and *maybe* "religion." Women, on the other hand, talk about shopping, children, social concerns, and *spiritual growth*. Women are more likely to ask, "What do you *feel* about this?" where a man is more likely to ask, "What do you *think* about this?"

We can see gender differences manifested in the way men and women function sexually. When it comes to sex, women are more likely to see it as being wrapped up with relationship, commitment, and their overall emotional makeup. Men are more gratification-oriented, localized in stimulation, and mechanical in physical expression. Who knows all the whys and wherefores, but men tend to be promiscuous and polygamous—whether in thoughts or in action—while women tend to be more chaste and monogamous.

Perhaps the most graphic exception to this generalization is the revealing apparel worn by many women, including Christian women. Women often dress seductively and act flirtatiously. Even so, men typically initiate actual sexual activity and, most important for our consideration, women call it to a halt. Women draw the lines of sexual conduct even when pregnancy and social stigma are not at issue. Although it should not be the case, sexual participation is a moral decision made far more often by women than men.

Women generally act on a higher moral plane in other ways as well. Look at the prison populations, for example. Men greatly outnumber women as criminals. Although in current culture the percentage of women offenders is escalating, the gender gap is still substantial. Not even the latest assaults on gender differences have changed the reality that men gamble more, drink more, and more often vent their anger with physical violence. Perhaps it is only cultural, but across the board in virtually *every* culture, women appear to be superior to men in basic moral behavior.

Most people would also agree that women tend to be more sensitive, tender, and nurturing. They are often more open to communicating about relationships and their emotions than are men. They are often better at handling the "C" word—commitment—which sends chills down the spines of many men. Perhaps that explains why a woman is more likely to feel comfortable seeking a personal, committed relationship with God in which there is intimate communication by prayer.

All these special qualities suggest that women tend to be more naturally inclined toward spirituality than men. The principle of male spiritual leadership notwithstanding, godly women keep the embers of spirituality from dying in society. For that reason, often it is women who keep the church alive when, worldwide and churchwide, men have abandoned their spiritual leadership roles in the home and in the church.

Women in the Forefront, Backstage

Evidence of women's pervasive spirituality can be found on every hand. For example, it surprises few of us to hear people say, "Church is for women and children," because it is women, not men, who occupy church pews in the greatest number. In dying European churches, women keep open what few churches remain. And it is women who knock themselves out being hospitable and aiding benevolent causes.

Who do we find most frequently engaged in Bible studies? Women. Occasionally we will run across a men's training class, or a men's Christian fellowship, but everywhere we turn we find women meeting together for Bible study.

Perhaps most obvious, women in their role as mothers spend more time with their children—telling them about God, teaching them to pray, and singing together those first little songs of praise. Where did *you* learn the most about God— from your father, or your mother? If your father was a strong Christian leader in the home, you are one of the fortunate few. In homes throughout the world and in virtually any church that one might point to, women of faith hold the fabric of religious life together— too often by default.

Why are women more likely to be spiritually oriented? Perhaps because of their maternal instinct. When it comes to giving birth, women experience the miracle of a new life created within their own bodies. Try as they might to relate to the process, men are basically spectators. Even before a young girl's sexual and maternal instincts have been awakened, she normally exhibits a gentler spirit than her roughhousing brothers and is likely to appreciate more fully her spiritual self.

If you are not so sure that women are more naturally spiritual than men, it may be because you have been fortunate to experience spiritually strong men in your life. (Any man reading this book is likely to be one himself.) Or perhaps you know a lot of women who don't fit the mold of the superspiritual wife and mother. Certainly, not every man is a spiritual wimp, nor is there any guarantee that womanhood equates with deep religious feelings or active church participation. There are both deeply religious men out there and materialistic women by the droves. But on the broad scale of human experience, women get the nod in the category of spiritual orientation.

Where men have been my greatest teachers in terms of biblical doctrine, I have learned a lot more about basic spirituality from women than from men. And it didn't come from women in the pulpit or teaching Bible classes (not unexpected, since only men have been in such positions). It came from women who shared their great faith over coffee in the kitchen, or around the table at lunch, or sitting on the beach together in the quiet of an ending day.

It may be just my feeling, but I see men most often proceeding from the *mind* and women most often proceeding from the *heart*. Our dominant qualities as men and women seem to correspond with the theological factors which contribute to spiritual growth. Where men are more like the rationality of *law*, women are more like the intuitive expression of *grace*. Where men tend to correlate more closely with the external ritual of *works*, women tend to correlate more closely with the internal strength of personal faith. If men are seen in the doctrinal structure of the *Word*, women more likely are seen in the free exercise of the *Spirit*.

As in our previous musical illustrations, where men provide the beat while women provide the melody, the symbiotic relationship between us makes the "music" of Christian work and fellowship harmonious. Balance is the key. And gender is the key to balance.

Openness: A Blessing and a Curse

From many letters I have received in response to *The Daily Bible,* I have discovered that there are two kinds of Bible readers. Perhaps owing to their traditional teaching role, men tend to *study* the Bible, or at least parts of it, in a more academic, structured way. Women, on the other hand, tend to *read* the Bible, often from cover to cover, with an openness to learn what God is telling them about a relationship with him.

This observation may highlight yet another spiritual difference between men and women: Women tend to be more open than men—more trusting. On the plus side, women are more open to the supernatural and spiritual realm—more willing to trust in the mystical and miraculous. On the minus side, many women go too far and succumb to fraudulent spiritual leaders and emotionally appealing but spiritually deceptive ideas.

This may have something to do with why Eve fell prey to Satan's temptation. Satan took advantage of woman's finest qualities—her desire for truth and her openness to spiritual leading.

Compared with women, men tend to be more skeptical and cautious, more analytical and closed-minded. On the minus side, men are less willing to admit to having a "weaker" emotional side, or to open themselves to a spiritual dimension that can't be tested in a test tube or verified by a computer program. On the plus side, men are ideally suited to be in positions of spiritual "authority." They provide a rational, cautious stability which, if sometimes overly entrenched, prevents spiritualism from running unbridled to its own destruction.

This may have something to do with Adam's sin in failing to protect Eve from Satan's temptation. He had a responsibility to guard against anyone betraying her spiritual openness and trust.

All this gives us reason to rethink the word "leadership" as it relates to the church. God has not said that Christian women are not to be leaders. Biblical leadership is male, but only between men and women. Women lead all the time! In accumulated teaching, example, word, and deed, they undoubtedly lead even more than men. But *how* they lead, *when* they lead, *whom* they lead, and *where* they lead are all important. Men are *designated* leaders in ways that play to their natural spiritual strength, just as women lead in areas that are consistent with their natural spiritual strength.

Nor should we downplay the way that wives can have a great influence *through* their husbands. Surely this helps explain why an elder is to have a wife. Did not God send out his disciples by two?

Not only will women "be saved through childbearing" (1 Timothy 2:15), but it is as mothers that they have their most lasting influence. It is in the nursery and during after-school cookie sessions (where those still exist) that some of the most meaningful spiritual leadership of all takes place.

This is not to suggest, of course, that a childless woman cannot be saved, or live a productive, Spirit-filled life. The reference here is to the normal role of wife and mother. In fact, Paul specially honors the single, childless woman whose life is wholly dedicated to Christian service (1 Corinthians 7:34).

Getting Back on Track

Picture the contrasting ways of leading in terms of a smoothly functioning train system. In all the "unofficial" ways in which they serve, Christian women provide the *locomotion* for the kingdom, while God put men in the home and church as the *rails* which keep that spiritual energy on track and guide it safely within the bounds of Scripture. If the rails of male spiritual leadership seem restrictive, they also provide freedom for female spirituality to go forward in the way that God intended for godly women to serve him.

Male spiritual leadership is not the honor of an exclusive men's club that many Christian men would like it to be. The rails in our illustration not only guide and lead in terms of direction, but they also bear the weight of responsibility. This is no time for condescending male superiority. Leadership is direction, yes, but first and foremost it is structure, foundation, and support.

What Christian women bring to the church is more than cleaning up behind the scenes. Their insight and encouragement is the backbone of the church. Their lifting up of God before their children secures the future. And godly women often provide the impetus needed to get career-oriented workaholic husbands to recognize their own spirituality and responsibility before God. God isn't taking away opportunities for service from women; he is adding responsibility to men.

The Reason for Male Leadership

The question which arises at this point is why God would place men in positions of spiritual leadership if women are more spiritually-oriented. Wouldn't spiritually oriented women make better spiritual leaders, or at least be qualified to share in leadership roles? It is always dangerous to presume God's reasons for clearly stated spiritual principles. We might guess the wrong reason entirely. It is enough that God has imposed a duty, whether or not we correctly understand his rationale. But I keep thinking that something in my experience as a teacher suggests a possible explanation.

Each year as I look out over a class of bright and eager first-year law students in my Criminal Law course, I am aware that many of them are much brighter than I am. Yet it never bothers me to know how bright they are, because I also know that I am much farther down the road of knowledge and experience than they are. Even if I were to discard my many years of teaching and the years I practiced law as a District Attorney, I still would have little to worry about. The real difference between us is the fact that I am the *teacher* and they are the *students.*

If I were to assign a case which neither they nor I had ever seen before, by class time I would know that case better than any student in the room. It's not a matter of intellect or experience; what matters is that I am the teacher. I *have* to know the case better! They *expect* me to know it better! My very position *dictates* that I know it better!

As I read the case the night before, I anticipate the penetrating questions that invariably come from bright students. The next day when I stand before them in the classroom, there is no one else to turn to. *I* am the expert. *I* am the one who must come up with all the answers. *I* am the teacher.

Conversely, as the students read the case, they too easily can skim through the material saying to themselves, "It's okay if I don't understand all the court is saying. Professor Smith will fill in the blanks. He will help me make sense of it."

The point is that a person in a leadership position is often the one who benefits most from the experience. Ask any teacher, and he or she will tell you that teachers learn more than their students. They *have* to. It goes with the position; it flows naturally from their leadership responsibility.

This rationale may be behind the principle of male spiritual leadership. Far from men being spiritually superior to women, and therefore exclusively entitled to occupy positions of spiritual leadership in the home and the church, I believe the reason is just the opposite. I suggest that men may be put in positions of functional leadership because they are *less* inclined to be spiritual than women, because they are not *naturally* as spiritually oriented as women. Therefore God thrusts them into leadership roles so that they may maintain spiritual strength through the ongoing exercise of spiritual responsibility. If we don't always see that principle working—and too often we don't—we can only ask how much worse the situation would be if it were not for the principle.

God calls men to *teach* so that they might *learn—not* because they already have superior knowledge or insight. He calls men to *lead* so that they might become better *followers—not* because they already have reached the destination. He calls men to be the *head* so that they might be better members of the *body—not* because they have earned their way to positions of authority.

This is not to say that God wants us to take the weakest man among us and appoint him as a spiritual leader—for his own good. Among other qualifications, an elder must not be a recent convert. He must manage his own family well and be able to teach (1 Timothy 3:2-7). The point is that active involvement at all levels strengthens Christian men. Those who have reached the highest levels of spiritual growth will be recognized as congregational leaders. Others will continue to grow as they take on increasing leadership responsibility.

Male spiritual leadership, as such, is not an award for out-standing service. It is not a certificate of merit. It is a call to responsibility before God, a duty imposed upon often-reluctant recipients. For many men it may be a chastisement and a rebuke. Leadership is for men needing more discipline, for men needing a closer walk with God and a closer relationship with their wife and children.

Seen in this light, male spiritual leadership may be God's way of balancing spiritual motivation between women, who already thirst for a relationship with God, and men, who would just as soon be fishing or watching Monday Night Football. (Yes, there are many women who would just as soon be shopping or watching the "soaps.") It gives men added incentive to become involved.

When men are active in church-leadership roles, they are more likely to grow in their personal relationship with God. When men take seriously their spiritual headship in the home, they are more likely to understand who they are in relationship with their own Head, Jesus Christ.

However, there's a catch here. In order for this rationale to hold true, Christian men must not only *hold* leadership positions, but they must *exercise* spiritual leadership. It will not be enough for men to wear the title without bearing the responsibility, any more than it would make sense for me to show up to class unprepared and uninterested. Nor will it do for men to *say* they are the head of the family when they don't have a clue as to how to lead their family toward God. It won't do for men to insist on exclusive authority in the church when they haven't the faintest idea how to nurture the family of God.

Yet another caution: Male spiritual leadership is the responsibility of *all* Christian men, not just those who may play central roles in religious ritual. In a congregation of 500 men, only 50 or so may be actively involved as elders, deacons, ministers, or teachers. What of the remaining 90 percent? Are they "off the hook"? Are they somehow exempt from the principle of male spiritual leadership? Someone will point out that most of the remaining men will be burdened with spiritual headship in their own families, and surely that ought to be the case. But we have done great disservice to men if we exempt them from leadership within the church as well.

Part of our problem is the popular distinction between "clergy" and "laity." No such distinction existed within the first-century church. While there were elders and deacons who were appointed only upon special qualification, and while there were evangelists who devoted most of their time to spreading the Gospel, the early church came much closer to being a mutual ministry than our present-day church structures, which so often resemble a corporate organization chart.

In the New Testament we see men active at every level of participation. You never get the idea that men (or women either, for that matter) were pew-sitters. There was work to be done by everyone in the church. The men were *involved*. They were all participants in the common worship. They all contributed to the functioning and worship of the church. And in such a participatory fellowship, they grew spiritually as God intended them to grow. They were strong men of God because they were busy in the kingdom—not just a few "clergy" types, but *all* the men.

The High Price of Well-Intended Salvage Efforts

As long as that occurred, the church remained strong. And Christian families remained strong. As long as that occurred, Christian women felt no need to take over leadership positions in the church or to wear the pants in the family. You didn't hear women bemoaning that *someone* has to take the lead because the men wouldn't! But that is the cry that often goes up when male spiritual atrophy sets in.

Whether it be in the home or in spiritually dead churches, women must exercise their natural spiritual strength to encourage men to assume the leadership roles which God has given them. They must encourage without themselves taking on that responsibility or pressuring their husbands into reluctant, "window-dressing" leadership. Otherwise, any temporary, short-term gains will be offset in the long run.

If women insist on equal participation in the church, the price they risk paying is spiritually weakened men on the home front. Just as family headship is a training ground for those who would lead the church as elders (1 Timothy 3:4, 5), male spiritual leadership in the church is a training ground for enhanced spiritual leadership in the home.

It is not a matter of men saying, "If I can't be the leader, I'm not going to play the game." It's a matter of *exercise*. If men aren't exercising spiritual leadership, far fewer of them will maintain the spiritual stamina to play the game.

Involved church participation brings a man more in touch with his own spiritual nature. It defines his authority in the home in terms other than brute strength or power politics. Church leadership reminds a husband of Christ's own sacrificial leading and concerned headship. Habits of spiritual shepherding formed in the work of the church become habits of the heart within the family.

Spiritual Headship—Not Decision-Making

My greatest fear in writing a book of this nature is that Christian men will see in it a biblical legitimacy for the traditional concept of male dominance in the home. I am afraid that too many men today feel they are the King of the Castle, the Head of the House, the Grand Decision Maker. "Do what I tell you to do and ask questions later," is the attitude of far too many men. And far too many of them would trace their entitlement back to the Bible!

If there is anything the Scriptures teach us, it is that such an attitude is un-Christlike. A man's wife is "bone of his bones, flesh of his flesh"! How can a man fail to understand that abusing his wife is as absurd as abusing himself? "Husbands ought to love their wives as their own bodies" (Ephesians 5:28).

"But we're not talking about *abuse*," someone says. "Isn't a wife supposed to obey her husband in the Lord?" No scripture says that. What the Scriptures teach is that the wife is to *submit* to her husband—meaning to her husband's *spiritual* leading. That is a long way from arbitrary authority on the part of a husband. It is a long way from saying that men are to make all the family decisions, even if they take into consideration their wives' feelings about the matter.

Have we overlooked what Paul told women to do? "I counsel younger widows to marry, to have children, to *manage* their homes and to give the enemy no opportunity for slander" (1 Timothy 5:14). How is a woman supposed to *manage* her home without making decisions concerning that responsibility? If men get upset at the thought of women entering their "domain" in the church, imagine how upset women get when men enter *their* "domain" in the home. A man's wife is not to be his robot. She is not to wait in breathless anticipation of his permission before she can think, speak, or act. To the contrary, she is expected to be independent and strong in her own realm of responsibility.

What then does male leadership mean? It means male *spiritual* leadership. The biblical word is *servanthood!* It means that a man's time is spent in the Word, so that he is at least as knowledgeable as his wife regarding what the Scriptures teach. That would be a major start for many men. It means being the initiator of family prayers, and not just at the dinner table. In fact it may call a man to abandon trite table prayers in favor of meaningful prayers on other occasions.

Male spiritual leadership means thinking of *God's* plan when considering *family* plans. "Where should we live?" (What would *God* want for our family?) "What job should I take?" (How best could I serve God and my family?) "What house should we buy?" (How can our family's financial resources best be used for the Lord?) "Where should our children attend school?" (What will be best for our children's spiritual development?)

When the husband begins asking those kinds of questions and involving his wife in those kinds of decisions, we will come much closer to male spiritual leadership in the home. Deciding which color of car to buy, when to pay what bills, and what magazines the family can order doesn't even come close to what God has called men to be.

We reach a more godly definition of leadership when the husband is asking how he can best reveal his own love for the Lord to his wife and children, and when he concerns himself with how he can nourish and edify his wife—spiritually, emotionally, mentally, and physically. The husband demonstrates undeniable spiritual leadership when he models a life of dependence on God and trust in his Word; when he exhibits a godly character; when he lives out his relationship with the Lord in a way that involves his wife in his inner life; and when he establishes priorities for his time that put his life in proper order. There is true spiritual leadership when the husband is responsible for the spiritual and emotional "environment" of his home.

The husband who understands what spiritual leadership is all about and puts it into practice is not likely to insist on making the "final decision" in matters which are crucial to the family, or to have a wife who is made to feel inferior. God calls men to *spiritual* headship, not dictatorship.

We began this chapter comparing men and women to a jazz ensemble in which each instrument plays an important part. We suggested that the man's role is like the percussion instruments, which set a tempo for the more free-spirited instruments. Instead of inhibiting or repressing those instruments, the percussion section provides a foundation for richer, fuller music to be expressed together.

In a marriage, and in the larger family of the church, conscientious Christian men provide a similar foundation for the fullness of faith which most women already have in abundance. Spiritual men nurture spiritual women. Spiritual men encourage spiritual women. Spiritual men protect spiritual women. In short, men are called to do for their wives what many of their wives are already doing for them. If there is not to be shared functional leadership, there *is* to be shared spirituality. When each person is playing the part that he or she has been called to play, what more beautiful harmony could there be?

Intensely Personal

We cannot close this chapter without identifying with the intensely personal situations faced by women whose men are either weak or unwilling to take seriously their God-given roles and responsibilities. Ideals are not always achieved. Are women supposed to stand by and watch their marriages and families self-destruct?

The problem is that a man simply can't be pushed into spiritual leadership. Prayer, not pushing, is the way to a man's heart. Only a wife's godly character and respectful submission has any chance of getting his attention. Attempting to take over family headship will only send a man in the opposite direction. Even alone, if necessary, a woman can lead her children to God. Even alone, by God's grace, a woman can lead her husband to be a man of strength. In such a case, God honors her spiritual leadership in the home.

This is where submission finds its ultimate meaning. Where turning to God through the Word and in prayer can bring the nurturing a husband does not provide. Where trust in God can bring dignity and assurance of self-worth. Where biblical examples of strong women of faith can inspire a woman of God to patience and steadfastness while God is working in the reluctant heart of her husband.

Study Questions

1. Does the principle of male spiritual leadership still apply if there are women who are seemingly more qualified to lead, either in the home or in the church?

2. What is the beauty and strength of having a division of clearly defined role responsibilities as between men and women?

3. What spiritual distinctions, if any, do you see between men and women?

4. Do you agree with the observation that, across the board, women are more naturally spiritual than men?

5. If not, how do you explain the apparent differences between men and women spiritually? If so, to what do you attribute that greater spiritual inclination?

6. If you believe that women are more naturally spiritual than men, why do you think God gave men the responsibility for spiritual leadership?

7. Which is more important: understanding why God has commanded us to live before him in a certain way, or obeying his will whether or not we can fully understand it?

8. What do we learn from the history of virtually every church that has changed from male leadership to a more gender-inclusive leadership?

9. In the most practical terms, what is male spiritual leadership all about—especially in the home?

10. What is a woman to do when the man in her life or the men in her church have reneged on their responsibility to be spiritual leaders?

16 *Where to Draw the Line?*

Applying the Principle

Questions, Questions, and More Questions

Once the principle of male spiritual leadership is acknowledged, we are faced with questions of application. For example, when do "boys" (whom women may teach) become "men" (whom women are not to teach in certain settings)? Is it wrong for a woman to lead a prayer in the home when the man of the house is present? Is it different if the man is not a Christian? May women lead the prayers in a mixed home Bible study or prayer meeting? Does it matter that she is specifically *asked* by a man to lead a prayer? May a woman read a passage of Scripture when called upon to do so in a class? How about in public worship? May she comment on its meaning?

Too often we feel a need for the rules to be spelled out neatly and precisely in black and white. Mature, responsible Christians ought to be able to know when the line of propriety is crossed. They should also know when taking a nontraditional role is a matter of meeting an explicit need or, on the other hand, is done to make a statement that God would never approve.

I don't mean to cop out at this point, but it is the main principle about which I am most concerned. When the principle itself is honored scrupulously, the lines will tend to be in sharper focus. Furthermore, I am reluctant to share my own line in each instance, for if a person were to disagree with where I draw the line, he or she might discredit altogether the principle itself, which came from God.

That said, we must ask ourselves whether we are taking pains to distinguish between God's will and what we might like to think the rule is in each case. Too much fuzzy interpretation of clearly stated biblical principles has surfaced for us to think that the present climate of women's liberation has not affected our thinking even in the church. The effect of *present* culture on what happens in the church should be as great a concern to us as the effect which *past* culture may have had on the early church.

If we cannot know all the answers with mathematical certainty, we can—and indeed must—honestly and humbly acknowledge the basic scriptural principle. Where we are tempted to draw no lines, Scripture tells us there are lines to be drawn. Where we are tempted to draw as few lines as possible, Scripture tells us there are more to be drawn than might suit us personally.

This is the real question: Are we drawing the lines without ever acknowledging the fundamental existence of the spiritual gender factor that God has called us to recognize? If so, we will inevitably draw the lines in the wrong places—our places, not God's.

For Want of a Nail

Changes in church participation seem petty on the surface. If women want to lead public prayers, someone might question, "What harm could it do?" No one questions that they can lead beautiful prayers and read Scripture passages, perhaps with even more feeling than many men. If women want to be recognized as deaconesses, who are we to say they shouldn't be? *And* as long as women can fill those roles, what objection could we have to appointing women as ministers and elders as well? Human thinking and current cultural norms would clearly ratify such a decision.

Yet you remember the old saying: "For want of a nail the shoe was lost; for want of a shoe the horse was lost; for want of a horse the rider was lost; for want of a rider the battle was lost; for want of a battle the war was lost." *Somewhere* along the line, the biblically mandated principle of male spiritual leadership is eroded. And *somewhere* along the line, the participation of women in roles God directed men to take is contrary to God's way. There are too many gender-related Scriptures to ignore that fact.

If it is not God's way, *somewhere* along the line the greater participation of women in the church will lead to a weakening, rather than a strengthening, of the church.

Even if lines are not drawn easily, they *must* be drawn. It won't do to draw the only line somewhere near the top of the leadership chart—even if a person conceded the inconsistency of drawing the line there. ("Neither male nor female" except at the top level?) If all we maintain of the principle is male exclusivity at the highest levels of church government, then we not only have created an illogical and unbiblical dichotomy which women would have every right to see as sheer discrimination, but we have robbed the church of its broader male strength. The responsibility of spiritual leadership for *all* Christian men must never be confused with the exclusive male hierarchy of just a few.

What Statement Are We Making?

Unfortunately, it is not *expediency* that lies behind the current push for equal access to roles which have been reserved for men within the church. The reason for the movement is not because no men are available to fill leadership roles. Instead, the stated reason is that, in Christ, women are given freedom to serve in every way men are. That very statement is the most troublesome. In fact, that statement may be exactly what Paul addressed in 1 Corinthians chapters 11 and 14. He was apparently talking to Christian women who had gotten the wrong message from "neither male nor female" and who were insisting that role distinctions had been tossed out of Christian worship.

When expediency doesn't demand it, overextended participation makes the wrong statement. Particularly in today's activist climate, the *reason* for such participation is precisely what Paul condemned. Unfortunately, the *timing* of any inroads into traditional male roles couldn't be worse. Now more than ever we need to reaffirm strong male leadership both in the church and in the home. The pressure of a secular society to bring sexual equality into God's kingdom ought to tell us that now is not the time for "shared spiritual leadership."

The mood of the moment ought to be a yellow light rather than green. A biblical principle should be permitted to be as pervasive as possible so that its purpose will have its intended effect. Accepting a principle in theory and then limiting its practical application to token lip service emasculates the principle and defeats its purpose. Women of God can appreciate a pervasive principle of male spiritual leadership which is consistently applied in the church and in the home. Few could appreciate being told that male spiritual leadership means nothing more than that women have been excluded from the highest leadership roles in the church. The *pervasive principle* approach answers the needs and desires of most women. The *restrictive rule* approach is a slap in the face to all women.

Crack the door open in biblically neutral areas of service, and we will soon find it to be a threshold to the biblically ordained leadership roles themselves. The slope is indeed slippery. As a lawyer I am well aware of "floodgate" arguments which seize upon improbable ultimate consequences as a reason for not doing something that is imminently reasonable. Floodgate arguments should be used with caution. But in this case we already have proof. Already we have seen churches which have made the rapid progression from women participating in "lower levels" of public worship to being appointed deaconesses, pulpit ministers, and elders.

Why should women join with men in leading "lower level" worship activities? "Because," we are told, "there is neither male nor female." If that is true, then it is also true that women should be allowed to join men in the pulpit. Accepting that rationale for shared participation in seemingly innocent areas of public worship leaves no room for line-drawing whatever. That is why the "floodgate" threat is so real.

The *statement* being made runs counter to biblical teaching. The *statement* being made is by no means insignificant, neutral, or harmless.

There is another statement which we would be making if women were permitted to serve in these less significant roles and never allowed to exercise more serious responsibilities. That statement would be that women are qualified only for servile positions in the church. It is not a statement I would want to make. When male spiritual leadership is demonstrated from top to bottom, as it were, we run less risk of implying that Christian women are somehow inferior to Christian men. Top-to-bottom male spiritual leadership allows the gender factor to be God's universal factor. Arbitrary linedrawing near the top of some hierarchical church structure ("Women can do everything except serve as elders") ironically ends up being reduced to no more than strict legalism. *Chauvinistic* legalism!

Keeping Men in the Lineup

I cannot say that I have learned profound leadership lessons from passing communion trays. I doubt if leading congregational singing provides much understanding about *spiritual* leading. And reading the Scripture in worship doesn't greatly enhance my ability to shepherd the flock. But all these forms of service do set a tone for what is ultimately important: male spiritual leadership. Men need to be utilized in every way possible. It is God's way of encouraging us, teaching us, reminding us— calling us to our most important responsibility.

Maintaining a high male profile in everything that the church does reminds us of the greater principle: It is not what women *could* do, but what men *should* do.

Women are already involved in the work and service of God. Career-pressed, sports-lured, financially-distracted Christian men need all the encouragement they can get to become involved with spiritual service. If not all of them can be elders and deacons, let them pass the communion trays. Perhaps it will remind them of their greater need to serve. If not all of them can be pulpit ministers, let them read the Scripture. Perhaps it will remind them of their greater need to get into the Word more personally.

The real question, of course, is not where to draw the line. Being concerned about how much we can get away with and still be consistent with the principle misses the point altogether. The real question is whether we are prepared to accept the principle of male spiritual leadership as being of God, and, if so, how we may implement the principle to the fullest extent in the life of the church and in the daily outworking of relationships between men and women of faith. May God grant us judgment in our struggle to properly apply the principle. But may God first of all give us hearts of obedience and submission to his leading.

Study Questions

1. How is the principle of male spiritual leadership to be applied at the congregational level, particularly in areas where there is no explicit apostolic guidance?

2. In what way does one's attitude toward the principle itself affect one's drawing of difficult lines?

3. To what extent might petty arguments over line-drawing camouflage a more fundamental rejection of the principle itself?

4. Might the same level of participation be either acceptable or unacceptable depending upon whether a wrong statement is being made about male spiritual leadership?

5. Given the current climate of feminism and political correctness, is now the best time to push the envelope for a wider role for women?

6. To what extent have today's cultural norms dictated the agenda of the church?

7. What are the potential consequences of accepting cultural arguments which many are now using to gain wider acceptance of practicing homosexuals?

8. In what way does the question of what women may or may not do in the church mask the larger question of God has called men to be and to do?

9. What is the relationship between male leadership in the church and headship in the home?

10. At what point must fellowship be breached over issues involving gender roles?

17 Tempest in a Global Teapot

Looking at the Bigger Picture

Some time ago in London I happened upon a wonderful (though sadly, short-running) musical called "Winnie," which delightfully chronicled the war years of Winston Churchill. Churchill has always been one of my heroes, so the play naturally caught my attention. The music was terrific, the acting was superb, and the choreography was fun and exciting. But the story line itself stole the show. Here I was in a London theater across from Victoria Station reliving the bombing which during the war had threatened those very structures. I found myself caught up in a strange time warp.

On the way home from the play I took "the tube," as Londoners affectionately refer to their subways, and once again scenes from the play flashed before my eyes. As I descended the long escalators into the bowels of the underground system, I half-expected to find thousands of bomb-wearied Londoners fitfully sleeping alongside the tube tracks during seemingly endless overnight air raids. It was a picture of huddled masses which I could hardly imagine—fearful, cold, and crowded, with the stench of human odors hanging like a pall.

Later, as I lay warm and comfortable in my bed, I heard the carefree sounds of London on the sidewalk several floors below my room. People were laughing, talking, and having a good time, oblivious to the kind of terror which had gripped the city of London over 40 years earlier. In contrast, I tried to imagine what it was like to hear the bombs falling during the Blitz, what it was like to see historic buildings burning from Lambeth to the West End.

My thoughts then raced around the world to places where terror still reigns: to bombed-out rebel villages in Afghanistan; to bloodstained mud huts in Eritrea, where tens of thousands were being systematically eliminated in tribal massacres; to the decimated homes and businesses of those in Nicaragua who happened to be on the wrong side of the political fence; to scenes of twisted men, women, and children who were victims of Iraqi mustard gas. My mind reeled from the horrors of war.

I was touched by the suffering which must have taken place during the Blitz of London, and by the agony of the German people when British and American planes dropped retaliatory bombs over their crumbling cities. And how can we begin to contemplate the inhumanity of the Holocaust? Or the plight of political refugees around the world? Or the millions who starve in Ethiopia? War, hunger, pollution, crime, and disease vied for attention as I lay there, overwhelmed with the life-and-death issues which reach out to us from the front page each day. "What are we to do?" I wondered. "What are the answers? How can we turn it all around and forever put an end to the problems which plague us?"

And then it hit me. Instead of doing anything about any one of those threats to a suffering humanity, I was writing a book about whether Christian women could pass out communion or lead a prayer or be deaconesses in the church. Somehow, on that night in that place with those thoughts, my book on the role of women in the church hardly seemed to matter.

Who cares who does what in a worship service, when there are people starving because they don't have even the bread or the few drops of wine that we take in memory of our crucified Lord? Who cares whether a woman can lead a prayer in the company of Christian men, when half a world away there is a mother who has just watched her baby being hacked to death by some crazed soldier? And who cares whether a woman can serve as a deaconess, when in Bangladesh a cyclone has has killed thousands of women who will never find out the answer, or even the question, for that matter?

I know the issues and potential solutions are completely different, but sometimes I wonder what affluent, well-educated, and abundantly blessed Christian women are thinking about when they invest time and energy trying to win the right to share devotional thoughts in the setting of Sunday worship, or preach a sermon, or wear the title of deaconess. Are they oblivious to the plight of women in the world around them? At other times I wonder what I myself am thinking about to spend months of my time writing a book in response to calls for liberation of women within the church. Am I completely oblivious to more serious concerns that beg for my attention?

I can't answer for those who are pressing for a wider role for women in the church (although I can appreciate the legitimacy of their concerns), but I have thought prayerfully about the significance of this book. I'm convinced that, in the big picture, the issues are far greater than who can lead a prayer or who can preach. Much more is at stake than whether some ecclesiastical body will permit women to be priests, elders, deaconesses, or ministers; or whether women can be called upon to read the Scriptures during worship.

In fact, the basic issue is not at all about Christian women, but about Christian men. It is not about what women may or may not do, but about what men *are* or *are not* doing.

Beyond that, the issue is the direction the church is going— uphill or downhill? Will the church remain strong in the next generation, or will it deteriorate for lack of male participation? Beyond even that, the issue is the prospect for strength in families around the world. Will the trend toward family disintegration continue, or is there some way to turn it around so that the family unit is strong enough to support the fabric of a global society torn apart by the forces of evil?

What are the solutions to the seemingly insurmountable problems facing the world? Do they lie in political policies, economic strategy, or military might? As Christians we believe that God has a better way to solve the problems facing the family of man. The corporate body of believers must show the way through lives filled with Christlike love, peace, and sharing.

We haven't even mentioned the greatest problem of all—the problem of sin. Sin is the world's greatest terror, and we as the church must tell the world about the solution to sin, Jesus Christ.

But for all of this to happen, the church must remain strong. We need all hands on deck. If women have already enlisted—as they always have—it is the men whom we must draft. It is the men who must assume the responsibility which God has given them. It is the men who must come to fully appreciate the gender factor and the principle of male spiritual leadership.

Little Issues Become Big Issues

In the big picture, the impact of the church on a world torn by evil and destruction depends directly on its own internal strength, and its strength in turn depends upon the uncompromising viability of male spiritual leadership. What seem to be such innocent inroads into this biblical bastion may in fact have far-reaching consequences.

I am not so naive as to think that we are normally inclined to stretch very far in considering all the adverse possibilities which might result from a dramatic shift in roles within the church. Certainly proof of such potentially negative results is hardly possible. But wisdom would suggest that we look far beyond the more immediate questions. Perhaps two perspectives can demonstrate the greater concerns.

Impact on Abortion

The most crucial moral issue of our time—the battle over abortion—may itself be in some respects a spinoff of the battle over gender roles. Abortions obtained in order to maintain a given lifestyle are often a direct result of the now-fashionable demeaning of motherhood, seen both in the elevation of careers over homemaking and in the disdain among a growing number of younger women for the burdensome role of having children. In many sectors of society today, motherhood is no longer as American as baseball and apple pie. Equality in gender roles, particularly in the workplace, has fostered the belief that having children is now an option, whether it be through legitimate family planning (in advance of pregnancy) or, if need be, through abortion (regardless of its deadly impact on the child who is already developing in the womb). Feminism in support of abortion rights is inevitably tied to feminism in support of gender equality.

What happens in the church with respect to gender may be even more crucial than what happens in society generally. Gender equality in the work and worship of the church fosters the idea that *God* is gender neutral in all respects. When there is, as argued, "neither male nor female," then no distinctions can be made by gender, and hence roles—whether within the church or without—are indistinguishable. At that point, traditional gender functions, including motherhood itself, are skeptically considered to be as inappropriate as the abandoned gender distinctions themselves. The progression is not difficult to see. Once *gender* distinctions breakdown, *role* distinctions deteriorate. Once *role* distinctions deteriorate, *functional* attitudes change.

Bigger issues are at stake when there are those who press gender equality with an altogether different agenda in mind.

Surely, the last thing Christians ought to be doing is contributing to the undermining of motherhood in any way which might lead to greater acceptability of the already infinitely shameful killing of millions of unborn babies each year. Far from being a matter of seeming insignificance, male spiritual leadership may actually be a matter of life and death.

Breakup of the Family

Yet another crucial issue regarding the struggle over gender equality is the effect it may have on the already widespread disintegration of the family. Sadly, history is repeating itself in an ironic way. During the days of slavery in America, the most common feature of black families was the forced separation of the father from the mother and her children. Through slavery, the family unit was torn apart in such a way that the children were almost invariably raised by the mother alone. The unhappy results were a number of long-term repercussions related to male spiritual leadership.

Without the presence of the father in the home, for instance, it was the mother who became the spiritual leader. She *had* to be the leader. Unfortunately, this became the pattern followed even after slavery, owing in part to the fact that black men—robbed of the opportunity to be a strengthening influence in the home—had not learned *how* to lead, spiritually or otherwise.

The problem then became self-perpetuating. Without the father in the home, or without his leadership even if he was physically present, there was no strong male influence serving as a model for boys on their way to becoming men. When they themselves grew up to be fathers, they had little idea of anything remotely akin to male spiritual leadership, and thus a matriarchal society has continued to the present time. As one small reminder of that fact, black athletes are notorious for their "Hi, *Mom!*" greetings when the television cameras catch them in a moment of jubilation. Their maternal bonding far exceeds paternal bonding.

Without casting aspersions at blacks in general—and certainly not upon black women, who have coped as best they could when all too often left to do the work of *both* parents—it is clear that the high drug abuse and crime rate among young black men is attributable to the dysfunctional family structure as much as to any other factor, including economic and educational bias. In the black community, the absence of strong male leadership has led to an unparalleled social upheaval.

What involuntary slavery did for black families, voluntary divorce is beginning to do for white families. The disintegration of the family unit is having disastrous consequences for the children of divorce—especially young men. Like their black counterparts, young white boys are now also growing up without models of strong male leadership in the home. Children of divorce, like the children of slavery before them, typically live with their mothers. Increasingly, mothers are having to shoulder the entire responsibility of single parenting. And while they may perform that role as conscientiously as possible, there is no way that they can provide both their own maternal nurturing and the kind of male leadership which ought to be borne by the father.

Is it any wonder, then, that drug use, truancy, homosexuality, and criminal activity have soared among young whites throughout society, even without the economic and educational bias often faced by young blacks? With so much at stake, is now the time to abandon the last vestiges of male spiritual leadership? Or indeed has the time come to reaffirm more than ever the need for family leadership which men have been called to provide?

The sad thing, of course, is how often divorce itself has been caused by either husbands *abusing,* or wives *refusing,* the biblical principle of male spiritual leadership. Show me a family where the principle of male spiritual leadership is dishonored and I'll show you a family torn by the tensions of crisis and conflict. If male spiritual leadership tends to be an academic doctrinal controversy in the church, it becomes incredibly real and terribly practical when it comes to family harmony and stability. And as the family goes, so goes society.

Wrapping Up

What the Scriptures tell us from beginning to end is that men and women were purposely created to be different in both form and function. Neither male nor female was an afterthought and neither was in any way inferior to the other. Each was a perfect match for the other. Men and women were given those special characteristics which are most suitable to the unique roles to which God has called them.

God called men to be the spiritual heads of their wives—to nurture them, to protect them, and to serve them through the Word and through lives of personal strength and honor. God called women to submit to their husbands' spiritual leading as they go about their family-oriented responsibilities and in everything else they do.

Within the church the functions of men and women are also governed by Scripture. Just as men are to exercise spiritual headship in the home, they are to exercise spiritual leadership in the church. God has called men as elders, to be spiritual overseers in local congregations. And the formal responsibilities of deacons (who, like the elders, must meet specific biblical qualifications) are also given to men, although women, as well as other men, may serve informally in similar ways through their service to others.

Whether it be in the exercise of an elder's spiritual authority through his personal example and ministry of the Word, or in the moral authority assumed in the teaching of the Gospel by evangelists and Bible-class teachers, it is *men* who are called to that task, not women. Even though women *are* called to teach—the older women to teach the younger, and mothers to teach children—God's intent is clear and unmistakable: Women are not to teach men in the assembly of the church or to exercise authority over them.

One of the beautiful things about the writing of this book is the fact that, as a man, I have been able to draw from the spiritual understanding and advice of many women as well as men. I have learned much from these women of God as they prayerfully reviewed various drafts of the manuscript and shared their thoughts about the material presented. Both you and I have been the beneficiaries of their rich insight, because in many ways they "taught me the way of the Lord more perfectly" regarding these issues. If God has not called women to positions of functional leadership, he has certainly called them to opportunities for leading.

If we are given fewer guidelines than we might hope for regarding other specific functions within the church, we nevertheless are bound by the overarching principle of male spiritual leadership. Any involvement of women which threatens that principle is contrary to God's will. Sadly, today's call for a wider role for women in the church appears to be just such a threat. The statement being made to justify such inroads, that "there is neither male nor female," is a dangerous statement as thus misused, and is unworthy of clear biblical teaching.

Two ideas must be put to rest once and for all. The first is that the principle of male spiritual leadership was part of a patriarchal system no longer relevant to our situation—that it was simply a matter of custom in a culture foreign to our own. Nothing in Scripture supports that assumption. The principle of male spiritual leadership found its genesis *in* Genesis, before culture or custom began. It was established in the process of Creation as a part of Creation and will continue until God's New Creation in heaven.

The second idea which must be abandoned is that role distinctions in the church violate human rights, equality, and fair play. What seems so natural to a rightsconscious society at the end of the twentieth century is surprisingly foreign to Scripture. The church is not a secular organization to be governed by an Equal Rights Amendment. The church is the spiritual body of Christ. In the kingdom of God, personal rights give way to responsibilities, and personal freedoms yield to the leading of the King.

Submission Below; Submission Above

The welcome surprise is that yielding and forbearance in the kingdom—captured best in the word "submission"—are always for the good of those who submit. Through male spiritual leadership—when conscientiously exercised—women of faith are honored, served, and protected. And men of faith are strengthened, motivated, and called to a spiritual orientation which doesn't always come naturally to them. These benefits alone would be reason enough to appreciate the gender factor in the home and in the church. But there's more.

A woman's submission to the spiritual leading of her husband and her respect for the leadership of godly men in the church is a training ground for a far more important role of submission. Undoubtedly that is why Paul wrote, "Wives, submit to your husbands *as to the Lord"* (Ephesians 5:22).

Likewise a man's submission to his responsibilities as spiritual head of the family and as leader in God's spiritual family, the church, is also a training ground for a far more important role of submission. The spirit of that role is captured in Paul's instruction "Husbands, love your wives, just as Christ loved the church" (Ephesians 5:25).

Through the practice of submission in our respective gender roles, we are taught the greatest lesson of all: submission to God, who thereby leads us ever closer to himself.

Lord, help us to see your divine wisdom in all that you ask us to do. Help us to see that your commands are bridges, not walls. Forgive us for abusing positions of leadership which you have entrusted to us, for confusing domineering attitudes with spiritual headship and servanthood. Forgive us for abandoning the responsibilities which you have laid before us and for coveting roles to which you have called others. Unify your church through your Word. Help us to be strong men and women of God, humble and submissive to your will. Let your kingdom come into our lives and, through us, into the whole world.

Study Questions

1. What is the danger of viewing gender roles as a matter of political equality, or discussing it in terms of "rights?"
2. How is the principle of male spiritual leadership different from sex discrimination?
3. What difference does it make to think in terms of a pervasive principle rather than specific rules or lines?
4. How are the issues concerning gender roles refocused when we talk about the responsibility of men rather than the freedom of women?
5. How, if at all, does the discussion about gender roles affect such issues as motherhood or even abortion?
6. What relationship does male spiritual leadership—or perhaps the lack of it—have to the breakdown of the family?
7. To what extent does a lack of male spiritual leadership affect the broader society?
8. What lessons can be drawn from the experience of slavery and the black American family? What parallels can be seen increasingly in the white American family?
9. If you are a woman, what advantages or disadvantages do you see in the principle of male spiritual leadership?
10. If you are a man, in what ways do you feel you have either honored or dishonored the principle of male spiritual leadership?

CPSIA information can be obtained at www.ICGtesting.com
Printed in the USA
LVOW04s0407190315

431166LV00002BA/2/P